Freedom after Kant

Also available from Bloomsbury

Joy and Laughter in Nietzsche's Philosophy, edited by Michael J. McNeal and Paul E. Kirkland
Kant's Rational Religion and the Radical Enlightenment, by Anna Tomaszewska
The Parallel Philosophies of Sartre and Nietzsche, by Nik Farrell Fox
The Politics of Immortality in Rosenzweig, Barth and Goldberg, by Mårten Björk

Freedom After Kant

From German Idealism to Ethics and the Self

Edited by
Joe Saunders

BLOOMSBURY ACADEMIC
LONDON • NEW YORK • OXFORD • NEW DELHI • SYDNEY

BLOOMSBURY ACADEMIC
Bloomsbury Publishing Plc
50 Bedford Square, London, WC1B 3DP, UK
1385 Broadway, New York, NY 10018, USA
29 Earlsfort Terrace, Dublin 2, Ireland

BLOOMSBURY, BLOOMSBURY ACADEMIC and the Diana logo are
trademarks of Bloomsbury Publishing Plc

First published in Great Britain 2023
This paperback edition published 2024

Copyright © Joe Saunders and Contributors, 2023

Joe Saunders has asserted his right under the Copyright, Designs and
Patents Act, 1988, to be identified as Editor of this work.

For legal purposes the Acknowledgements on p. vi constitute an
extension of this copyright page.

Cover image: Immanuel Kant, c. 1765 (Hulton Archive / Getty Images)

All rights reserved. No part of this publication may be reproduced or
transmitted in any form or by any means, electronic or mechanical, including
photocopying, recording, or any information storage or retrieval system,
without prior permission in writing from the publishers.

Bloomsbury Publishing Plc does not have any control over, or responsibility for,
any third-party websites referred to or in this book. All internet addresses given in this
book were correct at the time of going to press. The author and publisher regret any
inconvenience caused if addresses have changed or sites have ceased to exist,
but can accept no responsibility for any such changes.

A catalogue record for this book is available from the British Library.

A catalog record for this book is available from the Library of Congress.

ISBN: HB: 978-1-3501-8775-7
PB: 978-1-3501-8899-0
ePDF: 978-1-3501-8776-4
eBook: 978-1-3501-8777-1

Typeset by Integra Software Services Pvt. Ltd.

To find out more about our authors and books visit www.bloomsbury.com
and sign up for our newsletters.

Contents

Acknowledgements	vi
Notes on contributors	vii
Introduction	1

Part I   The eighteenth century: Kant and his contemporaries; freedom and normativity

1	Freedom, radical evil and 'ought implies can': A problem for Kant *Robert Stern*	11
2	Reinhold on free will and moral obligation: A Kantian response *Jochen Bojanowski*	27
3	Kant and the fate of freedom: 1788–1800 *Owen Ware*	45
4	Fichte on self-sufficiency and teleology *Gabriel Gottlieb*	63

Part II   The nineteenth century: The post-Kantians, idealists and pragmatists; nature, politics and experience

5	The feeling of freedom: Schelling on the role of freedom in grasping nature *Dalia Nassar*	83
6	Is autonomy sufficient for freedom? *Charlotte Alderwick*	95
7	Freedom and Hegel's theory of the state *Christoph Schuringa*	113
8	'In and through their association': Freedom and communism in Marx *Andrew Chitty and Jan Kandiyali*	127
9	Mill on freedom, normativity and spontaneity *Christopher Macleod*	141
10	Practical grounds for freedom: Kant and James on freedom, experience and an open future *Joe Saunders and Neil Williams*	155

Part III   The twentieth century: New developments; freedom, the self and others

11	Levinas and finite freedom *James H.P. Lewis and Simon Thornton*	175
12	Rethinking existentialism: From radical freedom to project sedimentation *Jonathan Webber*	191
13	Murdoch and freedom *Ana Barandalla*	205

Index	220

Acknowledgements

I would like to thank everyone involved with this book.

The idea for this collection came about at a workshop on 'Morality after Kant', organized by James Clarke, Gabriel Gottlieb and Elisabeth Thorsson at the University of York in 2017. It was a good workshop. And lacking in imagination, I suggested that 'we should do something similar on *freedom* after Kant'. Afterwards, James Clarke, Jeremy Dunham, Simon Thornton and Owen Ware, all exchanged encouraging messages about the project with me, and I owe them thanks for that. I think the idea probably would have remained at the after-workshop dinner if it wasn't for them.

The contract was officially accepted by Bloomsbury in April 2020, and I owe a big thank you to Jade Grogan for her help with that, and everything since.

Of course, April 2020 was a strange time, and this book has taken shape during the course of a global pandemic. This was a trying time for everyone involved, in different ways. I'm really grateful to all the authors for the work they produced over this period and the conversations that we've had about freedom after Kant. Let's keep them going!

Finally, I also owe a large thanks to Bob Stern. I am grateful for numerous helpful conversations and feedback he's offered throughout the whole process and for getting me interested in freedom after Kant in the first place.

Notes on contributors

Robert Stern is Professor of Philosophy at the University of Sheffield, UK. He has published widely on Kant and German Idealism, including *The Routledge Guidebook to Hegel's 'Phenomenology of Spirit'* (2002, 2nd edn 2013), *Hegelian Metaphysics* (2009), *Understanding Moral Obligation: Kant, Hegel, Kierkegaard* (2012) and *Kantian Ethics* (2015). He has also published *The Radical Demand in Løgstrup's Ethics* (2019) and is currently working on Luther's influence on philosophy.

Jochen Bojanowski is Assistant Professor of Philosophy at University of Illinois Urbana-Champaign. His main areas of research are moral and political philosophy. He is the author of *Kant's Theory of Freedom (Kants Theorie der Freiheit)* and *Fraternal Justice (Geschwisterliche Gerechtigkeit)*.

Owen Ware is Associate Professor of Philosophy at the University of Toronto. Author of *Kant's Justification of Ethics* (2021) and *Fichte's Moral Philosophy* (2020), his work has appeared in venues such as *Mind, Philosophy and Phenomenological Research, Philosophers' Imprint* and the *European Journal of Philosophy*.

Gabriel Gottlieb is Associate Professor of Philosophy at Xavier University (Cincinnati, OH). He is the editor of *Fichte's Foundations of Natural Right: A Critical Guide* (2016) and, with James A. Clarke, co-editor of *Practical Philosophy from Kant to Hegel: Freedom, Right, and Revolution* (2021). In addition to publishing on Fichte, he has published on Schelling and the philosophy of action.

Dalia Nassar is Associate Professor of Philosophy at the University of Sydney. She works on the history of German philosophy, aesthetics, the history of science and environmental philosophy and ethics. She is the author of *The Romantic Absolute: Being and Knowing in German Romantic Philosophy* (2014), and more recently, *Romantic Empiricism: Nature, Art, and Ecology from Herder to Humboldt* (2022). She is editor and co-editor of a number of volumes, including *Women Philosophers in the Long Nineteenth Century: The German Tradition* (with Kristin Gjesdal; 2021).

Charlotte Alderwick is Associate Head of Department and Senior Lecturer in Philosophy at the University of the West of England, Bristol. Her research interests are primarily in metaphysics, specifically the metaphysics of freedom and agency and theories of nature. She is author of *Schelling's Ontology of Powers* and co-investigator on the AHRC-funded Philosophical Life of Plants network. When she is not thinking about Schelling, freedom and nature, Charlotte likes to exercise her own freedom by being in nature, swimming in rivers and seas, eating and drinking delicious things and dancing at any possible opportunity.

Christoph Schuringa is Associate Professor in Philosophy at New College of the Humanities in London. His chief interests are in the history of European philosophy, especially Aristotle and German Idealism, in the Marxist intellectual tradition and in social and political thought. He is currently working on two monographs, *A Social History of Analytic Philosophy* and *Karl Marx and the Actualization of Philosophy*. He is the editor of the *Hegel Bulletin*.

Andrew Chitty has published widely on Hegel and Marx. He is co-editor of *Has History Ended?* (with Christopher Bertram, 1994) and *Karl Marx and Contemporary Philosophy* (with Martin McIvor, 2009). He is Emeritus Senior Lecturer in Philosophy at the University of Sussex.

Jan Kandiyali is Assistant Professor in Political Theory at Durham University. His interests are in social and political philosophy. His recent work includes 'Sharing Burdensome Work' (*Philosophical Quarterly*, forthcoming), 'Marx, Communism, and Basic Income' (*Social Theory and Practice*, forthcoming), 'Should Socialists Be Republicans?' *Critical Review of International Social and Political Philosophy*, forthcoming), 'Is Marx's Thought on Freedom Contradictory?' (*Critical Review*, 2021) and 'The Importance of Others: Marx on Unalienated Production' (*Ethics*, 2020). He is the editor of the book *Reassessing Marx's Social and Political Philosophy: Freedom, Recognition and Human Flourishing* (2017).

Christopher Macleod is Senior Lecturer in Philosophy in the Department of Politics, Philosophy and Religion at the University of Lancaster, UK. He works mainly on the philosophy of John Stuart Mill: the foundations Mill offers for his theory of practical and theoretical reason, and his connections to the Kantian, post-Kantian and Romantic traditions.

Joe Saunders is Associate Professor of Philosophy at Durham University. He primarily works on ethics and agency in Kant and the post-Kantian tradition. He also has interests in the philosophy of love and media ethics.

Neil Williams works as a Senior Lecturer in Philosophy at the University of Roehampton, London. He specializes in American pragmatism, post-Kantian idealism and environmental philosophy.

Simon Thornton is a teaching associate in the Department of Philosophy at the University of Sheffield.

James H.P. Lewis is a Leverhulme Early Career Fellow in the Department of Philosophy at the University of Birmingham.

Jonathan Webber is Professor of Philosophy at Cardiff University and President of the UK Sartre Society. He is the author of *Rethinking Existentialism* (2018) and *The Existentialism of Jean-Paul Sartre* (2009), editor of *From Personality to Virtue: Essays on the Philosophy of Character* (2016) and *Reading Sartre: On Phenomenology and Existentialism* (2011), and translator of Sartre's book *The Imaginary* (2004). He has published numerous articles on existentialism, phenomenology, character and virtue.

Ana Barandalla is an independent scholar specializing in ethics and metaethics.

Introduction

Kant marks a break in the history of thoughts on freedom. He introduces distinct new ideas, concepts, arguments and insights into the nature of freedom. Kant saw thinking as involving a certain sort of freedom or spontaneity. He also thought that morality involves a special kind of freedom and linked both our moral agency and moral status to such freedom. This freedom involves an independence from being determined by natural necessity. To complicate matters further, Kant argued that this independence from natural necessity was itself compatible with natural necessity. Kant's views are compelling, confusing, intriguing and insightful. And they were taken up by his contemporaries, successors and critics, who both build upon and also depart from his understanding of freedom.

This book brings together a combination of established experts and emerging scholars to reflect upon some of the different ways that freedom developed after Kant.[1]

In this, two main themes have organically emerged. These concern

1. the relationship between freedom and normativity (especially morality) and
2. the relationship between freedom and what lies outside the freedom of the agent.

Kant has plenty of things to say on these topics, holding compelling and distinctive views about both of these relationships. On the first, he maintains that 'ought implies can'[2] and that freedom and the moral law are intimately connected.[3] On the second, he views freedom as involving an independence from anything external to it and sees self-legislation or autonomy as the fullest expression of freedom.[4]

The relationship between freedom and normativity is taken up by almost all of the thinkers discussed in this collection. Reinhold, Fichte, Schelling, James, Mill, Sartre, Beauvoir, Levinas, and Murdoch, in their own different ways, all look to draw connections between freedom and normativity. But in doing so, they each depart from, or look to develop some aspect of, Kant's views on this topic.

The second major theme concerns how freedom relates to things that (appear to) lie outside the freedom of agents. This is taken up in the chapters on Schelling, which consider how freedom and nature relate, as well as in the chapters on Hegel and Marx, which explore the relationship between freedom, politics, and the state. We can also see this issue at play in thinking about how a free person relates to the freedom of others, or even their own previously freely chosen projects, an issue that gripped Sartre and Beauvoir. In working through these topics, we explore how far freedom extends, and whether morality, the state, others' freedom and our own projects are external to freedom or not.

These are the two major themes of the book, and they weave throughout the collection. The book itself is structured chronologically and divided into three sections. The first roughly covers the eighteenth century and deals primarily with Kant, his contemporaries, and his immediate successors. It explores new ways of understanding Kant's views on freedom, new challenges to these views, and how freedom began to develop immediately after Kant in the work of Reinhold, Fichte and Schelling.

The second section considers how views on freedom developed in the nineteenth century. It begins by looking at Fichte's views on self-sufficiency, before turning to consider Schelling's account of how freedom and nature relate, and his treatment of Kant. The section then turns to consider some of the political implications of freedom, exploring how freedom was taken up by Hegel and Marx and how their ideas of self-determination differed from Kant's. And finally, the section compares and contrasts Kant's views on freedom with Mill's and William James', looking at how these two different empiricists incorporated, but also attempted to move beyond, some of Kant's insights about freedom.

The final section of the book considers the development of freedom in the twentieth century, and in particular how ideas about freedom from Kant (and the post-Kantian tradition) were taken up, developed, and criticized by Sartre, Beauvoir, Levinas and Murdoch. In doing so, it explores, among other things, how a free being relates to their own self and others.

With these three sections, we hope to open up discussion of freedom after Kant, focusing not only on his immediate successors but also on how Kant's ideas, concepts, arguments and insights into the nature of freedom came to shape and develop the history of philosophy more broadly.

Allow me to say a little bit more about each chapter.

Part 1. The eighteenth century: Kant and his contemporaries; freedom and normativity

The collection begins with a chapter by Robert Stern, on freedom, radical evil and the 'ought implies can' principle in Kant. Here, Stern appeals to Luther's understanding of 'ought implies can' and argues that this causes serious problems for Kant's understanding of this principle, his account of freedom, and his project in his *Religion* book.

The second chapter considers Reinhold's views on free will, and the notorious issue of whether Kant is committed to thinking that we are unfree when we act immorally. In this chapter, Jochen Bojanowski develops what he calls a *capacity* reading of free will, where even when we fail to exercise our capacity for moral agency, we are still free because we remain in possession of this capacity. In doing so, Bojanowski looks to help us further understand Kant's views on freedom, and the link between freedom and reason.

The collection then turns to further consider the fate of freedom after Kant, and in particular the way in which the concept of freedom started to develop in the years 1788 to 1800. In this chapter, Owen Ware explores Fichte's and Schelling's attempts to provide a genesis or history of freedom. In doing so, he advances our understanding of this period, and of two important early attempts to overcome a seeming dilemma in Kant's theory of freedom, where he seems to be torn between thinking of freedom as involving independence from laws, but at the same time, not lawless.

The next chapter continues to explore this development, with Gabriel Gottlieb's providing a new understanding of self-sufficiency in Fichte's *System of Ethics*. In doing so, he looks to overcome objections to Fichte's account and also to clarify a sense in which Fichte's ethical theory is teleological. Through this, Gottlieb develops a novel understanding of freedom in Fichte and its relationship to normativity and morality.

Part 2. The nineteenth century: The post-Kantians, idealists and pragmatists; nature, politics and experience

The book then turns to the nineteenth century, beginning with Schelling's work on freedom.

Dalia Nassar looks at Schelling's *Ideas for a Philosophy of Nature* to think through the relationship between freedom and nature. In doing so, she makes the case that Schelling came to think that freedom and nature are mutually dependent. This would allow Schelling to overcome a possible 'gulf' (V: 175. 36) between freedom and nature that came to trouble Kant.

This is followed by a chapter by Charlotte Alderwick, where she asks whether autonomy is sufficient for freedom. Alderwick argues that while the early post-Kantians focused on our ability to rationally self-determine, they overlooked that this ability is tied to freedom from external determination. But she claims this is key for Kant; that is, his dualistic separation between rational agency and deterministic nature is central to his conception of freedom and is therefore a crucial part of what enables us to be autonomous. She then looks to Schelling's *Naturphilosophie* to draw out some of the implications of this.

The next two chapters move from nature to politics, reflecting upon the relationship between freedom, the state, and labour in Hegel and Marx.

Christoph Schuringa explores Hegel's claim that the state is the 'actualization of concrete freedom' (PR §260) in the *Philosophy of Right*. With this claim, Hegel hopes to move beyond what he sees as the empty formalism of Kant's conception of rational self-determination. Schuringa asks difficult questions of Hegel here, honing in on a tension in Hegel's thoughts, through looking at compelling claims and arguments that he made in some of his earlier writings that pull against his claim in the *Philosophy of Right*. In doing so, he looks to expose a threatening dualism at the centre of Hegel's thoughts on freedom.

Jan Kandiyali and Andrew Chitty argue that Marx's thoughts on freedom incorporate two key Kantian insights, namely that genuine freedom involves both expressing one's own essence and also treating others with a certain positive regard. In addition, they unpack how Marx develops these ideas in his own distinctive way, where his conception of our essence and the kind of treatment he thinks we owe others are different from Kant's. Alongside these two differences, Marx also argues that genuine freedom is only possible in a future communist society. Kandiyali and Chitty lay out why this is, that is, why a future communist society enables genuine freedom, and why capitalism prevents it.

The final two chapters of this section consider how freedom was taken up by two empiricists, J. S. Mill and William James.

Chris Macleod considers freedom, normativity and spontaneity in the works of Mill. In doing so, he shows various advances on these topics that Mill made upon the other British empiricists, in his attempt to do justice to the agency of human beings, and how Mill's thoughts on this topic draw from and develop ideas of freedom from Kant and the post-Kantian tradition.

Neil Williams and I then contrast Kant's views on freedom with William James'. Both Kant and James reject a compatibilist conception of freedom and do so (at least in part) for practical reasons. However, we note two important differences between their accounts. For James thinks that freedom requires the possibility of an open future and that morality hinges on the real possibility that the future can be affected by our actions. Kant, on the other hand, seems to maintain that we can still be free, even if the future is not open. The second difference between them is related and concerns the location of freedom. Kant views experience as determined by natural necessity and locates freedom outside of it. James has a richer conception of experience than Kant and holds that we can locate an incompatibilist conception of freedom within experience.

Part 3. The twentieth century: New developments; freedom, the self and others

The final section of the book considers how the concept of freedom continued to develop in the twentieth century. In this section, we see an emphasis on how a free being relates to their self and others. With this, the thinkers discussed here pick up on an important aspect of freedom that was crucial both in Kant's theory but also in the development of our understanding of freedom in the nineteenth century.

The section begins with a chapter on Levinas and finite freedom by James H.P. Lewis and Simon Thornton. They argue that, for Levinas, it is not enough for the individual to feel free from arbitrary external determination, as an individual must also stand in a fraternal, but *non-Utopian* relation with the other. Lewis and Thornton contend that, with this, Levinas differs from other comparable views in the post-Kantian tradition, in that he holds that the social relations that are constitutive of mature freedom can be non-utopian or even antagonistic.

In the next chapter, Jon Webber considers Beauvoir's idea of project sedimentation, that is, how our projects, even when freely chosen, come to be gradually sedimented over time. He explores how this poses a challenge to Sartre's radical conception of freedom, where one should be able to change projects instantaneously. Webber argues that Sartre was right to revise his theory of freedom in line with this idea of Beauvoir's, for it helps explain what it is to be *committed* to a project, but also how there can be cultural – rather than just individual – values.

The collection then turns to consider Iris Murdoch's views on freedom. Ana Barnadella explores freedom in Murdoch, as it relates to the self and morality. She puts forward a constitutivist reading of freedom and value in Murdoch, where, despite Murdoch thinking that she needed to move away from Kant, she ends up quite close to Kant and contemporary Kantians like Korsgaard.

In the end then, we are left with questions. For puzzles remain concerning both the relationship between freedom and normativity and how freedom relates to things that appear external to it – and indeed how far freedom extends, that is, what things are actually external to freedom.

Perhaps that is where we must remain: in a difficult position, forced to ask questions about freedom, but unable to settle upon answers. Allen Wood (2008: 124) thinks this is key to understanding Kant on freedom – that 'Kant's greatest insight regarding the problem of freedom may be that it is insoluble and a source of permanent torture to philosophy'.[5] I agree with Wood that this is a difficult topic, but I do not think the situation is as hopeless as he makes out. By comparison, Michelle Kosch, at the start of her book *Freedom and Reason in Kant, Schelling and Kierkegaard*, remarks:

> The point of these chapters is not to present a unified interpretation of Kant's thinking on freedom. Were such a unified interpretation readily available, the post-Kantian development could not have taken the form that it did.
> (Kosch 2006: 15)

That seems right to me. Kant's genius lies in how he introduced compelling new ideas, concepts, arguments and insights into the nature of freedom, not that he somehow managed to do this *and* settle all of the issues and complications that arose. But I don't think this is just a failing, or like Wood, that questions about freedom are insoluble and tortuous. Kant's work on freedom is messy, fluid and full of tensions, but that is part of what makes it so fertile and generative.[6]

For freedom is a difficult concept, but it's also a crucial one, that goes to the heart of our condition, who we are, and how we relate to ourselves, others, and nature. And I think the chapters in this collection show that a variety of different philosophers have made some progress in thinking about these issues. In Reinhold, we learn more about the relationship between freedom and reason. In Fichte, we gain a more radical understanding of what it means to be self-determining. In Schelling, we find a way to bring freedom and nature closer together than Kant did. In Hegel, Marx, Mill and James, we see different accounts of how freedom might best be realized in this world. And in Levinas, de Beauvoir and Murdoch, we learn more about how we ought to treat the freedom of others. My hope is that these chapters, and this collection in its own small way, can help us think through these difficult issues at the heart of a crucial concept and to better understand freedom after Kant.[7]

Notes

1. See Josifović, S. and Noller, J. (2018) for another recent collection which also looks at the development of freedom after Kant; see also Ware (2019) for discussion of how freedom developed immediately after Kant in Reinhold, Maimon and Fichte.
2. See, for instance, A807/B835, V: 143n, VI: 50. 19-21 and VI: 380. 7-12. For further discussion of this principle in Kant, see Stern (2004) and Stern's chapter in this collection.
3. See IV: 447. 6-7, IV: 450. 24, V: 29. 24-5.
4. See, for instance, his remarks at the beginning of the third section of the *Groundwork*, at IV: 446.7– 447. 7.
5. Cf. Hegel's remark that: 'No idea is so generally recognized as indeterminate, ambiguous, and open to the greatest misconceptions, to which therefore it actually falls prey, as the Idea of *freedom*, and no Idea is in common circulation with so little consciousness of it' (*Philosophy of Mind*, §482Z, p. 215).
6. Richard Velkley makes a similar point about Dieter Henrich's work on Kant: 'Many of Henrich's studies of Kant locate within his principal arguments areas of tension, or "fractures", which are revelatory not of Kant's logical negligence but of his penetration into the fundamental and necessarily problematic sources of human questioning. [...] The most central passages of a philosopher's thought, Henrich avers, are necessarily the most difficult and resistant to interpretation. They are also the passages that are the most fertile soil for future philosophical developments' (Velkley 1994: 10).
7. I would like to thank Jeremy Dunham, Irina Schumski, Bob Stern and Neil Williams for helpful comments on this introduction.

References

Hegel, G. W. F. (2007), *Philosophy of Mind*, ed. and trans. M. Inwood, Oxford University Press.

Hegel, G. W. F. (1991), *Philosophy of Right*, trans. H. B. Nisbet, Cambridge University Press.

Josifović, S. and J. Noller (2018), *Freiheit nach Kant: Tradition, Rezeption, Transformation, Aktualität*, Brill.

Kant, I. (1998), *Critique of Pure Reason*, ed. and trans. A. Wood and P. Guyer, Cambridge University Press.

Kant, I. (2019), *Groundwork for the Metaphysics of Morals*, ed. and trans. C. Bennett, J. Saunders and R. Stern, Oxford University Press.

Kant, I. (1996), *Practical Philosophy*, ed. and trans. M. Gregor, Cambridge University Press.

Kant, I. (1998), *Religion within the Boundaries of Mere Reason, and Other Writings*, ed. and trans. A. Wood and G. Di Giovanni, Cambridge University Press.

Kosch, M. (2006), *Freedom and Reason in Kant, Schelling and Kierkegaard*, Oxford University Press.

Stern, R. (2004), Does 'Ought' Imply 'Can'? And Did Kant Think It Does? *Utilitas*, 16 (1): 42–61.

Stern, R. (2023), 'Freedom, Radical Evil, and "Ought Implies Can": A Problem for Kant', in J. Saunders (ed.), (2023) *Freedom after Kant*, Bloomsbury.

Velkley, R. (1994), 'Introduction: Unity of Reason as Aporetic Ideal', in D. Henrich (ed.), *The Unity of Reason: Essays on Kant's Philosophy*, 1–15, Harvard University Press.

Ware, O. (2019), 'Freedom Immediately after Kant', *European Journal of Philosophy*, 27 (4): 865–81.

Wood, A. (2008), *Kantian Ethics*, Cambridge University Press.

Part One

The eighteenth century: Kant and his contemporaries; freedom and normativity

1

Freedom, radical evil and 'ought implies can': A problem for Kant

Robert Stern

In his late work *Religion within the Boundaries of Mere Reason Alone*, Kant wants to take evil seriously enough to require a role for divine assistance or grace in overcoming it but not in such a way as to undermine freedom – and this whole project is held together by an appeal to 'ought implies can'. And yet, while offering a position that is implicitly critical of more orthodox Lutheran thinking on these issues, Kant does not consider Luther's radical take on the principle of 'ought implies can'. I will suggest in this chapter that broadly Lutheran concerns about the principle can be used to raise serious doubts about the cogency of Kant's project in the *Religion* book, which leaves that project in disarray. I will begin in §1 by setting out how Kant tries to balance evil, grace and freedom by appeal to the principle that 'ought implies can'. I will then show in §2 and §3 how Lutheran considerations can be used to throw doubt on the way Kant uses that principle, which then puts pressure on Kant's whole strategy on these fundamental issues and particularly on his conception of freedom as it relates to evil and to grace.

1. Evil, grace and freedom – and 'ought implies can'

As I understand the basic structure of Part One of the *Religion* book, it operates as follows: Kant in effect sets up what looks like an inconsistent triad, but he then uses the principle that 'ought implies can' to claim that while the triad may seem to be inconsistent to us, it must somehow be possible to put the various elements of the triad together coherently, although limitations on our understanding of the world (which transcendental idealism can account for) mean we cannot ourselves see how. Nonetheless, 'ought implies can' gives us every reason to think this could be done from a standpoint higher than our own, which is all we need in the circumstances. Kant's appeal to 'ought implies can' is therefore pivotal to his project here. I will first show how the appearance of inconsistency arises and then how Kant's appeal to 'ought implies can' is designed to show that it must be resolvable in principle, even if we cannot really see how.

The first element in the triad is the fact that we are *evil*. Unlike what Iris Murdoch nicely calls the 'unambitious optimism' of much philosophy of our time (Murdoch 1997: 340) and what he calls the 'heroic faith in virtue' of his ('The End of All Things' 8:332),[1] Kant takes a dim view of human beings and so takes seriously the nature of our imperfections, just as Murdoch does. Kant does not deny that we can do good actions, or even that we can do them out of the right motivations of duty and respect for the moral law, but that in all of us, this goodness can be overthrown; Kant is thus happy to treat the bon mot that 'every man has his price, for which he sells himself' as an updated version of the Pauline claim that we are 'all under sin' (*Relig* 6:38). This is why Kant speaks of a universal *propensity* to evil, for while it may not be being actualized, it is always there to be brought out, if the price is right. There are two aspects to this propensity. First, what it is to be evil here, Kant argues, is to reverse the priority of the moral law and the law of self-love, so that rather taking the former to check our self-interested drives or incentives [*Triebfeder*], we view things the other way round and so adopt the moral law for the reason that it furthers our interests – and this is something any of us can come to do (*Relig* 6:36–7). But second, the reason Kant calls it a 'propensity' rather than just a capacity is that once we have exercised it, we may find it hard to go back – just as someone who has a propensity for drink may find it hard to stay sober once they have tried it (cf. *Relig* 6:29 note). Kant has caused problems for readers by making quite a lot of the apparently empirical grounds for taking this propensity to be universal as an inductive claim, but while also suggesting it can be given an a priori proof of some kind[2] – where it is then hard to see how any merely inductive or empirical argument could give him the universality he needs. Nonetheless, while Kant doesn't make it very clear, I think an a priori argument can be based on the Kantian claim that qua human beings we have a capacity for choice and so have the capacity to choose evil as well as good, and the equally conceptual claim that having chosen evil over the good, one's will is then so corrupted that this stands in the way of going back again, like the desire for intoxication that has been aroused in the potential alcoholic who has taken their first drink. These are just constitutive features of the human will, as opposed to the holy will which has no capacity to choose evil and hence has no problem of overcoming its corruption; and these features seem to provide an adequate basis for Kant's assertion of the universality of a human propensity to evil, understood in this way.

Given the deep divergence between the good will and the evil will, which hinges on giving the moral law and the law of self-interest a distinctive ordering, it follows that it is hard to see how the agent themselves could make any transition from evil to good and thus how they could take any steps in this direction, much less hope to be fully successful. This then brings us to the second concept in Kant's triad, namely *grace*. Kant introduces grace as one of the 'parerga' or additions to religion within the boundaries of pure reason, as something we have grounds to 'admit' or make space for [*einräumen*], even if we cannot comprehend it theoretically or have any use for it practically, while we should also be careful not to overplay it, as this can potentially lead to enthusiasm [*Schwärmerei*] and thaumaturgy. Nonetheless, Kant acknowledges the pressure to introduce some idea of grace, precisely given how his conception of what it is to be evil is thoroughgoing and radical 'since it corrupts the ground of all maxims' (*Relig* 6:37) and so shapes the fundamental outlook of the evil agent at the root (radix), leaving them with no real resources with which to turn back to the good. Kant puts the difficulty in very Lutheran language when he writes: 'How it is possible that a naturally evil human being should make himself into a good human being surpasses every concept of ours. For how can an evil tree bear good fruit?' (*Relig* 6:44–5).[3] It is true that on Kant's account, the evil agent still has some relation to the moral law, in the sense that they are still conscious of it and do not derive their motivations simply from wanting to reject it entirely (as does the diabolical will) (*Relig* 6:35–6), and so they feel some need to take it into account – but they precisely do so by making 'morality into a secondary interest, an interest that is pursued only, and to the extent that, it is compatible with one's inclinations' (Grenberg 2005: 29–30). Given this ordering and the difficulty in seeing how an agent would come to reverse it, therefore, there is a pressure to give grace a role in two respects: as introducing an external mechanism to bring about the transformation that apparently cannot be carried out from within the evil agent, precisely because they are evil (sometimes called sanctifying grace),[4] and a radical forgiveness that renders the agent blameless regardless of their efforts (usually called justifying grace).

However, of course, this then makes it hard to see how we can attribute any *agency* to such an evil will in becoming good and thus impute the move from evil to good to the subject themselves, where such agency is required if we are to call them good or evil in the first place. This then brings us to the third concept in Kant's triad, namely *freedom*, and Kant's claim that '[t]he human being must make or have made *himself* into whatever he is or should become in a moral sense, good or evil. These two [characters] must be an effect of his free power of choice [*Willkür*], for otherwise they could not be imputed to him and, consequently, he could be neither *morally* good nor evil' (*Relig* 6:44). Kant's appeal to this power of free choice is taken to be central to his response to concerns associated with Reinhold that Kant's identification of morally good actions with autonomous actions means that morally bad actions are unfree, and so are not evil.[5] Kant's reply involved arguing that while morally bad actions are not autonomous, as in acting badly the agent follows their desires rather than what they have most reason to do, they still act freely and imputably, as this is a course they have chosen for themselves through opting to make the law of self-love prior to the moral law. The good and the evil agent must thus have chosen these different routes for themselves, if moral goodness or moral evil is to be imputed to them.

We have thus seen how Kant puts in place each element of the triad – evil, grace and freedom. But, of course, they also seem to be in deep tension with one another. For, if evil is as profound as Kant claims, how can the agent escape it without grace? But if the agent requires grace, how can the transition from evil to good be considered as a free choice? But if it cannot be considered a free choice, how can it be imputed to the agent? But if it cannot be imputed to the agent, how can they be considered evil in the first place, as then it is not really in their power to be good? But if it is in their power to be good, what role is there for grace? But if there is no role for grace, and the agent can make themselves good, can we really call them evil in any profound sense? And around we go again. It seems that we are caught in an aporia which we cannot satisfactorily resolve, an aporia Kant himself puts as follows:

> Now if a propensity to this [inversion between the law of self-love and of morality] does lie in human nature, then there is in the human being a natural propensity to evil; and this propensity itself is morally evil, since it must ultimately be sought in a free power of choice, and hence is imputable. This evil is *radical*, since it corrupts the grounds of all maxims; as natural propensity, it is also not to be *extirpated* through human forces, for this could only happen through good maxims – something that cannot take place if the subjective supreme ground of all maxims is presupposed to be corrupted. Yet it must equally be possible to *overcome* this evil, for it is found in the human being as a being who acts freely.
>
> (*Relig* 6:37)

It would seem, therefore, that we are caught between a triad of concepts that are in deep tension with one another, but no one of which Kant feels able to give up.

However, one of the fascinating features of Kant's transcendental project is that it gives him some room to manoeuvre when faced by a puzzle of this kind. For, that project makes space for the following two claims: on the one hand, our theoretical reason is limited by certain constraints placed upon it by our human perspective, but on the other hand, as long as theoretical reason does not show a view to be impossible, practical reasons might be able to give us grounds to believe it is true, even though we cannot really explain it and hence properly understand it. Thus, in this case, Kant argues that even though we cannot see how, while of course our propensity for evil cannot ever be entirely extirpated or wiped out [*vertilgen*], nonetheless even when it has been exercised and the rightful order in our principles of action has been reversed, our being evil must still leave some room for us to make some steps towards the good; although because they are necessarily limited, these steps require supplementation by grace, but a grace that can be earned as a result of those steps we have taken for ourselves, and which can thus be imputed to us. Of course, we certainly cannot really understand how it is we make those first steps, as this seems ruled out by what it is to have exercised our propensity to be evil on Kant's account, whereby we will have 'corrupted the ground of all maxims'. Nonetheless, we know it must be possible somehow – because evil though we are, we still acknowledge that we are under an obligation to take those steps, and ought implies can. An appeal to the latter principle thus turns out to be crucial to Kant's position here.

In this respect, clearly, there are parallels with the strategy Kant adopted in a previous case, namely when he was faced by the threat that causal determinism appears to pose to our freedom. In addressing this issue in the *Critique of Practical Reason*, Kant's argument centres on the example of a man who is asked to give false testimony, on pain of immediate execution. Kant argues that the man will be conscious that he ought to overcome his love of life and refuse to give false witness, but because ought implies can, he must also hold that he is free to act in this way, even if in fact he might not do so because he could be tempted to do other than he ought to do. Kant takes this example to confirm that 'morality first discloses to us the concept of freedom' (*CPrR* 5:30), rather than the other way round, and so is the '*ratio cognoscendi* of freedom'. Thus, Kant argues, despite all the difficulties in understanding how this is possible which result from the limitations of our theoretical reason, nonetheless from the fact that we find ourselves under obligations (a fact which in good conscience we cannot deny) and thus based on the evidence of our practical reason, we can come to see that we are free, on the grounds that ought implies can.

Likewise, in *Religion*, Kant is happy to use the same grounds to argue that an evil agent must be able to take some steps towards the good, even though the depth of that evil again makes it hard to see how that is possible, alongside the general difficulty (raised in the *Critique of Practical Reason* above) of understanding how any moral action can fit into the temporal and causal order of nature: 'For if the moral law commands that we *ought* to be better human beings now, it inescapably follows that we must be *capable* of being better human beings' (*Relig* 6:50). Kant thus uses the principle of 'ought implies can' to support the following view: while human evil means there must always be some room for the idea of grace, nonetheless the principle of 'ought implies can' shows that we must also be able to take some steps towards goodness for ourselves, which entitles us to receive this assistance – though how this is possible, given the corruption in the ground of all maxims and hence radical reversal in our commitments to the laws of self-love and morality that occurs once we are evil, remains beyond the understanding of creatures such as ourselves, though (we can assume) not for God, who responds to our efforts accordingly.

Kant's position on this issue thus ultimately comes out as a doctrine of cooperative grace, whereby we do what we can to restore the order of our incentives, and God then assists us in our efforts:

> Granted that some supernatural cooperation is also needed to his becoming good or better, whether this cooperation only consists in the diminution of obstacles or be also a positive assistance, the human being must nonetheless make himself antecedently worthy of receiving it; and he must *accept* this help (which is no small matter), i.e. he must incorporate this positive increase of force into his maxim: in this way alone is it possible that the good be imputed to him, and that he be acknowledged a good human being.
>
> (*Relig* 6:44)[6]

While it remains hard for us to see precisely how a bad tree can bear good fruit in this way, we at least know it must be possible, as 'the command that we *ought* to become better human beings still resounds unabated in our souls; consequently we must also be capable of it, even if what we can do is of itself insufficient and, by virtue of it, we can only make ourselves receptive to a higher assistance inscrutable to us' (*Relig* 6:45). It is thus by appeal to the principle that 'ought implies can' that Kant tries to conjure a way out of his apparently inconsistent triad.

We will now turn to consider whether Lutheran considerations can be used to cast doubt on whether Kant's strategy here can be successful.

2. 'Ought implies can': Rebutting the argument from pointlessness

Although Luther's name is not mentioned explicitly in *Religion*, there are several implied references,[7] and of course, as Kant would have known full well, this whole topic of grace and its relation to our own efforts or 'works' is full of Lutheran resonances.[8] It is doubtless the case that Kant would have seen himself as making a stand in debates that can be traced back to the Reformation and beyond and would have realized that he was adopting a stance that Luther would have rejected. There are three central features of Kant's position that make it problematic from a Lutheran perspective. First, Kant attributes free choice to the will, which is something questioned by Luther most extensively in his debate with Erasmus in *De servo arbitrio* – which can be translated as 'the enslavement [or bondage] of free choice'. Second, Kant offers a picture of cooperative grace, with echoes of the Scholastic doctrine that grace can be attained and earned through our efforts by 'doing what in us lies' (*facere quod in se est*).[9] Luther saw such positions as forms of semi-Pelagianism, which accepted that divine assistance was needed to fully overcome sin, but nonetheless wrongly held that something could be done to earn that assistance. Thirdly, and consequently, Luther objected that this led to a 'pactum' conception of our relation to God, as an arrangement whereby if we do our side of the bargain, God can be expected on to do his; but for Luther, this was to reduce our relation to God to a matter of commercial exchange and to bind his will.[10] Instead, Luther argued, God's grace should be seen as a matter of his gratuitous promise to us, which has nothing to do with our works.

Now, again without saying so explicitly, it is clear in Kant's text that he shared two familiar worries about this Lutheran position, which led him to adopt his picture of cooperative grace instead. First, as we have seen previously, Kant has the worry that if free choice is denied, then there is a problem of imputing actions to agents and thus conceiving of them as good or evil at all (*Relig* 6:44). Second, again like many other critics of Luther, Kant is worried about a problem of motivation: namely that if the Lutheran picture is taken to heart, we will lose any impetus to take actions to better ourselves, as we will simply rely on grace to do everything for us; but for Kant this makes this idea of grace practically incoherent, as it cannot be incorporated into a maxim regarding what we should do, as it tells us to do nothing.[11] Given these fundamental concerns, Kant clearly feels warranted in defending a less radical position than Luther's and arguing for cooperative grace instead.

At the same time, we have seen, Kant does acknowledge Lutheran concerns about this position of cooperative grace: namely how can we cooperate in this way, if we are evil – for how can a bad tree bring forth good fruit of any kind, that might be sufficient to constitute our contribution to the process? It is at this point, as we have also seen, that while allowing it cannot really be made comprehensible (any more than can the transition the other way, from good to evil), Kant argues that this must nonetheless be possible on the grounds that 'ought implies can' (see *Relig* 6:44–45).

Now, it is not my intention here to consider how Luther might defend himself against Kant concerns over imputation and motivation; rather, I want instead to go in the other direction and consider what arguments Luther might give against Kant's position above, and in particular Kant's use of the principle that 'ought implies can' as a route out of the inconsistent triad which was set out in the previous section. For, one of the curious things about the *Religion* book is that while as we have seen Kant implicitly criticizes the Lutheran position on grace, he does not consider possible Lutheran criticisms of his own position at all – which is particularly intriguing, for as I will now discuss, in his dispute with Erasmus, Luther had in effect considered a strategy rather like Kant's and offered arguments against it which Kant ignores and so simply does not address.[12] It is therefore those arguments which I want to consider now, as I think they can be developed to represent a telling challenge to Kant's position. I will first present Luther's own argument regarding 'ought implies can' but then turn to a further development of that argument in the Lutheran tradition found in the work of K. E. Løgstrup, which is needed to deal with a possible Kantian response to Luther's own position.

When it comes to Luther himself, as has been mentioned, his own views on this issue were largely developed and articulated in his debate with Erasmus in *De servo arbitrio*, where Erasmus had appealed to the principle of 'ought implies can' to argue that we must have some degree of free choice. However, unlike Kant who simply appeals to the principle without clearly explaining why it holds, or on what basis it can be supported,[13] Erasmus offers two key arguments in support of the principle, which Luther then addresses – what I will call an argument from pointlessness (discussed in this section) and an argument from justice (discussed in the next). Assuming that Kant has in mind similar arguments, by looking at Luther's response to Erasmus, we can see how Luther might respond to Kant as well.

Turning to the first of his arguments, one part of Erasmus's basic strategy is to point to numerous biblical examples of God commanding and admonishing us to do various actions and to argue that these examples would not make sense unless it was assumed that we have some ability to decide whether or not to act on these orders and to carry them out. In particular, Erasmus suggests, unless we had free choice, these commands and other forms of exhortation would be *pointless*, as we would be being told to do something which we cannot in fact achieve but which can only be accomplished by God himself. He thus asks Luther: 'What is the point of so many admonitions, so many precepts, so many threats, so many exhortations, so many expostulations, if of ourselves we do nothing, but God in accordance with his immutable will does everything in us, both to will and to perform the same?' (Erasmus 1969: 87).

In response, however, Luther argues that even if a command or admonition is unfulfillable by an agent because they lack free choice, nonetheless the command or admonition can still have a value and a purpose – in precisely showing the agent where their incapacities lie. This use of the law has come to be known as its 'convicting' or 'pedagogic' use and is explained by Luther as follows:

> [B]y the command to love [God] we are shown the essential meaning of the law and what we ought to do [*debeamus*], but not the power of the will or what we are able to do, but rather what we are not able to do; and the same is shown by all other expressions of demand [*verbis exactionis*] ... [T]he words of the law are no evidence of free choice, but show what we ought to do [*debeamus*] and cannot do.
> (Luther 1955–86: 33:133–4)

For Luther, this convicting use of the law plays an essential role in his 'theology of the cross', where it is through despair at our own sinfulness and incapacities that we are finally opened up to God and to his promise to us – just as a parent might tell a child to do something knowing full well they cannot, in order to reveal to the child how dependent they are on the parent (cf. 1955–86: 33:120). Luther thus frequently quotes Paul's writing: 'Through the law comes knowledge of sin' (Romans 3:20), claiming that '[t]he words of the law are spoken, therefore, not to affirm the power of the will' (as Erasmus claims) 'but to enlighten blind reason and make it see that its own light is no light and that the virtue of the will is no virtue' (1955–86: 33:127). Thus, in response to Erasmus's argument from pointlessness, Luther insists that the convicting use of the law gives a clear point to uttering admonitions and commands to an agent who has no ability to follow them: 'The commandments are not, however, either inappropriate or purposeless, but are given in order that blind, self-confident man may through them come to know his own diseased state of impotence if he attempts to do what is commanded' (1955–86: 33:128), which is necessary to put him in the right relation to God.

Having seen how Luther offers this response to Erasmus, the question now is whether a similar reply could be given to Kant's arguments in *Religion*? Luther's key claim is that one cannot infer from 'ought' qua command to 'can' qua action on the basis of pointlessness because there are circumstances where it can make perfect sense to issue a command knowing that the subject of that command is unable to comply. Let us assume for the sake of argument that Luther's claim works against Erasmus: can it also be made to work against Kant? I will consider three worries the Kantian might raise in response.

A first response might be to say that while in their debate on this, Erasmus and Luther are considering the 'ought' to be a kind of command or admonition issued by an authority, our conception of the moral ought does not have to take this form – in which case this debate is irrelevant. For example, one might take a natural law view of the moral law and its obligatory power, which does not trace that obligatory force back to any commander. However, the difficulty with this response is that Kant himself *does* put the issue in terms of command, as that is his way of understanding the imperatival force of the moral law which makes it an 'ought' in the first place, as reason exercises its authority over our non-moral desires.[14] Given this conception of the ought, it then does seem that considerations over the nature of the command which constitutes the ought are relevant to Kant's thinking on this issue.

A second response might be to accept this general point but to argue that nonetheless Kant's conception of the command involved is very different from that of Erasmus and Luther, so again different considerations apply. For, of course, for Erasmus and Luther, the commander in question who makes the law obligatory is God, and a God with certain powers – for example, the power to help us if we fail to follow what is commanded. It could be argued, however, that while Kant has a commander, because this is not God but reason,[15] this puts things in a very different light. For, as we have seen, in his response to Erasmus, Luther takes it for granted that he can attribute various purposes and capacities to God, as a way of explaining why issuing an unfulfillable order still makes sense – but, the Kantian might argue, attributing these kinds of purposes to reason is much less clear, so the Lutheran cannot run a parallel argument in the Kantian case, to explain why reason might issue commands that the agent cannot fulfil.

Now, of course, it is true that one obstacle to comparing the positions here might be based on the claim that God is an agent of some kind, whereas reason is not – it is just a faculty or capacity, which we should be careful not to anthropomorphize, and if we refuse to do so, then it will be hard for the Erasmus/Luther debate to make sense in a Kantian context. One response to this might be to observe that insofar as Kant *himself* speaks of reason as a commander issuing orders – but then, perhaps this is just a manner of speaking that he could and should have avoided. However, it can be replied, it is in fact not necessary to anthropomorphize reason in order to raise issues that parallel those raised by Erasmus and Luther: for, we can ask, what *would be the point of a reason* that generated unfulfillable demands, meaning what basis would we have to take it seriously, without thinking reason does this self-consciously, in the manner of a divine agent – just as we can ask of some apparently useless organ or capacity, why we should not just dispose of it or ignore it.

Nonetheless, the Kantian could respond: while he may attribute some value to reason, he can do so without attributing to reason the kinds of capacities and role which Luther attributes to God, and so we cannot use Lutheran arguments to show why Kantian reason would issue unfulfillable demands, as the two are radically different.

Now, to some extent this will certainly be true. For, on Luther's account, God is said to issue these demands to help turn us towards him in our despair, so that we might finally accept his promise of salvation – and of course, the role of Kantian reason is not to do anything of this kind. Nonetheless, the basic Lutheran strategy could still be applied to the Kantian conception if it can be plausibly claimed that *some* purpose could be found for a Kantian reason which issues unfulfillable demands on us, as this would defeat an argument from pointlessness – it doesn't have to be *Luther's* precise purpose, which requires God rather than reason to be the source of these demands. One way of conceiving this might resemble Luther's own: namely, we should take these oughts seriously because by issuing them, reason teaches us both 'the essential meaning of the law' and also a fundamental humility with regard to our relation to that law. In response, the Kantian might then challenge the nature and desirability of this humility, arguing perhaps that it would cause us to give up actively trying to follow the law and instead despair. But, of course, this would be to beg the question against their Lutheran opponent, who holds that the Kantian exaggerates the extent of our moral agency in the first place and has every reason to doubt it given Kant's own account of radical evil. Moreover, the secular Lutheran might reject the claim that this will result in despair, as what enables us to escape that evil may be said to come from outside us in a different way, that does not require God – such as Murdoch's suggestion that despite our 'fat, relentless ego', the good is still able to cut through despite of and not necessarily because of ourselves.[16] It would seem, then, if Kant is read as adopting an argument from pointlessness for ought implies can, it can be questioned from a broadly Lutheran standpoint.

Thirdly, however, I now want to consider a final Kantian response to the Lutheran argument we have been discussing: namely that Kant's basic argument for why ought implies can is *not* in fact an argument from pointlessness at all, so that even if Luther's replies to Erasmus on this score go through, they cannot be employed to cast doubt on Kant's position. For, it could be argued, the argument for ought implies can is not really a pragmatic one but is *normative*: namely that a commander who issues an unfulfillable demand loses their *authority* qua commander, as they are requiring a person to do what cannot be done, and this is *unfair* or *unjust* in a way that undermines their legitimacy qua commander and thus the legitimacy of this command, meaning it is no longer really a command at all, but something merely coercive.

Now, as mentioned above, Kant nowhere explicitly explains *why* he takes ought to imply can, but it is certainly possible for the Kantian to abandon the argument from pointlessness and instead offer this second argument for 'ought implies can', namely the argument from justice; and as Erasmus also offers this argument, we can see how in his debate with the latter, Luther offers considerations that can defuse this argument as well and so can consider whether these considerations too can be used against Kant.

3. 'Ought implies can': Rebutting the argument from justice

While we have discussed Erasmus's argument from pointlessness above, and shown how Luther addresses it, other passages in Erasmus raise more normative considerations against the idea of commands that cannot be fulfilled, particularly if they have sanctions attached, by claiming that they would be unfair and unjust and thus would make a divine being who acted in this way morally problematic and abhorrent. For example, Erasmus writes:

> [A]nyone would deem a master cruel and unjust who flogged his slave to death because his body was too short or his nose too long or because of some other inelegance in his form. Would not the slave rightly cry out to his master under the blows, 'Why am I punished for what I cannot help?' and he would say this with still more justice if it were in his lord's power to alter the bodily blemish of his slave, as it is in the power of God to change our will.
>
> (Erasmus 1969: 88–9)

Erasmus's concerns here are clearly from the perspective of theodicy, and whether a God who commands us to do what we cannot do would represent a kind of moral evil which cannot be vindicated.

Turning to Luther's response to this challenge, while this response is theologically orthodox in certain respects, it will doubtless appear disappointing to the more contemporary reader. For, he argues that while indeed God's actions here may appear morally problematic to us, we cannot apply our moral standards to God, and so this argument from justice cannot be used in this context. Luther thus again appeals to Paul's words, this time from Romans 9:20: 'Who are you, to answer back to God?' (Luther 1955–86: 33:140).[17]

Now, while in their own way (as we have seen), the Kantian too is willing to place limits on our understanding and perspective, they can nonetheless be expected to reject the strategy as it is adopted in this particular context, as Kant famously treats moral considerations as applying even to God, who is also required to operate within the moral law[18] – and many contemporary ethicists and even theologians might be inclined to agree. Similarly, while a contemporary consequentialist might say that there are consequences which flow from God's actions here which could in the end make them justified, even if we cannot perhaps see what those good consequences are from our perspective, the Kantian may be expected to reject any such consequentialist approach and argue simply on deontological grounds that it is wrong to apply considerations of blame and hence of obligation to an agent who cannot do what is being required of them, as violating a kind of natural justice. It may thus appear that using this second argument from justice, the Kantian can respond to Luther's attempt to reject 'ought implies can'.

However, I now want to suggest that the situation is more complex and that in fact even the argument from justice can be overturned, ironically on the basis of certain key Kantian assumptions regarding our freedom – although in making this case I will not be drawing on Luther himself[19] but on a philosopher and theologian working in the Lutheran tradition, namely K. E. Løgstrup.[20]

Løgstrup's relevance here arises from the fact that he treats the ethical demand that lies at the centre of his ethics as *unfulfillable*, for the reason that if we are conscious of it as a demand, we have already failed to love the other person, so if we are faced by an ethical demand we have already gone wrong and so cannot act in the right way.[21] The most we can do is therefore fulfil a demand qua demand – but then we will not be acting out of love, but instead a sense of duty, which is no more than a substitute for genuine care for the other.

Now, in the course of this discussion, Løgstrup recognizes the worry that this may leave his view vulnerable to a challenge based on 'ought implies can': namely if the latter principle holds, how can we be under a demand that we cannot fulfil? He thus raises the question whether our ethical outlook is fundamentally contradictory: on the one hand, we feel under an obligation to love the other person, but at the same time we know that precisely because it seems to be an obligation, any such love is impossible for us, as to love is incompatible with feeling bound or constrained in this way.

What is now of interest to us here is how Løgstrup responds to this challenge, which he does as follows. First, Løgstrup suggests, one key way to deal with this contradiction is to accept that insofar as we are faced with an unfulfillable demand, *this is our fault*, for only because we have made the demand unfulfillable *ourselves*, though a failure of ours to feel love, does it still stand as a demand: 'We combine the assertion of existence that its demand is fulfillable with our assertion that it is unfulfillable – by taking on the unfulfillability as our guilt and thus conceding that existence is in the right' (Løgstrup 2020: 143). Thus, Løgstrup then argues, while it may be the case that 'ought implies can' in general, nonetheless if the reason we cannot act is down to the fault of the agent themselves, the 'ought' remains intact. In this way, he suggests, if we accept this guilt on ourselves, we can feel the full force of the demand and not dismiss it as a sham or inapplicable to us, even while recognizing its unfulfillability. Thus, it is necessary for us to remain 'standing in the contradiction by taking on the full responsibility for the unfulfillability of the demand as our own' (Løgstrup 2020: 144).

As a way of understanding the limits of 'ought implies can' as a principle, Løgstrup's position seems plausible.[22] To take an example: Imagine a student who has left writing their essay too late, so that they cannot fulfil their obligation to submit the essay tomorrow. If the reason they have no time, is because they chose to go partying or visiting friends instead, it seems plausible to say that the obligation on them to submit the essay still stands and that they can be justly punished for failing to do so, even though they cannot submit the essay in the time available. Put another way, their inability seems to give the student no excuse for escaping the obligation, as the inability was self-imposed, and thus enforcing sanctions remains fair.

Finally, then, if we accept the general cogency of Løgstrup's approach, how does this apply to Kant? Could the Lutheran use it to rebut the argument from justice, but in a way that avoids Luther's rather unsatisfactory attempt to put God outside the moral realm?

It seems to me that Kant would find it hard to dismiss Løgstrup's argument, precisely because his commitment to freedom among his triad of concepts, and in particular his conception of Willkür, means that he must accept the key consideration Løgstrup introduces: namely that the inability of the agent to act as they should comes about through their own choice. For, as we discussed above, this is central to Kant's claim that we are evil and also to the kind of imputation which he wants to emphasize – so if evil were not down to us, something for which we could be held responsible, this whole side of Kant's account would collapse. However, if this is the case, then it can be argued that there is a limit here to 'ought implies can', given that our inability to do the good is our fault – and so Kant's argument from ought implies can must fail.

To put the point more schematically, Kant's argument might be presented as follows:

1. We choose to be evil [Kant's thesis of radical evil].
2. But we ought to be good.
3. Therefore we can be good.

But the response is this:

4. But 'ought' does not imply 'can' if the inability to act is one's own fault.
5. The choice to be evil is our own fault [Kant's thesis of radical evil].
6. Therefore 3 does not follow from 2.

So Kant's argument fails to go through, and the Lutheran can offer an acceptable response to the argument from justice.

It might be said, however, that there remains something problematic about the Lutheran position: for, if we can choose to be evil, surely we must also be able to choose to be good, so that we can now deduce our capacity for good from this feature of our situation directly, without having to go via 'ought implies can' at all.

However, it seems to me that Kant's conception, precisely because it is a conception of *radical evil*, makes it possible for the Lutheran to insist on the following asymmetry here: while we can choose evil and so can be blamed for taking this option, *once we have done so* we have lost the capacity to do good. For, as discussed above, Kant's conception of evil involves a thoroughgoing transformation in the priority we give to the law of self-love over the moral law, such that once we have settled on this order of fundamental maxims and established this as the basis of our character [*Gessinung*], it is hard to see how we could change things back to the right order – which is exactly the problem Kant himself raises, of how a bad tree can produce good fruits, of making itself good rather than bad. As we discussed, Kant allows that we cannot make sense of this, precisely because once we have chosen the bad, it is not clear on what basis will we be able to choose the good, as our values will now be the opposite of what they should be and seemingly must be to make this reversal possible. Indeed, this then is why Kant appeals to 'ought implies can' to show that there must nonetheless be some way out for us, even though the route above is apparently closed.

But, it could be said, while Kant himself was pessimistic on this score, he need not have been, as no matter how far we have gone astray, the idea of Willkür always still means we can choose the good, as Willkür is conceived by Kant as a capacity of choice that is not constrained by our practical reasoning, in the manner of Wille – and so is always able to take another route, whichever option it has selected previously. Thus, while Wille as autonomous follows the moral law and hence the good, Willkür as free can opt either for the good or for evil and, thus having chosen one, can always equally well choose the other.

This, however, brings us to a final Lutheran point that is also raised by Luther in his disagreement with Erasmus: namely that this idea of Willkür is barely intelligible. For, he argues, our capacity for choice does not reside in a normatively neutral space, as able to go the one way as the other on a whim.[23] Thus, if it is not to be mere random arbitrariness, any choice must be guided by what the agent takes to be the good, and which it thus has most reason to do – and if it has gone in the direction of the bad in the thoroughgoing way suggested by Kant, what is bad will now seem to it to be good, which will then make it impossible to turn away from the bad through its own efforts, given the choice it has made. Kant is thus right to see that his only way out of this conundrum is to appeal to 'ought implies can' – but wrong to think that this appeal can succeed, for reasons we have discussed.

Notes

1   Cf. *Relig* 6:19–20, where Kant speaks of the 'recent … heroic opinion' that 'the world steadfastly … forges ahead … from bad to better'.
2   On the one hand, Kant writes: 'We can spare ourselves the formal proof that there must be such a corrupt propensity rooted in the human being, in view of the multitude of woeful examples that the experience of human *deeds* parades before us' (*Relig* 6:32–33); on the other hand, he also suggests an a priori argument is also needed at 6:35, but which he then does not clearly offer in what follows. Further discussion of this issue with references to the literature can be found in Indregard 2020.

3   See for example Luther, *The Freedom of a Christian*, 1955–86: 31:362–3.
4   There is thus a difference between understanding how an agent who has chosen evil over good can come to reverse that choice and how an agent can come to choose to put the moral law ahead of their sensuous nature and hence choose the good in the first place, where Kant suggests that this is less of a mystery, and here no appeal to grace is required: cf. *Conflict of the Faculties* 7:58–9, though Kant suggests that even this remains an object of 'wonder'.
5   For a detailed discussion of the historical complexities of this debate, see Guyer 2018.
6   Kant adopts a similar view in *The Conflict of the Faculties* (7:43–4).
7   See for example: *Relig* 6:42, the reference to Romans 5:12 is found in Luther's German Mass (1955–86: 53:66); *Relig* 6:47, the reference to John 3:5 is discussed extensively in Sermons on St John (1955–86: 22:277–81); and as noted above, the reference to the good/bad tree from Matthew 7:18 at *Relig* 6:44–5 is a common reference point for Luther also. For a more general discussion of Luther's influence on Kant in this text, see Auweele 2013.
8   Cf. Adams 1998: xi note 6: '[Kant] grapples with Luther's central theological concerns (and seems to understand them better) than Leibniz, for example, despite the latter's vast theological erudition and ostensibly more orthodox Lutheranism.'
9   Cf. *Relig* 6:51–52, where Kant makes this the basis of his distinction between '*religion of rogation* (of mere cult)', which he rejects for holding we can be made happy by God without doing anything, or merely asking to be made happy, and '*moral religion*, i.e., the religion of *good life-conduct*', which he endorses: 'According to moral religion, however (and, of all public religions so far known, the Christian alone is of this type), it is a fundamental principle that, to become a better human being, everyone must do as much as in his power to do; and only then, if a human being has not buried his innate talent (Luke 19:12–16), if he has made use of the original predisposition to do the good in order to become a better human being, can he hope that what does not lie in his power will be made good by cooperation from above.'
10 For a pithy exposition of these themes, see *Heidelberg Disputation*, §16 (1955–86: 31:50–1).
11 Cf. *Relig* 6:53: 'For the employment [of the idea of grace] would presuppose a rule concerning what good we ourselves must *do* (with a particular aim [in mind]) in order to achieve something; to expect an effect of grace means, however, the very contrary, namely that the good (the morally good) is not of our doing, but that of another being – that we, therefore, can only *come by* it by *doing nothing*, and this contradicts itself.'
12 There is of course an interesting historical question here, about why Kant chose to ignore these arguments, and felt entitled to do so, where the influence of Pietism on his thinking may play a role, as may fears of censorship: but to investigate this issue is not possible within the bounds of this chapter. For some comments on these issues, see White 1990: 1–3.
13 White 1990: 16–43 goes through various places in Kant's text trying to find hints of Kant's argument for 'ought implies can', while noting all are very brief and do not amount to a significant defence of the principle.
14 Cf. *Groundwork* 4:405, where Kant speaks of the 'commands of duty', and of how 'reason issues its commands unrelentingly'; and 4:413: 'The representation of an objective principle insofar as it is necessitating for a will is called a command (of reason), and the way this command is formulated is called an *imperative*.'
15 Contra divine command readings of Kant, such as Hare 2001: 87–119.

16 Cf. Murdoch 1997: 369, and her famous example of how seeing the beauty of a kestrel can act as a form of involuntary 'unselfing'. For some further discussion of how this relates to Lutheran themes in Løgstrup, who is discussed below, see Stern 2021.
17 Cf. also Luther 1955–86: 33:145-7, 173-4, 289-92. Luther is fully aware that '[r]eason in her saucy, sarcastic way' will feel cheated and dissatisfied by this response, but he insists it has biblical authority (146).
18 *The Conflict of the Faculties* 7:48: '[I]t is only by concepts of *our* reason, insofar as they are pure moral concepts and hence infallible, that we can recognize the divinity of a teaching promulgated to us.'
19 It is an interesting question, which cannot be explored here, whether Luther himself could have also taken this option or is just confined to the approach outlined above, given his other commitments, for example concerning the fall and free choice, and thus how far he could hold us responsible for sin and how far this too is attributable to external forces.
20 For an earlier representative of this view in the Lutheran tradition, see for example the *Heidelberg Catechism*, complied by Zacharius Ursinus in 1563, and his response to question 9: 'Doth not God do injustice to man by requiring of him, in his law, that which he cannot perform?', to which the reply is: 'Not at all: for God made man capable of performing it; but man, by the instigation of the devil, and his own willful disobedience, deprived himself and all his posterity of those divine gifts.' In the exposition on this reply, the text goes on: 'He who requires what is impossible is unjust, unless he first gave the ability to perform what he requires; secondly, unless man covet, and has of his own accord brought this inability upon himself; and, lastly, unless the requirement, which is it not possible for man to comply with, be of such a nature as is calculated to lead him to acknowledge, and deplore his inability. Wherefore if man, by his own fault and free will, cast away this ability with which he was endowed, and brought himself into a state in which he can no longer render full obedience to the divine law, God has not for this reason lost his right to exact the obedience which man in his duty is bound to render him' (Ursinus 2019: 66).
21 Cf. Løgstrup 2020: 127: '[W]hat is demanded is that the demand should not have been necessary'; and Løgstrup 2007: 69, where he contrasts the ethical demand with responding to the sovereign expressions of life (such as love and compassion), which do not involve any such demand: 'The sovereign expression of life is indeed realized, but spontaneously, without being demanded. The demand makes itself felt when the sovereign expression of life fails, but without engendering the latter; the demand demands that it be itself superfluous. The demand is the correlate of sin; the sovereign expression of life is that of freedom.' For further discussion of this issue, see Stern 2019: 94-9.
22 For an experimentally informed study that seems to show this intuition is widely shared, see Chituc et al 2016.
23 Cf. Luther 1955–86: 33:115: 'It is, moreover, a mere dialectical fiction that there is in man a neutral and unqualified willing, nor can those who assert it prove it.'

References

Adams, R. M. (1998), 'Introduction', in Kant 1998: vii–xxxii.
Auweele, D. V. (2013), 'The Lutheran Influence on Kant's Depraved Will', *International Journal for Philosophy of Religion*, 73: 117–35.

Chituc, V., P. Henne, W. Sinnott-Armstrong, and F. De Brigard (2016), 'Blame, Not Ability, Impacts Moral "Ought" Judgments for Impossible Actions: Towards an Empirical Refutation of "Ought" Implies "Can"', *Cognition*, 150: 20–5.

Erasmus, D. (1969), 'On the Freedom of the Will', trans. E. G. Rupp and P. S. Watson in *Luther and Erasmus: Free Will and Salvation*, Philadelphia: Westminster Press.

Grenberg, J. (2005), *Kant and the Ethics of Humility*, Cambridge: Cambridge University Press.

Guyer, P. (2018), 'The Struggle for Freedom: Freedom of Will in Kant and Reinhold', in E. Watkins (ed.), *Kant on Persons and Agency*, 120–37, Cambridge: Cambridge University Press.

Hare, J. E. (2001), *God's Call: Moral Realism, God's Commands and Human Autonomy*, Grand Rapids: Eerdmans.

Indregard, J. J. (2020), 'Every Man Has His Price: Kant's Argument for Universal Radical Evil', *Inquiry*, DOI: 10.1080/0020174X.2020.1724564.

Kant, I. (1998), *Religion within the Boundaries of Mere Reason, and Other Writings*, ed. and trans. A. Wood and G. Di Giovanni, Cambridge: Cambridge University Press.

Luther, M. (1955–86), *Luther's Works* (American edition), ed. H. Lehmann and J. Pelikan, 55 vols, Philadelphia: Fortress Press/St. Louis: Concordia Publishing House.

Løgstrup, K. E. (2007), *Beyond the Ethical Demand*, trans. S. Dew and H. Flegal, Notre Dame: Notre Dame University Press.

Løgstrup, K. E. (2020), *The Ethical Demand*, trans. B. Rabjerg and R. Stern, Oxford: Oxford University Press.

Murdoch, I. (1997), *Existentialists and Mystics*, ed. P. Conradi, Harmondsworth: Penguin.

Stern, R. (2019), *The Radical Demand in Løgstrup's Ethics*, Oxford: Oxford University Press.

Stern, R. (2021), 'Murdoch and K. E. Løgstrup: "*Can* We Make Ourselves Morally Better?"', in M. Hopwood and S. Panizza (eds), *The Murdochian Mind*, 331–44, London: Routledge.

Ursinus, Z. (2019), *The Commentary of Dr. Zacharias Ursinus on the Heidelberg Catechism*, trans. G. W. Willard, reprint edn., Eugene: Wipf and Stock.

White, R. (1990), '"Ought" Implies "Can": Kant and Luther, a Contrast', in G. M. Ross and T. McWalter (eds), *Kant and His Influence*, 1–72, Bristol: Thoemmes.

2

Reinhold on free will and moral obligation: A Kantian response

Jochen Bojanowski

Carl Leonard Reinhold's conception of free will was initially meant as a response to what Reinhold called the 'friends of Kantian philosophy'. He developed this conception in his (untranslated?) 'Eighth Letter' of the second volume of his *Letters on Kantian Philosophy*. According to Reinhold, these so-called 'friends' fundamentally misunderstand the 'spirit' of Kant's writings, even though their interpretation accurately represents their 'letter' (Reinhold 1792: 285 f.). If their literal interpretation of Kant's writings was correct, Kant's theory of free will would entail a contradiction: morally evil actions would not be free. This problem has come to be known as the Reinhold problem. Some also refer to it as the Reinhold-Sidgwick problem because Henry Sidgwick supposedly pointed to the same problem roughly 100 years after Reinhold (Sidgwick 1888). In fact, these problems are similar but not identical (see Guyer 2018: 120 f.). So, for clarity's sake, I will simply speak of the Reinhold problem in what follows. Reinhold's theory of free will should be understood as an attempt to solve this problem without giving up on the core of Kant's moral philosophy.

The stumbling block for Reinhold is what Henry Allison has accurately dubbed Kant's reciprocity thesis: 'A free will and a will under the moral law are one and the same' (GMM, 4:447). According to Reinhold, the literal meaning of this thesis is that an act of volition is free if and only if it is morally good. This reading generates the Reinhold problem, which Reinhold attempts to solve by giving up on the literal meaning. He proposes a definition of the negative and the positive concept of freedom that avoids the contradictory implications. Other Kantians responded to Reinhold's proposal, many of them attempting to preserve the letter of Kant's thesis against Reinhold. Let us call them 'Kantians in letter' to distinguish them from Reinhold, who is merely a 'Kantian in spirit' on the topic of free will. Kantians in letter embrace Reinhold's criticism. In their view, however, Reinhold's theory of freedom is compatible both with Kant's spirit *and* with his letter.

According to the standard story, the reciprocity thesis merely implies that a free act of volition is always normatively bound by the moral law. Moreover, with his so-called incorporation thesis and his distinction between *Wille* and *Willkür*, Kant can account for what Reinhold wants him to account for: evil actions that are an act of free choice. I believe that this attempt to reconcile Kant with Reinhold comes at a high price. The

Kantians in Spirit, Reinhold, and the Kantians in letter must ultimately give up on some of the central tenets of Kant's moral philosophy. If freedom essentially consists in our 'capacity of self-determination for or against the practical law through choice' (Reinhold 1792: 272), how can freedom be of inner and unconditional value (Kant, MS 6:434)? If freedom essentially consists in our capacity to choose for or against the moral law, how can it be the 'ratio essendi' of the moral law (Kant CPrR, 5:4)? Finally, if freedom is defined in terms of choosing for or against the moral law, how does 'transcendental freedom' only get its 'objective reality' through the moral law (CPrR, 5:3 f.)? I don't think that Reinhold can satisfactorily answer any of these questions, and to the extent that Kantians in letter are committed to Reinhold's solution, they will fail to answer these questions as well. Moreover, what is perhaps most worrisome is the inability of both Kantians in letter and Kantians in spirit to deliver a unified theory of free will that can explain why free will essentially consists of autonomy. Reinhold's definition of freedom ultimately undermines Kant's conception of autonomy. I believe that this merits the claim that Reinhold's theory of free will is neither Kantian in letter nor Kantian in spirit. To the extent that Kantians agree with Reinhold's definition of freedom, they are Reinholdians, not Kantians.

This chapter will develop and defend a capacity reading of free will (Paton 1947; Potter 1974; Wood 1984; Engstrom 2002; Bojanowski 2006; Benson 2010). I believe that the Reinhold problem is rooted in the ambiguity of the terms 'Wille' and 'Willkür'. This ambiguity also affects the notions of 'autonomy' and 'heteronomy'. These notions can refer to particular acts or to capacities. I will call this the 'capacity–act ambiguity'. Disambiguating the 'capacity–act ambiguity' will also help us to disambiguate the reciprocity thesis and to dissolve the Reinhold problem. According to my reading, 'autonomy' and 'heteronomy' are not two ways of exercising what Reinhold believes to be our essentially two-way capacity of volition. Kant's claim is not that we *act* heteronomously when we act immorally. 'Heteronomy' is a term that describes the causality of the volitional capacity of non-human animals. The human *capacity* of volition as a capacity for moral agency, by contrast, never loses its autonomy. This capacity, the capacity for rational volition, self-consciously recognizes the normative priority of moral commands over desires that are contrary to it. Only in virtue of our autonomous capacity can we be said to be governed by categorical imperatives, and only in virtue of this capacity do deviant exercises of our volition count as deficient. Even when this capacity is exercised in a deficient way, however, this outcome was in no way causally determined.

This chapter is divided into four parts. I will first develop Reinhold's revisionary theory of free will, before turning to the attempts by the Kantians in letter to accommodate Reinhold's revision. I will show why these attempts cannot explain why Kant defines freedom as the 'capacity of pure reason to be by itself practical' and why they are thus unable to hold on to the conception of an autonomous capacity of volition in Kant's sense. In the third section, I will propose the capacity account of rational volition, which is supposed to preserve, against Reinhold, Kant's reciprocity thesis, his conception of autonomy and, consequently, his definition of free will. Finally, I will respond to Reinhold's objection against a corollary of the capacity reading: the incapacity thesis. Reinhold and contemporary Reinholdians believe this objection to be detrimental to the capacity account. Defending the capacity account against this objection will help us to better grasp the connection between free will and rational volition.

1. Reinhold's definitions of free will

Reinhold's criticism in his 'Eighth Letter' is officially directed at the 'friends of Kantian philosophy'. These 'friends' are his own colleague in Jena, Johann August Heinrich Ulrich, and Ulrich's student, Erhard Schmid. In his book *Eleutheriology, or on Freedom and Necessity*, Ulrich rejects Kant's conception of freedom as the autonomy of pure practical reason. The identification of freedom of the will and the effectiveness of pure practical reason implies *determinism*, not freedom (Kant-Correspondence, 339, 19.01.1788). Ulrich's student, Erhard Schmid, author of the *Dictionary for an Easier Use of the Kantian Writings* and another friend of Kantian philosophy, comes to the same conclusion. In contrast to Ulrich, however, this conclusion leads him to assert an 'intelligible fatalism' (Schmid 1788: 250). Both Ulrich and Schmid agree that Kant's theory of freedom implies that freedom of the will is impossible. Reinhold's own conception of freedom should be understood as an attempt to avoid these deterministic or fatalistic implications. Although Reinhold doesn't mention Ulrich's and Schmid's names explicitly, he leaves no doubt about the targets of his criticism.

Reinhold's intention in the 'Eighth Letter' is to work out a theory of freedom that saves Kant's theory from absurdity. He attempts to preserve the 'spirit' of that theory by sacrificing the 'letter' (Reinhold 1792: 263 f.). His argument proceeds as follows. He first considers two definitions: a definition of the will in general and a definition of the morally good or pure will. In each case, he points to the property that makes the will free. Both properties, Reinhold argues, articulate a necessary but not sufficient condition of freedom of the will. He then turns to his own alternative conception of free will. Let us take a closer look at both Reinhold's criticism and his alternative. Reinhold's definition of the 'will in general' is as follows:

> WG: [A will in general is] the capacity of the person to determine himself to the realization or non-realization of the commands of the selfish drive.
>
> (Reinhold 1792: 264)

The selfish drive (SD) is understood as a 'drive for pleasure'. According to Reinhold, the flaw in this position is that it mistakes a 'singular mark of freedom' for the whole of freedom. We can call this the hedonic negative concept of free will (HNF).

> HNF: A will is free only if the person is 'independent of the commands [of the selfish drive]'
>
> (ibid.).

This singular mark is only necessary but not sufficient for free will, for if we abstract merely from the commands of the selfish drive, what remains are the commands of 'rational desire' (vernünftiges Begehren) or, as Reinhold also calls it, the 'unselfish drive' (USD):

> USD: An unselfish drive is a 'drive for pleasure guided by the power of reason (Denkkraft)'
>
> (Reinhold 1792: 307)

According to this definition, the will is still dependent on its drive for pleasure. The main difference between SD and USD is merely that between 'immediate' and 'mediate' determination (Reinhold 1792: 265). Moreover, if freedom of the will is merely understood in the negative sense of HNF, the will is still determined by USD in the absence of the selfish drive. In the absence of the selfish drive, an 'act of will is nothing but the expression of a drive for pleasure guided by the power of reason' (Reinhold 1792: 265). Again, Reinhold's main point is that HNFW is only a necessary but not a sufficient condition for free will.

Turning now to Reinhold's definition of the pure or moral will:

> PW: [A pure will is] the capacity of the person to determine himself to the realization or non-realization of the commands of the selfish drive according to the commands of the unselfish drive (or the practical law).
>
> (Reinhold 1792: 266 f.)

We can now articulate what we might call a deontic negative concept of free will:

> DNF: A will is free only if the practical law (reason) can determine the will 'absolutely independently […] of pleasure and pain.'
>
> (Reinhold 1792: 267)

DNF is also merely a necessary condition for freedom of the will. It is crucial not to equate possible determination with actual determination or the will's realization of a given demand in action with necessity. Reinhold explicitly considers the activity of reason as a solely legislative function here: '[The] free act of practical reason, – which only gives the law, – [is not to be confused] with the act of the will' (ibid.). This confusion, according to Reinhold, is the source of the problem that would later be named after him, for if the will were free if and only if it acted from the moral law, the impure or immoral will would not be free and hence would not be immoral or evil (Reinhold 1792: 270).

Reinhold's solution to this problem is simple: He distinguishes between the 'declaration' (*Aufstellung*) of the law through practical reason and its 'execution' (*Ausführung*) through the will. Freedom only pertains to the will, not to practical reasoning, and the 'autonomy' of the will consists in its capacity of 'self-determination […] for this law to which [the will] binds itself' (Reinhold 1792: 271). With this distinction in tow, Reinhold can now put forward his own negative and positive definitions of free will.

> RNF: A will is negatively free if and only if the person determines herself 'independently of:
> (i) the coercion (Zwang) of instinct, [...]
> (ii) the necessitation of our involuntary desire modified by reason [...], and
> (iii) the necessitation of practical reason itself'.
> (Reinhold 1792: 272)

Reinhold's positive definition then proceeds as follows:

> RPF: A will is positively free if and only if the person has the 'capacity of self-determination for or against the practical law through choice' (*Willkür*)
> (ibid.).

Every reader of Kant familiar with the introduction to the *Metaphysics of Morals* will have already noticed a significant connection between Reinhold's definition and a well-known passage from the introduction. In this passage, Kant writes:

> Free will cannot be defined, as some have attempted to do, as a capacity for choice for or against the law.
> (Kant, MS 6:226)

Let's call this the 'Reinhold Passage', for there are at least three points of connection between this passage and Reinhold's 'Eighth Letter'. Firstly, Reinhold's letter is an attempt to provide an accurate *definition* of free will. The Reinhold Passage is a response to that attempt. The Reinhold problem is only properly understood if it is viewed as a quest for a consistent definition of 'free will'. Secondly, Reinhold's positive definition of free will (RPF) is precisely the definition that Kant considers in the Reinhold Passage. Kant rejects this definition because it casts our pure practical capacity in 'the wrong light' (Kant, MS 6:227). Still, he also introduces his own positive and negative definitions of freedom (Kant, MS 6:213 f.). Both of Kant's alternative definitions show that Kant was unconvinced by Reinhold's criticism. This makes it all the more compelling to read this passage as Kant's response to Reinhold. Kant addresses this same problem and proposes alternative negative and positive definitions of free will. Finally, Reinhold's distinction between the lawgiving function of practical reason, and the executive function of the will comes at least very close to Kant's distinction between 'Wille' and 'Willkür' (Kant, MM 6:226). The difference seems to be that Reinhold is unwilling to locate the lawgiving function within the will. The introduction to MM is the first time Kant introduces the distinction between 'Wille' and 'Willkür' as a sharp terminological distinction. Reinhold's 'Eighth Letter' could very well be the influential factor here.

We do not know whether Kant in fact read Reinhold's 'Eighth Letter'. We know that he confirmed, in a short personal letter to Reinhold, the arrival of the second volume of Reinhold's book. With that said, Kant did not comment on the content of Reinhold's book at all in this personal letter (Correspondence XI, 399 (12/21/1792)). We also know that Reinhold explicitly expressed a strong interest in Kant's verdict on the seventh and eighth letters. If Reinhold was convinced he'd found a devastating criticism, he was respectful enough to hide it. He writes that he merely hopes for 'a hint [...] dropped down in a few lines', which could 'instruct him about the protonpseudos' or confirm that he is indeed 'on the right track' (Kant, Correspondence 9:410 (01/21/1793)). We have no evidence that Kant ever sent a response to this request, but we do have a letter from Kant dated more than a year later in which he apologizes in a rather long-winded way to Reinhold for not engaging with the philosophical substance of his writings (Kant, Correspondence 9:494 (03/04/1794)). Considering the three connecting points of the Reinhold Passage, however, it seems likely that Kant ultimately attempted to give Reinhold the 'hint' he had asked for in the introduction to the *Metaphysics of Morals*. This hint, however, was an attempt to instruct Reinhold about the 'protonpseudos' of his theory, as Reinhold put it in his letter to Kant. It was not the confirmation or the admission that Reinhold had likely hoped for. Before we turn to a close analysis of Kant's argument against Reinhold's NF and PF, however, let us first examine what I consider to be the standard response in the Kant literature.

2. Embracing Reinhold's theory of free will

Reinhold's objection has not remained unanswered. Defenders of Kant's theory usually point to what Henry Allison has called the 'incorporation thesis' (Allison 1990):

> [T]he freedom of choice is of the very peculiar quality that it cannot be determined to action through any inner spring [Triebfeder] *except so far as the human being has incorporated it into its maxim* […]; in this way alone can an inner spring, whatever it may be, coexist with the absolute spontaneity of the capacity of choice [Willkür] (freedom).
>
> (Kant, Rel., 6:23 f.)

The concessive clause emphasized by Kant is decisive here: The inner spring does not directly determine our action as a cause of nature. The inner spring instead determines our action only if we have 'incorporated' it into our maxim, hence the term 'incorporation thesis'. Morally evil actions are attributable to us, and they are imputable to us only because we freely chose a maxim contrary to the moral law. The same holds for morally good actions: It is not the case that pure reason as a 'rational drive' directly determines our actions; instead, the morally good action is also only attributable to us because we have freely opted to act on a morally good maxim. With the incorporation thesis, so the argument goes, Kant solved the Reinhold problem by integrating into his theory of free will the missing link to decision-making.

With this solution to the Reinhold problem, however, a new, hermeneutical problem arises: How is the freedom of choice in Kant's incorporation thesis in the *Religion* compatible with his conception of autonomy from the *Groundwork* and the second *Critique*? The Reinhold problem now seems to be a Reinhold/Kant-of-the-*Religion* problem, for in the *Groundwork* and the second *Critique*, Kant identified freedom with autonomy (Kant, GMM, 4:447; CPrR, 5:29). An autonomous will is a will the maxim of which is guided by the universal law and not by self-love. Even if the incorporation thesis permits Kant to declare acts of self-love as free, it remains unclear how this claim is compatible with his earlier claim, his so-called reciprocity thesis:

RT: 'A free will and a will under the moral law are one and the same.'
(Kant, GMM, 4:447)

Reinhold takes the reciprocity thesis to imply that a will is free if and only if it is morally good. So, even if the incorporation thesis can solve the Reinhold problem, another problem is lurking: How is this solution compatible with Kant's reciprocity thesis? Call this the hermeneutical problem. Kantians in letter typically have a two-step response to it: They first point out that RT only states that a free will is 'under' moral laws, not that it necessarily acts from them. This interpretation leaves room for the possibility that a free will is determined by something other than the moral law. In a second step, they appeal to a distinction that Kant first introduced even after he wrote the *Religion*, in the introduction to the *Metaphysics of Morals* of 1797: the distinction between *Wille* and *Willkür*. This distinction points to an internal differentiation within our capacity of volition:

The laws proceed from the will; from the faculty of choice (*Willkür*) the maxims.
(Kant, MM 6:226)

This distinction is supposed to explain how an autonomous will can be determined by principles that are not in line with the moral law. Kantians in letter now believe they can both solve the Reinhold problem *and* hold on to Kant's conception of autonomy, which would then also solve the hermeneutical problem. While the will as the legislative function only prescribes the law, the faculty of choice as the executive function can still respond to the law in one way or the other. Morally good and evil actions are both based on the free choice of a particular maxim through *Willkür*. This act is an expression not of autonomy but of absolute spontaneity. On the other hand, autonomy pertains to the legislative function, i.e., the will (Carnois 1987; Allison 1990; Willaschek 1992; Hudson 1994; Beck ³1995). The will in general thus has two functions: a legislative and an executive one. The executive function takes care of the Reinhold objection; the legislative function preserves Kant's idea of autonomy.

Introducing the distinction between *Wille* and *Willkür* as a solution to the Reinhold problem turns out to be a Pyrrhic victory, however, for Kant explicitly claims in MM that the will in its legislative function cannot correctly be called free:

[T]he will [...] can neither be called free nor unfree, because it does not refer to actions, but directly to the legislation for the maxim of actions.
(Kant, MM 6:226)

Suppose autonomy merely pertains to the will in its legislative function and that the legislative function cannot be called free. How could this possibly be compatible with what seems to be at the core of Kant's theory of free will, namely the claim that a free will and an autonomous will are 'one and the same'? According to this interpretation, only the spontaneity of the faculty of choice seems to qualify as free. Thus the hermeneutical problem remains unsolved.

There is a well-known move in Kant scholarship for when Kant's published writings don't match one's desired interpretation. One can move away from Kant's published work and turn to his unpublished texts, i.e., his 'reflections', his 'preparatory work' and the lecture notes of his students. Let us call this move 'alternative philology'. Some interpreters who push the *Wille–Willkür* distinction use alternative philology to make their case, finding a source in Kant's preparatory work, his '*Vorarbeiten*', to the *Metaphysics of Morals*. This passage confirms their response to the Reinhold objection:

> Willkür is, therefore, free to do or not to do what the law commands. But the will is free in a different way because it is lawgiving not obedient.
>
> (Kant, MS-Vorarbeiten, 23:249)

Lewis White Beck claims that this 'different way' of conceiving of freedom refers to autonomy as the positive concept of freedom. Autonomy does not consist in the ability to 'start a new causal series'. Instead, it signifies the original 'genesis of the law through the subject'. Accordingly, positive freedom consists in nothing more than the original genesis of the moral law. By contrast, freedom of choice as negative freedom is the causal ability to 'start a new causal series' in the world (Beck ³1995: 172Fn10, 186). Let me make this distinction even more explicit by distinguishing between Beck's positive sense of freedom (BPF) and his negative sense (BNF):

> BPF: The will is free in the positive sense iff it generates the moral law.

> BNF: The faculty of choice is free in the negative sense iff it has the capacity to initiate a causal series.

It is unclear in what sense of 'negative' the capacity to initiate a causal series is negative, but let's leave this aside here. The point is that alternative philology yields two concepts of freedom that Kant failed to make explicit in his published writings. He even equivocated between *Wille* and *Willkür* in his earlier work (Beck 1995: 169). However, with the incorporation thesis in the *Religion*, the distinction between *Wille* and *Willkür* in the *Metaphysics of Morals*, and the distinction between positive and negative freedom from the *Vorarbeiten*, Kant provided the key to resolving the Reinhold objection, thus saving his theory from the inconsistency charge. The false belief that Kant fully identified morally good actions with free actions is based on the false belief that there is only one function of the faculty of volition and only one kind of freedom (Beck 1995: 193).

This response to the Reinhold objection is revealing. On the one hand, it shows how little this supposedly 'Kantian' solution differs from Reinhold's own. On the other hand, it also reveals that this solution is even further removed from Kant's published work than Reinhold's solution. Reinhold believed that Kant confused the self-activity of reason with free will. Reinhold resolved this confusion by distinguishing between free will on the one hand and the self-activity of reason on the other (Reinhold 1792: 281). In contrast to alternative philology, Reinhold did not claim that the 'self-activity of reason' ought to be signified with the term 'freedom'.

It is well known that Kant's unpublished writings contain many claims that are incompatible with his published work. Elsewhere, I outline a philological procedure for how to handle these inconsistencies and what use we should make of Kant's unpublished work (Bojanowski 2006). Suffice it to say, Reinhold's response to the Reinhold objection is closer to Kant's response than that of the alternative philologists who defend 'Kant'. Kant and Reinhold agree that the mere act of legislation, or the 'self-activity of reason', is not to be called free. But they disagree as to how free will ought to be defined. This definitional issue is at the centre of Reinhold's criticism. So Kant is not shifting the topic to the definitional problem in the Reinhold Passage; he is simply responding to Reinhold's request.

Before we take up their disagreement in the next section, let's take a closer look at their agreement. Reinhold's and Kant's denial that the will as the legislative function is free gives rise to a hermeneutical problem: If spontaneity is the feature that distinguishes the executive function (free *Willkür*) from the legislative function (*Wille*), and if the legislative function, by contrast, cannot be free, why does Kant then characterize free will as autonomy, and autonomy as freedom (Kant, GMM, 4:447)? With this account of the *Wille–Willkür* distinction, it seems that we must reject Kant's reciprocity thesis from the *Groundwork* and the second *Critique*. Even alternative philology does not help us much here, for even if one accepts the claim from the *Vorarbeiten* that the will is free 'in a different way', i.e., 'autonomous', it remains unclear how the will as the legislative function could be a law to *itself*. The will generates the law, but it cannot obey or disobey it. So how could it be a law to itself?

Henry Allison's unified interpretation of the *Wille–Willkür* distinction can help us to make a decisive step forward. His unitary account also distinguishes between the spontaneity of our faculty of choice and the autonomy of the will. However, there are two senses of 'will' that need to be kept distinct. If *Wille* and *Willkür* are two aspects of one and the same faculty of volition, this faculty of volition in general can also be called 'will' or 'will in general'. We can then distinguish between 'will' in the narrow sense, i.e., the legislative function, and 'will' in the broad sense, i.e., the will as the faculty of volition in general. This broader sense includes both the legislative and the executive function (Allison 1990: 130 f.). Distinguishing between a narrow and a broad sense of 'will' is crucial because only the will in the broad sense can be legitimately called autonomous. Only if the will contains both the legislative and the executive function can it be a law to *itself* (Allison 1990: 131; see Kant, GMM, 4:447).

I believe that Allison's unitary account is a decisive move in the right direction. It can help us to arrive at an adequate understanding of Kant's use of 'autonomy'. With 'autonomy', Kant does not mean the mere act of lawgiving. Instead, 'autonomy' refers to our volitional capacity in general, which contains both functions, the legislative and the executive. However, even Allison unnecessarily falls back into the Reinholdian line, for he also distinguishes between the spontaneity of our faculty of choice and the autonomy of the will. Without availing himself of alternative philology, Allison flat-out asserts that Kant's positive concept of freedom as 'the capacity of pure reason to be by itself practical' fails because it entails the identification of free and morally good actions. Kant mistakenly identifies autonomy and positive freedom (Allison 1990: 132). Instead, Kant should have defined the positive concept of freedom in the following way. Call this Allison's positive concept of freedom (APF):

> APF: [T]he positive concept of Willkür is its capacity to act on the basis of the dictates of pure reason or, equivalently, pure Wille.
>
> (ibid.)

This definition only entails that the faculty of choice has the ability to select universalizable maxims. It leaves room for the free selection of immoral maxims. According to Allison, the will in general is only autonomous if the faculty of choice does in fact select maxims that are universalizable. Autonomy becomes a success term for a capacity of volition that is able to act from universalizable maxims. In the next section, we will see why this act reading of autonomy is the main flaw of Allison's argument. Allison's solution to the Reinhold problem crucially depends on the claim that it is the spontaneity of the faculty of choice that decides whether pure reason becomes practical or not (Allison 1990: 133; see also Allison 1996d). Again, the unitary account is a step in the right direction. However, Allison openly admits that his interpretation is ultimately incompatible with Kant's official definition of freedom in the *Metaphysics of Morals*. He also fails to explain why Kant takes acting from the moral law to be the distinguishing feature of a free capacity of volition.

Moreover, Kant leaves no doubt that it is his positive concept of freedom, i.e., autonomy, that first gives the idea of 'transcendental freedom', i.e., absolute spontaneity, its 'objective reality' (Kant, CPrR, 5:3 f.). So both alternative philology and Allison's unitary account are incompatible with Kant's text. Even if Allison's response satisfactorily responds to the Reinhold objection, the hermeneutical problem remains. This problem presents itself to Allison and alternative philology in the following way: Why does autonomy give transcendental freedom or absolute spontaneity 'objective reality' if even heteronomous acts are acts of transcendental freedom? But the problem only presents itself to them in this way because it is based on an act reading of autonomy that I will reject in the next and the final section. Alternative philology and Allison are unwilling to make autonomy the essential definitional mark of the free will. Therefore, Allison's Kant's theory of freedom is, with regard to this crucial aspect, not Kant's theory of freedom but Reinhold's.

3. Resisting Reinhold's theory of free will

In this section, I will show that the Reinhold objection is rooted in the ambiguity of the terms *Wille* and *Willkür*. This ambiguity also spreads to the notions of 'autonomy' and 'heteronomy'. The terms *Wille* and *Willkür* can both be understood as acts or capacities. Kant's phrase in the reciprocity thesis 'a will under moral laws' can mean 'a capacity of volition under moral laws' or 'an act of volition under moral laws'. The same holds for the term *Willkür*. Call this the 'capacity–act ambiguity'. The English translation of the Cambridge edition renders *Willkür* in the crucial passage consistently as 'choice', not as 'faculty' or 'capacity of choice' (Kant, MM, 6:213 f.). This translation is misleading. It suggests, as we will see, the Reinhold problem.

The capacity reading I am proposing here is not new (it goes back at least to Paton 1947), but its implications have not been fully worked out. Part of the novelty of my response to Reinhold consists in its extension of the capacity reading to Kant's conception of autonomy. Autonomy and heteronomy are not two ways of exercising what Reinhold believes to be our essentially two-way capacity of volition. Kant's claim is not that we *act* heteronomously when we act immorally. Kant's claim is instead that the human *capacity* of volition is autonomous. As a capacity for moral agency, it never loses this autonomy. Only in virtue of our autonomous capacity are we governed by categorical imperatives. Animals, by contrast, have a different kind of capacity of volition. They have a capacity of choice, but they lack the capacity to choose and to act from self-imposed laws. This is what makes their capacity of volition merely heteronomous. The distinction between 'autonomy' and 'heteronomy' is not supposed to cash out two kinds of human acts but two different types of capacities of volition. My central claim is that Reinhold and the Reinholdians in Kantian clothing have been misled by an act reading of 'will' and 'autonomy'. Even proponents of the capacity reading fall prey to the act interpretation of autonomy (Wood 1984: 81). I will attempt to develop a non-concessive response to Reinhold by explaining how evil actions are possible without giving up on Kant's positive concept of freedom. Moreover, I will show why Reinhold's definition of freedom leads him into a dilemma: He must give up either categorical obligation or his voluntarist definition of freedom.

This section is divided into three parts. First, I will analyse Kant's definitions that do not run into the Reinhold trap and are compatible with his reciprocity thesis. I will then need to explain why my response does not fall prey to the standard objections. Finally, I will show why Reinhold, with his definition of freedom, runs into what I call the obligation problem.

In the introduction to the *Metaphysics of Morals*, Kant draws his distinction between a negative and a positive concept of freedom (KNF, PNF):

KNF: x is free in the negative sense iff x is "independent from the determination of sensuous impulses."

KPF: x is free in the positive sense iff x's "pure reason has the capacity to be by itself practical"

(MS, VI 213 f.).

Let me briefly explain why neither definition excludes the possibility of moral evil actions. Let me begin with KNF. If we were determined by sensuous impulses such that the action did not depend on our choice, the action would not be free. This captures conditions (i) and (ii) of RNF. What about condition (iii), i.e., '[t]he independence of the necessitation of practical reason itself'? Reinhold's description of the 'necessitation of practical reason itself' as an 'unselfish *drive*' is misleading. The word 'drive' implies that the necessitation, just like the determination of the selfish drive, is one of causal necessity. Reinhold is even more explicit: Free will cannot be saved by liberating the will from the 'slavery of instinct' and instead making it a 'slave of the force of reason (Denkkraft)' (Reinhold 1792: 294). However, the necessitation of practical reason is one of obligation, not causal necessity. This is even true of merely instrumentalist accounts of practical reason. 'Obligation' already implies that it is possible to choose otherwise. Reinhold's condition (iii) does not belong to the definiens of 'free will' because necessitation through reason (imperatives) does not exclude but rather entails free will (see, CPR, GMM).

The real touchstone of Kant's conception of free will is his positive definition. The capacity reading of KPF leaves it open whether reason will become practical or not (Paton 1947; Potter 1974). The realization of pure practical reason is a possibility, not a causal necessity. The problem for Kant's account seems to be that only if pure reason *is* practical (i.e., causally efficacious) are our actions also autonomous. And only if pure reason is practical are our actions also morally good. So again, autonomous and morally good actions seem to be the same. Conversely, if it is not the case that pure reason is practical, then our actions are not morally good and thus not autonomous. If only autonomous actions are free, and if heteronomous actions are causally determined such that we could not have chosen otherwise, then the Reinhold trap snares us yet again. This move, however, is based on the act reading of 'will', and it is precisely this move that the capacity reading blocks.

Let us consider the origin of the act reading. It begins with a misrepresentation of the reciprocity thesis and then exploits the capacity–act ambiguity of 'will' in its criticism:

(a) RT: A free will and a will under the moral law are one and the same.
(b) RT*: A free will is free iff it is morally good.
(c) RT**: A free will is free iff it wants what is morally good.
(d) RT**: A free act of volition is free iff it wants what is morally good.
(e) RT****: Actions are free iff they are morally good.

Now compare R**** with the capacity reading of RT:

> CRORT: A capacity of volition is free, iff it has the capacity to act from the representation of the moral law.

CRORT does not entail that the free capacity of volition loses its freedom if it doesn't act from the moral law. It leaves room for the possibility of choosing against the moral law. Reinhold wants to make this possibility of choosing independently of the necessitation of both nature and reason the definitional mark of a free capacity of volition. Why does Kant believe that this is mistaken, and why does he instead define free will in terms of pure reason's ability to be practical? Kant's argument against Reinhold's definition of freedom in terms of an undetermined choice is that it portrays free will 'in a false light' (Kant, MS 6:227). As we will see in a moment, one of the advantages of the proposed capacity reading is that it can make good sense of this argument.

Our will is a capacity of volition guided by reason. The main claim of Kant's moral philosophy is that the moral law is the constitutive and a priori principle of this capacity. It demands that the particular principles of our volition (maxims) be universalizable. Not every instance of the exercise of our capacity of volition is a full realization of this capacity. But every instance of the realization is informed by or performed with our consciousness of the moral law. Otherwise, acts that are contrary to the law could not be called 'evil'. Reinhold does not want to reject the categorical imperative as a principle of practical reason. What he does question, however, is that the moral law is constitutive of *willing*. Instead, he believes that there are two 'drives': the selfish drive and the unselfish drive. And both of these drives are somehow external to our will. Only by denying or affirming the content of the selfish or the unselfish drive do we allow them to determine our will.

In choosing between the two, we are free because neither of the two necessitates us. Let us remember that 'necessitate' is ambiguous here. It can mean 'causal necessitation' or 'obligation'. Rational determination is not causal determination. This explains why KNF does not contain the absence of *rational* necessitation but is only defined in terms of 'independence from being determined by sensible impulse'. The obligatory force of reason, i.e., 'necessitation' as 'obligation', is no threat to but rather entails free will. And our consciousness of moral obligation does not exclude but is a necessary condition for our actions' counting as evil.

Suppose we define the freedom of our capacity of volition, as Reinhold does, as the capacity to choose for or against the 'unselfish' drive. In that case, we deny that the moral law has normative authority for this capacity. We deny that the moral law is an expression of our self-consciousness as practical cognizers (Kant, CPrR 5:29). And we deny that the 'moral ought is a will from our own perspective as rational beings' (Kant, GMM 4:455). Reinhold's picture of two competing drives suggests that both drives have a claim on us that we recognize as equally valid. In making a moral judgment, however, we know the universalizable maxim to be of unlimited goodness. We also know that all of our competing desires that are not compatible with what is universalizable are at best of limited goodness. So, as beings who have a capacity of rational volition (will), we believe that the moral law has authority over our particular desires and interests. To say that the capacity consists in the ability to choose for or against the moral law is, as Kant says, to put it 'in a false light' because the goal of this capacity is to act from an idea of pure reason, i.e., the idea of universalizability.

Reinhold rejects Kant's distinction between *Wille* and *Willkür* (Reinhold, Vermischte Schriften 366). He believes that the moral law has its origin in reason and is thus not part of the will. The will, by contrast, is confined to the activity of maxim selection. These maxims are chosen in light of the commands of reason. But in willing, we decide whether we want to make the commands of reason the determining ground of our will (Reinhold, Vermischte Schriften 368). In effect, Reinhold excludes the legislative function from our capacity of volition.

This move is philosophically problematic and leads to the obligation problem: If the moral law is external to the capacity of volition, how can it get a grip on the agent? If the moral law is merely a law of reason to which we can position ourselves qua choice approvingly or disapprovingly, then only through our choice does the moral law become an object of our volition. However, if the moral law only becomes an object of our volition through choice, it is not good independently of that choice, and it would still be a legitimate question why we ought to do what the moral law commands us to do (see Zöller 2005). Since, on Reinhold's account, the moral law is outside of our capacity of volition, our faculty of choice would need to find some desire that hooks on to what is morally right. This would undermine categorical obligation (see Ameriks 2012: 84), for categorical obligation obliges us to do *x* regardless of our given desires. Categorical obligation is only possible if the moral law is not merely a cognitive representation of reason, as Reinhold has it. Categorical obligation also requires consciousness of that law's efficacy because it is the law. The practicality of reason does not merely consist in prescribing imperatives that presuppose given desires. In this case, reason would only be the administrator of our desires but not *by itself* practical (Kant, GMM 4:441). For reason to be 'by itself practical', the law has to be an 'inner spring', a *Triebfeder*, of our action.

Reinhold faces the following dilemma: Either his talk of an 'unselfish drive' implies that it is already an inner spring (*Triebfeder*) of our capacity of volition (Breazeale 2012: 107 f.), or, if it is only through choice that the moral law becomes a *Triebfeder*, reason is not practical but, as Hume has it, 'inert' (Hume, T 2.3.3.4). For Kant, the moral law has an immediate 'humiliating' and 'elevating' effect on us (CPrR 5:79-81). This feeling is the psychological side of moral cognition, and it precedes any particular choice of maxims. Kant calls this feeling 'respect for the moral law' (ibid.). It is humiliating because it strikes down claims from within us that are at best of limited goodness. It is elevating insofar as we realize that we can act independently of our particular desires and from what we ourselves judge to be of unlimited goodness. In short: Placing practical cognition outside of our faculty of volition, as Reinhold has it, deprives this cognition of its practicality.

If our capacity of volition is practical reason, as Kant claims (Kant, GMM 4:412), it would be misleading to define the freedom of this capacity as the capacity to choose between good and evil. It is this capacity that considers reason to be normative for inclinations. And it is this capacity that considers moral reasons to be normatively binding. In choosing what is morally good, the capacity does what it 'deep down' or 'a priori' wants to do. That our capacity of volition can be weak willed and act against its better judgment does not mean that it loses the capacity to do what it believes to be good all things considered, nor does it mean, pace Reinhold, that it is no longer accountable.

4. Response to critics

In this final section, I will defend the capacity response to Reinhold against recent critiques. What I call the capacity reading Courtney Fugate calls the 'current' or the 'popular' reading (Fugate 2015: 352, 359). As proponents of this reading, Fugate references Engstrom (2002), Potter (1974) and Wood (1984). It is puzzling why three not-so-recent articles merit the term 'current' or 'popular'. Admittedly, both 'current' and 'popular' are relative terms, but Fugate's Reinholdian reading is not only more popular but also more recent. Suffice it to say that none of the four more recent commentaries on the *Groundwork* uses the capacity reading (Allison 2011; Schönecker and Wood 2015; Timmermann (2007); Horn, Mieth and Scarano 2007). Wood's article can hardly be read as an attempt to *develop* the capacity reading. It is merely a sketch of a response to the Reinhold objection. The article's main target is the compatibilism debate about free will. Allison still defends Kant's reciprocity thesis against Reinhold by pursuing the argument based on the *Wille-Willkür* distinction and the incorporation thesis (Allison 2011: 296–300). I considered that argument in § 2, where I showed why this response is Reinholdian in spirit and fails to explain Kant's resistance to Reinhold's proposal. Timmermann acknowledges the seriousness of the Reinhold objection and believes it to be on target (Timmermann 2007: 164–7). Schönecker and Wood believe that the reciprocity thesis can only be rescued if one pursues one of the following two options: One can either read 'under the moral law' as merely expressing obligation, in which case acting against the moral law is still possible or, alternatively, 'will' can be read as referring not to the human will but to the holy will, which cannot possibly be evil. Hence the Reinhold objection is mute. This latter line is also pursued by Mieth (Horn, Mieth and Scarano 2007: 272 f.).

All four recent commentaries take the Reinhold objection seriously. Even where they seemingly agree with Kant, they do not raise the capacity reading, which Fugate misleadingly dubs the 'recent' or 'popular' reading, as a response. This is a minor point, however. Fugate pays more attention to the capacity reading than these commentaries do. As a result, he is also one of the few who have launched a philosophically powerful objection against the capacity reading. I will only respond to the objection that is relevant to the capacity reading as presented here, for it can help us to develop this reading further. Following Reinhold, Fugate criticizes Kant's incapacity thesis (IT) in the Reinhold Passage and turns it into his fundamental objection:

IT: Only freedom with regard to inner legislation of reason is really a capacity [*Vermögen*]; the possibility of deviating from it is a lack of a capacity [*Unvermögen*]. How, then, can this possibility be used to define freedom?

(Kant, MM 6: 226)

Earlier, we saw how Kant defines the positive concept of freedom (KPF) as the 'capacity of pure reason to be by itself practical' (Kant, MM 6:213 f.). With IT, Kant holds that 'deviating from legislative reason' is, by contrast, 'a lack of that capacity [*Unvermögen*]'. Against this claim, Fugate objects that if the 'lack of the exercise of this [capacity]' is to be understood as a 'free withholding of the [capacity] of freedom', then the so-called 'free withholding cannot be an exercise of that [capacity]' (Fugate 2015: 362). And if this withholding is not an exercise of this capacity (free will), then it cannot, after all, be free, and thus it cannot be evil. Fugate arrives at the same conclusion Reinhold had reached in his response to IT: '[T]he capacity to act *immorally* is not only an incapacity but also impossible' (Reinhold, Vermischte Schriften II, 399; Fugate 2015: 362). Moreover, Fugate presents additional, philological evidence for Kant's use of 'incapacity' in other contexts where it also means 'impossibility'. So, with IT, Kant seems to fall, yet again, back into the Reinhold trap.

Here is a reading of IT that gets Kant out of this trap. Take the organ analogy: The heart has the capacity to pump blood. In cases of heart failure, we might say, 'This heart lacks the capacity to pump blood.' We only register this as a lack and as a failure or deficiency in light of a conception of the heart's proper or eminent function. The terms 'deficiency' and 'failure' are only apt if there is a proper or eminent function. Analogously, we can say that our free capacity of volition (practical reason) is the capacity to act from the moral law. Only in light of the proper or eminent function of this capacity do we register the deviations from the moral law as a deficient exercise. The moral law is normative for this capacity, just as pumping blood is normative for the heart. To say 'the heart has the *capacity* not to pump blood' would be strange, even though it is possible for it to fail. Again, 'capacity' captures the proper or eminent use, not the deficient one.

The critical difference between the two cases is that failure to exercise the capacity is, in the heart case, not an act of free choice. Thus 'blame' in the strict sense, where it implies personal guilt, is out of place in the heart case but not in the case of our capacity of volition. A 'deficient exercise' of this capacity does not need to imply, as Fugate and Reinhold seem to believe, that it was 'impossible' to choose what one was morally required to do (Reinhold, Vermischte Schriften II, 399; Fugate 2015: 362). In IT, Kant explicitly states the opposite: 'The *possibility* to deviate [from the inner legislation of reason] is an incapacity' (Kant, MM 6: 226, my emphasis). Kant here explicitly admits that deviating is a possibility, and so reading 'incapacity' as 'impossibility' generates a straight contradiction. Here is a better reading: When we say, 'Paul ought to get up early', we imply that it is possible for him to get up early. But Paul might say: 'I wasn't able to do it' or 'I couldn't muster my will.' He was incapable of actualizing the capacity even though he potentially could have. The same can be said of moral choice: Paul ought to have acted from a universalizable maxim, but Paul couldn't muster his will to do it. He ought to have actualized his capacity, but he was incapable of doing it. Again, we only register Paul's incapacity to choose what is morally good as an incapacity in light of what he ought to do. Paul has the capacity to do it in the sense that he could do it, but Paul is incapable of doing it in the sense that he can't do it, given that he hasn't tried hard enough. If he were to try harder, he would be able to do what he ought to do. It's not impossible *tout court*. The 'free withholding', as Fugate puts it, is a deficient use of this capacity: We choose against something to which we are 'deep down', or rather 'a priori' as rational beings, committed.

Reinhold and Fugate turn the choice against the moral law into a definitional mark of our free capacity of volition. However, our rational capacity of volition is essentially directed at moral goodness. It is directed at the good not as a mere drive but as a capacity of practical cognition that acts not only according to laws but from the representation of them. We do not need to have the choice to act against the moral law to count as free. What we need instead is the ability to do what we want to do because we consider it to be of unconditional goodness. For Kant, having an alternative choice, though possible, is not a necessary condition of the freedom of the capacity of rational volition. This is where Reinhold and contemporary Reinholdians in Kantian clothing misconstrue free will or, what is the same, pure practical reason.

Conclusion

In this article, I have argued that both Reinhold and Kantians who embrace the Reinhold objection misconstrue Kant's reciprocity thesis and, ultimately, the essence of human freedom. The Reinhold problem is rooted in the capacity–act ambiguity of the terms *Wille* and *Willkür*. This ambiguity also transfers to 'autonomy' and 'heteronomy'. The capacity reading I propose here can avoid absurd implications and dissolve the Reinhold problem. I believe that Kantians should resist Reinhold's definitions of freedom. With RPF, Reinhold not only gives up on a unified theory of free will but also fails to explain why the freedom of our capacity of volition essentially consists in its autonomy. Moreover, in limiting our capacity of volition to a two-way capacity of choice, he places the moral law outside of our capacity of volition. With this move, Reinhold cannot explain how the moral law can possibly get a grip on the agent. On the Kantian picture, by contrast, it is the rational capacity of volition itself that recognizes the normative superiority of one 'way' over the other. It acknowledges that every morally evil action is an expression of a contradiction in willing. Hence, this exercise is a deficient exercise, one that it cannot fully or wholeheartedly approve of. This does not deprive our capacity of volition of its freedom, but defining the freedom of this capacity of rational volition merely in terms of choice fails to register the self-imposed normative direction.

References

Allison, H. (1990), *Kant's Theory of Freedom*, Cambridge: Cambridge University Press.
Allison, H. E. (2011), *Kant's Groundwork for the Metaphysics of Morals: A Commentary*, Oxford: Oxford University Press.
Ameriks, K. (2012), 'Ambiguities in the Will: Reinhold and Kant, Briefe II', in M. Heinz, M. Bondeli, and V. Stolz (eds), *Wille, Willkür, Freiheit: Reinholds Freiheitskonzeption im Kontext der Philosophie des 18. Jahrhunderts*, 71–89, Berlin and Boston: De Gruyter.
Beck, L. W. (1960), *A Commentary on Kant's 'Critique of Practical Reason'*, Chicago: University of Chicago Press.
Beck, L. W. (1995), *Kants 'Kritik der praktischen Vernunft'. Ein Kommentar*, München: UTB.
Benson, C. (2010), 'Autonomy and Purity in Kant's Moral Theory'. Unpublished doctoral dissertation. University of St. Andrews. http://hdl.handle.net/10023/937
Bojanowski, J. (2006), *Kants Theorie der Freiheit*, Berlin: de Gruyter.
Bondeli, M. and W. H. Schrader (2003), *Die Philosophie Karl Leonhard Reinholds*, Berlin: de Gruyte.
Breazeale, D. (2012), 'The Fate of Kantian Freedom: One Cheer (More) for Reinhold', in M. Heinz, M. Bondeli, and V. Stolz (eds), *Wille, Willkür, Freiheit: Reinholds Freiheitskonzeption im Kontext der Philosophie des 18. Jahrhunderts*, 71–89, Berlin: De Gruyter.
Carnois, B. (1987), *The Coherence of Kant's Doctrine of Freedom*, Chicago: University of Chicago Press.
Engstrom, S. (2002), 'The Inner Freedom of Virtue', in M. Timmons (ed.), *Kant's 'Metaphysics of Morals': Interpretative Essays*, 289–316, Oxford: Oxford University Press.

Fugate, C. D. (2015), 'On a Supposed Solution to the Reinhold/Sidgwick Problem in Kant's Metaphysics of Morals on a Solution to a Problem in the Metaphysics of Morals', *Eur J Philos European Journal of Philosophy*, 23 (3): 349–73.
Guyer, P. (2018), 'The Struggle for Freedom: Freedom of Will in Kant and Reinhold', in E. Watkins (ed.), *Kant on Persons and Agency*, 120–37, Cambridge University Press.
Horn, C., C. Mieth, and N. Scarano (2007), *Immanuel Kant, Grundlegung zur Metaphysik der Sitten*.
Hudson, H. (1994), *Kant's Compatibilism*, New York: Cornell University Press.
Hume, D. (2007 [1739–1740]), *A Treatise of Human Nature*: A Critical Edition, ed. D. F. Norton and M. J. Norton, Oxford: Clarendon Press.
Nöller, J. (2019), 'Practical Reason Is Not the Will: Kant and Reinhold's Dilemma', *European Journal of Philosophy*, 27 (4): 852–64.
Paton, H. J. (1947), *The Categorical Imperative*, London: Hutcheson.
Potter, Jr, N. (1974), 'Does Kant Have Two Concepts of Freedom?' in G. Funke and J. Kopper (eds), *Akten des 4 Intertationalen Kant-Kongress*, 590–6, Berlin: de Gruyter.
Prauss, G. (1983), *Kant über Freiheit als Autonomie*, Frankfurt am Main: Klostermann.
Rawls, J. (1971), *A Theory of Justice*, Cambridge, MA: Harvard University Press.
Reinhold, C. L. (1792), *Briefe über die Kantische Philosophie*, vol. 2, Leipzig: Göschen.
Reinhold, K. L. (2017 [1797]), 'Einige Bemerkungen über die in der Einleitung zu den metaphysischen Anfangsgründen der Rechtslehre von I. Kant aufgestellten Begriffe von der Freyheit des Willens', in M. Bondeli, and S. Imhof (eds), *Auswahl vermischter Schriften*. Zweyter Theil, 141–53, Basel: Schwabe.
Schmid, C. C. E. (1788), *Wörterbuch zum leichtern Gebrauch der Kantischen Schriften*, 2nd expanded, edn., Jena: Croker.
Scholten, M. (2020), 'Kantian Constructivism and the Reinhold-Sidgwick Objection', *European Journal of Philosophy*, 28 (2): 364–79.
Schönecker, D. (2015), *Immanuel Kant's 'Groundwork for the Metaphysics of Morals': A Commentary*, Harvard University Press.
Sidgwick, H. (1888), 'The Kantian Conception of Free Will', *Mind*, 13: 405–12.
Silber, J. (1960), 'The Ethical Significance of Kant's *Religion*', in Immanuel Kant, *Kant's Religion within the Limits of Reason Alone*, trans. T. M. Greene and H. H. Hudson, New York: Harper & Row.
Timmermann, J. (2007), *Kant's 'Groundwork of the Metaphysics of Morals': A Commentary*, Cambridge: Cambridge University Press.
Willaschek, M. (1992), *Praktische Vernunft. Handlungstheorie und Moralbegründung*, Stuttgart and Weimar: Metzler.
Wood, A. W. (1984), 'Kant's Compatibilism', in A. W. Wood (ed.), *Self and Nature in Kant's Philosophy*, 73–101, Ithaca and London: Cornell University Press.
Zöller, G. (2005), 'Von Reinhold zu Kant. Zur Grundlegung der Moralphilosophie zwischen Vernunft und Willkür', in *Archivo di Filosofia*, 73: 73–92.

3

Kant and the fate of freedom: 1788–1800

Owen Ware

Whence comes this free will for living things all over the earth, whence, I ask, is it wrested from fate?

– Lucretius.

1. Introduction

Twenty years ago, Karl Ameriks drew attention to the 'fate' of Kant's theory of autonomy:

> Just as modern religious apologists have been understandably accused of inadvertently corrupting, through their sincere but faulty arguments, the very faith that they sought most earnestly to defend, it can be argued that Kant's all-consuming effort to bring autonomy to the center of philosophy (and life in general) has had, in the long run, the unintended effect of leading to a widespread discrediting of philosophy (in its traditional special role) as such, and to an undermining of the notion of autonomy itself.
>
> (2000: 3)

In what follows I wish to show that Kant's theory of freedom suffered from an unusual fate of its own.[1] Yet I shall limit my discussion here to a more specific, and comparatively neglected, period in the reception of Kant's theory: the years 1788 to 1800. From the initial flurry of works published during this time, it is clear Kant's readers were troubled by the appearance of a dilemma hovering over his notion of freedom. On the one hand, they maintained, if we explain human actions according to laws or rules, then we risk reducing the activity of the will to necessity (the horn of *determinism*). But, on the other hand, if we explain human actions without laws or rules, then we face an equally undesirable outcome: that of reducing the will's activity to blind chance (the horn of *indeterminism*).

As we shall see, if there was anything like an unintended effect of Kant's theory during this period, it was not in the undermining of the notion of freedom itself, but in the unprecedented elevation it received in the hands of his two immediate successors,

J. G. Fichte and F. W. J. Schelling. My first aim in this chapter is to trace the history of this early reception, focusing on a number of lesser-known figures along the way. I will then explore the rise of a new approach to the problem of freedom, first with Fichte, who offers a 'genesis' of freedom, and then with Schelling, who offers a 'history' of freedom. Both Fichte and Schelling can be seen as inheriting the determinism/indeterminism dilemma from Kant, and their efforts to overcome it – whether successful or not – constitute a key chapter in the history of post-Kantian thought.

2. Kant and the causality of freedom

While scholars have debated over the issue, it is fair to say that Kant's views on freedom underwent several shifts during his career.[2] Arguably the most significant of these shifts occurred when he abandoned a Leibnizian view, according to which freedom exists alongside natural necessity, in favour of an incompatibilist view. By the time of the *Critique of Pure Reason* (1781, first edition), all traces of Leibnizian compatibilism have vanished, and in its place we find Kant speaking of a much stronger kind of freedom. This kind of freedom involves a form of spontaneity or what Kant defines as

> FREEDOM IN THE TRANSCENDENTAL SENSE:
> 'an **absolute** causal **spontaneity** beginning **from itself**' (A446/B474)

We find this definition in the section of the first *Critique* devoted to a contradiction, known as the Third Antinomy, which arises between the concepts of freedom (the thesis) and mechanism (the antithesis), both of which Kant says we must posit to understand events in the natural world. In framing this problem, however, Kant does not restrict the category of causality to the antithesis side of the contradiction: he speaks equally of a 'causality in accordance with laws of nature' and a 'causality through freedom' (A445/B473). The rule of mechanism, which explains the connection between natural events, is but a species of causality, of which spontaneity beginning 'from itself' is another kind. For Kant, this means that the threat facing transcendental freedom comes not from the idea of causality, but from the idea of unlimited mechanism. As we shall see, a unique aspect of Kant's position – and a cause for confusion among his early readers – is that the faculty of freedom is still law-governed, although law-governed in a non-mechanistic manner.

To clarify this point, consider how Kant sets up the Third Antinomy. The idea of freedom, he explains, seems to entail a type of liberty, not only from coercion but also 'from the guidance of all rules' (A447/B475). According to the antithesis, then, 'nature and transcendental freedom are as different as lawfulness and lawlessness' (A447/B475). But if that were true, we would have no basis to link the idea of freedom to a spontaneity under non-natural laws. So how shall we proceed? Kant's solution is to appeal to the doctrine of transcendental idealism and distinguish between things as they appear to us (phenomena) and things-in-themselves (noumena). On the basis of distinction, he argues, we can think of the causality of freedom in terms of its 'character', either as it manifests in the phenomenal order of appearances or as it lies at the noumenal ground of such appearances.

To say that every 'effective cause' must have a character, then, means only that it must operate according to a law, 'without which it would not be a cause at all' (A539/B567). And yet, as Kant points out, that leaves open the question of the law's status, whether it is mechanistic or not. When I get up from a chair, for example, I initiate an 'absolutely new series, even though as far as time is concerned this occurrence is only the continuation of a previous series' (A450/B478). My act of getting up is part of a chain of events extending indefinitely back in time to prior causal factors. Considered at the noumenal level, my decision does not lie 'within the succession of merely natural effects and is not a mere continuation of them' (A450/B478). And that is Kant's point: my decision counts as an 'absolutely first beginning of a series of appearances' (A450/B478).

While the doctrine of transcendental idealism serves to reconcile the concepts of freedom and mechanism, it does not serve to reject the sceptic's assumption that 'nature and transcendental freedom are as different as lawfulness and lawlessness' (A447/B475). It is possible at least that absolute causal powers lie at the basis of appearances, but that these causal powers operate independently from all rules, natural and non-natural alike. What this shows is that Kant's rejection of the idea of lawless freedom comes, not from his distinction between appearances and things-in-themselves, but from his claim that 'every effective cause must have a character ... without which it would not be a cause at all' (A539/B567). Indeed, this claim resurfaces at a crucial moment in the *Groundwork for the Metaphysics of Morals* (1785) when Kant connects the concept of freedom to the concept of the 'will' (*Wille*). And there he adds that 'the *will* is a kind of causality of living beings, insofar as they are rational, and *freedom* would be that property of such a causality as it can be effective independent of foreign influences *determining* it' (G 4:446).

Within the context of *Groundwork* III, moreover, Kant admits that this definition does not specify the essence of freedom, although he claims that a positive definition 'flows' from it:

> The explication of freedom stated above is negative and therefore unfruitful for gaining insight into its essence; but there flows from it a positive concept of freedom, which is so much the richer and more fruitful. Since the concept of causality carries with it that of laws according to which, by something that we call a cause, something else, namely the consequence, must be posited: freedom, though it is not a property of the will according to natural laws, is not lawless, but must rather be a causality according to immutable laws, but of a special kind; for otherwise a free will would be a non-entity [*Unding*].
>
> (G 4:446)

In my understanding, Kant's point is simply that for anything to happen, there must be a cause of its occurrence, and that cause must be explainable with reference to a character, i.e., with reference to a principle, rule or law that governs its activity. In effect, his claim is that once we characterize the will in terms of its independence from external influences, we must also posit the character of a free will in terms of its spontaneity under non-natural (and hence immutable) laws.³

But then the question becomes: what 'immutable laws' *could* govern the will's spontaneity in a way which is consistent with its independence? Consider what Kant says in reply:

> Natural necessity was a heteronomy of efficient causes; for every effect was possible only according to the law that something else determines the efficient cause to causality; what else, then, can freedom of the will be, but autonomy, i.e. the property of the will of being a law to itself? But the proposition: the will is in all actions a law to itself, designates only the principle of acting on no maxim other than that which can also have itself as its object as a universal law. But this is just the formula of the categorical imperative and the principle of morality: *thus a free will and a will under moral laws are one and the same.*
>
> (G 4:446; emphasis added)

In describing natural necessity in these terms, Kant's point is that the effects of a natural series are possible only according to efficient causes that lie outside of them. The character of natural causality is thus heteronomous or causality that operates 'from without'. By contrast, the causality of a free will must be autonomous or causality that operates 'from itself'. And once we reach this point of analysis, the rest of Kant's argument follows. Since he had already established a connection between autonomy and the principle of morality in *Groundwork* II – for reasons we need not rehearse here – all he has to do now in the context of *Groundwork* III is remind the reader that the rule of autonomy is the highest formula of the moral law. It then follows that the concepts of a free will and a will under moral laws are 'one and the same', as Kant says (G 4:446).

3. 'Necessity everywhere': Ulrich's charge

Such is the basic thrust of Kant's argument in the opening sections of *Groundwork* III. The idea of a lawless will amounts to a 'non-entity' (*Unding*), not because such a will is inconceivable, but because such a will would not amount to a causal power at all. In reply to the sceptic of the Third Antinomy, then, we can say that while the idea of causal spontaneity is free from coercion, and hence free from natural necessity, it is *not* thereby free 'from the guidance of all rules' (A447/B475).

Yet Kant's early readers were not so easily convinced, and the idea of lawful freedom would soon attract criticism when Johann August Heinrich Ulrich, professor of philosophy at the University of Jena, published a work titled *Eleutheriology or On Freedom and Necessity* (1788).⁴ One of Ulrich's counterarguments was that Kant, rather than protecting freedom from the forces of necessity, had merely reintroduced those forces *one level up*, that is, by making the will subject to the causal necessity of moral laws at the *noumenal* level. As Ulrich writes, Kant is committed to making natural necessity rule without exception over the world of appearances, including the empirical character of our will (1788: 32). Yet the empirical character of our will is, by Kant's own definition, grounded on an intelligible character whose causality must also operate according to laws without exception. We therefore have 'necessity with the immutability of the intelligible character (albeit not natural necessity in the Kantian sense)', the result being that 'necessity reigns here too'. Thus, Ulrich concludes, we have 'necessity everywhere' (*überall Nothwendigkeit*) (1788: 32).

Ulrich's *Eleutheriology* was influential for making the term 'indeterminism' (*Indeterminismus*) popular coinage among late eighteenth-century German writers. As Ulrich clarifies his choice of words, determinism views the operations of the will in terms of necessity, regardless of whether we locate those operations on a phenomenal level, with respect to one's empirical character, or on a noumenal level, with respect to one's intelligible character. By contrast, indeterminism views the will as *liberum arbitrium indifferentiae* (liberty of indifference) according to which the will is the power to choose equally between two courses of action. Curiously, Ulrich goes out of his way to deny that Kant's theory of freedom leads to indeterminism because he wants to argue that Kant's position 'denies' freedom by making the character of one's noumenal will governed by immutable laws (1788: 32).

At the same time, Ulrich's passing remarks about indeterminism proved to have lasting influence, notably his claim that a power to choose otherwise is a power without 'decisive reasons' and thus reduces the will to blind 'chance' (*Zufall*) (1788: 21). Other writers would soon use this distinction to place Kant's theory of will on the horns of a dilemma. As I mentioned earlier, their line of attack was to say that either Kant considers the will to be determined by rules (the horn of determinism), or he considers the will to be independent from such rules (the horn of indeterminism). 'There is no third option,' as one author puts it[5] – a claim Ulrich himself highlights in §6 of his *Eleutheriology*: 'There is absolutely no middle-way between necessity and chance' (*Es gibt schlechterdings keinen Mittelweg zwischen Nothwendigkeit und Zufall*).

Ulrich's denial of a middle way between necessity and chance would acquire near axiomatic status in the subsequent free-will debate that his work contributed to stimulating. In 1790, for instance, Carl Christian Erhard Schmid, one of Ulrich's younger colleagues in Jena, published a work titled *Attempt at a Moral Philosophy*, which he later reissued (in an expanded edition) in 1792. In this work Schmid uses the term 'intelligible fatalism' (*Intelligibler Fatalism*) to describe what he considers an unavoidable consequence of following Kant's definition of lawful freedom. Schmid takes a different route to Ulrich's conclusion, however, laying emphasis on the relationship between one's empirical actions and their intelligible grounds.

Still, Schmid's main line of argument is that while we cannot perceive those grounds, we can nevertheless think them, and thus the grounds of our actions 'are subject to rational laws of thinking, since like noumena these determining grounds are not subject to laws of sensibility' (1792: 357–8). Consequently, he argues, we are in no way permitted to ascribe the supersensible grounds of our actions to 'reasonless chance' or what amounts to the same, 'lawlessness' (*Gesetzlosigkeit*) or 'non-necessity' (*Nichtnothwendigkeit*) (1792: 357–8). Echoing Ulrich's axiom, he goes on to claim that 'there is absolutely no middle-way between the two', adding that the entire sphere of what is thinkable is 'limited to the concepts of necessity and chance' (1792: 358).

Ulrich and Schmid were a formidable pair, and their reactions to Kant would soon recruit a third member to their side, Christoph Andreas Leonhard Creuzer. To add to this growing tension, one of Kant's most influential advocates, Karl Leonard Reinhold, had already spilled much ink defending what he took to be a friendly amendment to Kant's theory of freedom. In his *Attempt at a New Theory of the Human Power of Representation* (1789), Reinhold distanced himself from the idea of self-determination according to immutable laws. And in its place he defined freedom as the ability to act without being constrained by the laws of reason or by the demands of sensibility, adding that someone displays free choice either by deciding to 'determine himself' by reason or to 'let himself be determined' by objects of sensibility (1789: 90).

Reinhold would reiterate this point in the second volume of his *Letters on Kantian Philosophy* (1792), writing that the will is 'the capacity of a person to determine itself to the satisfaction or nonsatisfaction of a desire, either according to the practical law or against it' (1792: 271–2). The implication is that freedom consists not merely in the 'independence of the will from the coercion of instinct' but also in 'the independence of a person from the necessitation of practical reason itself'. Correctly understood, Reinhold maintains, freedom *is* liberty of indifference: it is the capacity of 'choice' (*Willkür*) to act either 'for or against the practical law' (1792: 272). In saying this, however, Reinhold viewed himself as Kant's *defender*, although his modified account unwittingly brought Kant's theory of freedom once again under heavy fire.

4. The 'non-entity' of freedom: Creuzer's complaint

When Creuzer sat down to write his *Skeptical Reflections on the Freedom of the Will* (1793), the advantage of time was on his side, having both the written work of Kant's critics and sympathizers at his disposal. In addition to raising further objections against Kant, building upon the work of Schmid (who wrote the Preface to his book) and Ulrich before him, Creuzer criticized what he took to be Reinhold's 'transcendental indifferentism'. Reinhold was motivated to a liberty of indifference theory, as he makes clear in the second edition of his *Letters*, because he wanted to avert the pitfalls of subjecting the will to necessity at the noumenal level.

However, by characterizing the will in terms of the capacity to choose either 'for or against the practical law', Reinhold found himself saddled with all the problems Ulrich and Schmid had uncovered with indifferentism in general. In 1793, Creuzer was well positioned to bring these same problems to bear upon Reinhold's theory, arguing that the idea of a choice between reason and sensibility reduces to mere chance. It presents us with the concept of a will subject to two ruling forces, at one time reason, at another time sensibility, without any determining ground to explain what compels the will to choose one or the other (1793: 128n). In this context, too, Creuzer cites Letter 15 from Friedrich Jacobi's 1785 book on Spinoza, according to which a capacity that is completely lacking in determining grounds amounts to a 'non-entity'.

Creuzer's book also served to raise the stakes of the debate by entangling Kant's latest account of freedom in the horns of the determinism/indeterminism dilemma. Only one year prior, in 1792, Kant had published his essay 'On the Radical Evil of Human Nature' in the *Berliner Monatsschrift*, which became Part One of his *Religion within the Boundaries of Mere Reason* (1793). It is not evident whether Kant was responding to the rise of deterministic theories of freedom or whether he was reacting to Reinhold's liberty of indifference view. Yet it is clear that Kant's essay on evil marked a new phase in the presentation of his theory of freedom, since his essay contains an important distinction between the concepts of 'will' (*Wille*) and 'power of choice' (*Willkür*), which Kant had used interchangeably and even inconsistently in previous work.[6]

To the surprise of his critics, Kant now argued that the basic 'disposition' (*Gesinnung*) from which an agent selects her maxims is itself freely adopted. Clarifying his use of the term 'nature', he writes:

> By the 'nature of a human being' we only mean here the subjective ground for the use of his freedom as such (under objective moral laws), which lies antecedent to every deed that falls within the scope of the senses, the ground of which lies where it will. But this subjective ground must, in turn, itself always be a deed of freedom [*Actus der Freiheit*] (for otherwise the use or abuse of the human being's power of choice [*Willkür*] with respect to the moral law could not be imputed to him, nor could the good or evil in him be called 'moral').
>
> (R 6:21)

Highlighting this passage, Creuzer argued that Kant's 1792 essay contradicts his previous notion of lawful freedom, citing as evidence Kant's claim from *Groundwork* III that freedom 'though it is not a property of the will according to natural laws, is not lawless, but must rather be a causality according to immutable laws' (1793: 149). Having posited a form of indifferent choice at the noumenal level – where one freely adopts the subjective ground of one's maxims (whether good or evil) – Creuzer believes Kant saved his theory from the horn of determinism, only to get it caught – 'just like Reinhold' – in the horn of indifferentism, thereby reducing his concept of freedom to a 'non-entity' (1793: 147).

5. A 'higher legislation': Fichte to the rescue

With the publication of Creuzer's book, anyone following the free-will debate at the time would have seen Kant's opponents gaining an upper hand. Yet a sea change was looming on the horizon, the signs of which can be found in a review of Creuzer's book that Fichte wrote in 1793 for the *Allgemeine Literatur-Zeitung*.[7] What is evident upon reading this review is that Fichte, while sympathetic to the Kantian cause, was already expressing reservations towards Reinhold's theory of will. Beyond this, it is far from clear what Fichte's alternative amounts to. In one passage, for instance, Fichte speaks to the question of how an agent qua phenomenon can be in harmony with itself qua noumenon:

> For *determinate being*, as an appearance, some actual real ground in a preceding appearance must be assumed, in accordance with the law of natural causality. However, insofar as the determinate being produced through the causality of nature is supposed to *be in harmony with* the act of free determination (a harmony that, for the sake of a *moral world order,* also must be assumed), then the ground of such harmony can be assumed to lie neither in nature, which exercises no causality over freedom, nor in freedom, which has no causality within nature, but only in a higher law, which subsumes and unifies both freedom and nature.
>
> (CR 16: 414–15)

What is striking is that Fichte claims that the ground of the harmony between an agent's intelligible freedom and phenomenal nature lies 'as it were in a pre-determined harmony [*vorherbestimmten Harmonie*] of determinations through freedom with determinations through the laws of nature' (CR 16: 415).[8] And he even returns to this Leibnizian idea in the context of addressing Creuzer's complaint that Kant has left the connection between phenomenal effects and their noumenal grounds incomprehensible. 'What *is* incomprehensible', he replies,

> is how both of these objects [viz., thing in itself and appearance], which are completely independent of each other, could nevertheless be in harmony with each other. We can, however, comprehend why we cannot comprehend this harmony: namely, because we have no insight into the law that joins together freedom and nature. – Incidentally, it seems to this reviewer that this is also Kant's true opinion of the matter, and that the assertion, which is found in many passages in his writings, that freedom must possess causality within the sensible world is put forward only in a preliminary manner, pending closer determination of the proposition in question.
>
> (CR 16: 415)

Clearly nothing in this passage works to alleviate Creuzer's complaint, and Fichte's appeal to a predetermined harmony is more mystifying than clarifying.[9] Yet what is illuminating with respect to tracing the early reception of Kant's theory of freedom is that Fichte aligns the spirit of the Leibnizian doctrine with 'Kant's true opinion', referring to his recent essay on evil which entitles us to assume that 'our appearing, empirical character will harmonize with our intelligible character' by virtue of a 'higher legislation' (CR 16: 415). Beyond this Fichte says nothing to shed light on the higher legislation that serves to unite freedom and nature, though it would soon become the driving force behind his paradigm-shifting idea of a science of knowledge grounded in the concept of 'the I'.

6. The 'real issue' of freedom: Schelling in 1795

We do not find Fichte presenting a fully worked-out theory of freedom until his *System of Ethics* of 1798. Yet another, much younger sympathizer of Fichte's doctrine of science would attempt to fill in and develop some of the suggestions laid bare in the

'Creuzer Review'. Schelling, who had written his master's thesis on the biblical account of evil at the University of Tübingen, turned to the topic of freedom in one of his first major publications, *Of the I as the Principle of Philosophy* (1795). And what Schelling claims in this short but powerful essay is that the problem of transcendental freedom 'has continually suffered the sad fate of always being misunderstood' and that 'even after the *Critique of Pure Reason* has shed so much light on it, the real point in dispute does not yet seem to be fixed sharply enough' (SW I/1: 235; IP 122). In Schelling's view,

> The real issue never was absolute but only *transcendental* freedom, that is, the freedom of an empirical I conditioned by objects. What is incomprehensible is not how the absolute I should have freedom, but rather how the empirical I should have freedom; the question is not how an intellectual I could be intellectual, that is, could be absolutely free, but rather how it is possible that an *empirical* I could at the same time be *intellectual*, that is, could have causality through freedom.
> (SW I/1: 235; IP 122 – 3)

Schelling then argues that what we call the freedom of the empirical I is how the absolute I expresses itself under the conditions of finitude (a point we shall see Schelling develop in later work). Yet in 'Of the I' he admits right away that it is unclear how the empirical I's freedom could agree with the natural causality to which its actions are subject qua phenomenon. How, in other words, 'can the transcendental causality of the empirical I (as determined by absolute causality) agree with the natural causality of the same I?' (SW I/1: 237; IP 125).

Schelling's answer echoes Fichte's 'Creuzer Review' by framing the question in terms of a 'ground' that would join the pure I and the empirical I and bring the two into 'harmony' (SW I/1: 239; IP 125). And, like Fichte, he even characterizes this ground in Leibnizian terms, writing that our search brings us to 'a principle of preestablished harmony' (*prästabilierter Harmonie*) which, he adds, is 'merely immanent and determined only in the absolute I' (SW I/1: 239; IP 126):

> Because a causality of the empirical I is possible only within the causality of the absolute I, and because the objects likewise receive their reality only through the absolute reality of the I, the absolute I is the common center in which lies the principle of their harmony. The causality of objects harmonizes with the causality of the empirical I for the single reason that they exist only in and with the empirical I. But that they exist only in and with the empirical I stems from the one fact that both the objects and the empirical I owe their reality solely to the nonfinite reality of the absolute I.
> (SW I/1: 239; IP 126)

For Schelling, the absolute I secures a *pre-established* harmony between the freedom of the empirical I and its subjection to natural causality because both 'owe their reality' to this more fundamental ground. His reason for calling it an 'immanent' harmony is due to the fact that the noumenal and phenomenal aspects of the I are not opposed, as two distinct substances would be, but are rather different expressions of an original activity: the unlimited I itself.

Granted, this adds a few more brush strokes to the outline Fichte presents in the 'Creuzer Review', but in the end Schelling's essay raises more questions than it answers. In particular, his claim that the empirical freedom of the I is an identical yet limited (and hence finite) version of the I's infinite freedom does not directly address the dilemma of determinism and indeterminism. If anything, the outline before us demonstrates that Schelling wanted to find a reconciliation between the two. Yet on closer inspection it is not clear how he was able to avoid the charge of intelligible fatalism – where we have 'necessity everywhere' – given that his pre-established harmony assigns a primary role to the causality of the absolute I. If everything owes its reality to this absolute I, what room is left for any kind of choice at the empirical level?

7. The 'genesis' of freedom: Fichte in 1798

Among the many aims of the *System of Ethics*, it becomes clear that Fichte wants to redeem some version of the concept of *Willkür* or indifferent choice, if only to capture what he thinks is the element of truth in Reinhold's position. Interestingly, at one point Fichte calls attention to Kant's definition of freedom as the power to initiate a new state, saying that this is an 'excellent nominal explanation' but of limited value, 'since the concepts still in circulation regarding freedom are almost entirely false' (GA I/5: 52; SL 4: 37). In his view, a 'still higher question remains to be answered, namely: how can a state begin absolutely, or how can the absolute beginning of a state be thought?' (GA I/5: 52; SL 4: 37).

Not finding an answer in Kant or Reinhold, Fichte goes on to defend a 'genetic' model of how our consciousness of freedom unfolds from an initial state of 'indeterminacy', where we hover between a manifold of possible actions, to a state of 'determinacy', where we select one of these options and act accordingly. Along the lines of a genetic theory of freedom, we see that Fichte wants to preserve the idea of indifferent choice, but now qualified as a mere *stage* in the emergence of freedom. 'The will is a capacity to choose,' he explains, 'just as Reinhold correctly described it,' adding: 'There is no will [*Wille*] without the power of choice [*Willkür*]. One calls the will a power of choice when one attends to the above-mentioned mark, namely, that it necessarily arrives at a choice among several, equally possible actions' (GA I/5: 148 – 9; SL 4: 159).

As I have explained in more detail elsewhere,[10] Fichte's theory of freedom is novel by framing indifferent choice, or 'wavering' between a manifold of actions, as a state to be *overcome* through subsequent acts of reflection and resolution. Consider Fichte's distinction between our initial state of indeterminacy, what he calls '*formal* freedom', and the determination of our will through higher acts of reflection, what he calls '*material* freedom' (GA I/5: 132; SL 4: 139). On the basis of this distinction, Fichte speaks of formal freedom as the precondition for our power to choose between different actions, and he argues that we are always 'free' by not being determined by anything outside of us. Formal freedom so understood is similar to what Kant calls negative freedom in *Groundwork* III, the will's independence from external forces. To the extent that Reinhold characterized the will as enjoying this kind of indeterminacy, Fichte thinks his account is correct.

But when we step back to consider all the details of Fichte's alternative in the *System of Ethics*, it is clear that Reinhold's position does not reveal the whole truth about freedom. After all, Fichte maintains, overcoming a state of wavering between options is what advances the will's development, first in the form of determinate rational agency and then in the form of determinate moral autonomy, two higher stages of 'material' freedom. To achieve these higher stages, Fichte argues, an agent must 'tear loose' from her natural drive by projecting an *end* for its satisfaction and then (in yet another act of reflection) by projecting the idea of her own *freedom* as an end.[11]

At this point we must ask: to what extent has Fichte's genetic account succeeded in avoiding the dilemma of determinism and indeterminism? Compared to Schelling's 'Of the I', which traces the freedom of the empirical I back to the freedom of the absolute I, Fichte's theory seems to have the advantage of doing justice to real indifference of 'choice' (*Willkür*). On the other hand, his model seems to postpone, rather than pre-empt, the problem of intelligible fatalism, since it yields an account of the will's development into higher stages of *material* freedom, whereby the will ultimately determines itself according to the necessary laws of morality.

To complicate matters, Fichte seems to side with Kant in characterizing morality in terms of a 'constant and unchangeable – in other words, a lawful and necessary – thinking', the content of which he says expresses the following norm: 'that the intellect has to give itself the *unbreakable law* of absolute self-activity' (GA I/5: 61; SL 4: 48; emphasis added). Insofar as the genetic model leads to what Kant calls positive freedom in *Groundwork* III, where a free will and a will under the 'immutable' laws of morality are the same, one might worry that Fichte's position ends up in the snare of determinism. Nor does it help Fichte's case when he claims that it is 'absolutely impossible and contradictory that anyone with a clear consciousness of his duty at the moment he acts could, in good consciousness, *decide not to do his duty*' (GA I/5: 176; SL 4: 191). Does this not entail that our consciousness of duty leaves us *no choice* to act otherwise?

As it happens, Fichte is aware of this problem and he even addresses it in the following passage from the *System of Ethics*:

> The situation is thus as follows: if one constantly reflects upon the demand of the law, if this demand always remains before one's eyes, then it is impossible not to act in accordance with this demand or to resist it. If the law disappears from our attention, however, then it is impossible for us to act in accordance with it. *Hence necessity reigns in both cases*, and we seem to have become caught up in some kind of intelligible fatalism, though of a somewhat lower degree of the usual kind.
>
> (GA I/5: 177; SL 4: 191; emphasis added)

What Fichte calls intelligible fatalism of the 'usual kind' – referring to Schmid and Ulrich – is one in which an agent is determined to act by the moral law with the force of causal necessity at the noumenal level. Fichte thinks this kind of fatalism is 'averted by means of the important insight that the moral law is by no means the sort of thing that could ever be present within us without any assistance from us, but is instead something that we ourselves first make' (GA I/5: 177; SL 4: 191). As Fichte had explained earlier, 'all types of fatalism' share the same shortcoming of treating the law of mechanism as a supreme principle of thinking, thereby imposing mechanism onto the concept of the will (GA I/5: 150; SL 4: 161).[12] In the passage under discussion, however, the worry is that 'either one remains continually conscious of the moral law, in which case a moral action necessarily ensues, or else such consciousness disappears, in which case it is impossible to act morally' (GA I/5: 177; SL 4: 191).

This much, I think, is now clear. Even if we accept Fichte's point that the moral law is something we freely sustain in our minds, such that it does not bind our will with causal necessity, the puzzle remains how immoral action is possible. After all, Fichte is emphatic that it is *impossible* to act contrary to one's duty with *clear consciousness* of it. What is possible, he believes, is that one 'renders obscure within oneself the clear consciousness of what duty demands' (GA I/5: 177; SL 4: 191). That is to say, because our consciousness of duty is a product of self-activity, it follows that this consciousness 'endures only through the continuation of this same act of freedom' (GA I/5: 177; SL 4: 191). Rather than lose our awareness of duty against our will, Fichte's claim is just the reverse: that we *freely* render this awareness *obscure*, creating just enough distortion in our minds to rationalize acting contrary to morality. 'The appearance of fatalism disappears,' he concludes, 'as soon as one notices that it is *up to our freedom* whether such consciousness continues or becomes obscured' (GA I/5: 177; SL 4: 191; emphasis added).

This is no doubt helpful, but the question stands: how does Fichte's theory of freedom in the *System of Ethics* fulfil the promise of the 'Creuzer Review', namely, to articulate the harmony between one's empirical and intelligible character? At one point we find Fichte speaking to the problem of how nature and freedom can agree in a single subject, writing that 'the hypothesis of pre-established harmony, as it is usually understood, does not commit itself on this issue but leaves our question just as unanswered as it was before' (GA I/5: 127; SL 4: 133). On inspection, I think, Fichte's caveat is significant: the Leibnizian hypothesis does nothing to illuminate this question as it is 'usually understood'. The thesis guiding Fichte's doctrine of science is that there is nothing essentially dual in the self, no set of heterogenous powers, one natural and the other free, but rather a single ground of activity, the absolute I, and its subsequent self-limitations. From a transcendental standpoint 'we by no means have anything twofold' – and where there is no duality, Fichte remarks, '[T]here can be no talk of harmony nor any question concerning the ground of such harmony' (GA I/5: 127; SL 4: 133).

All this might lead one to think that Fichte has softened, if not released, his attachment to the idea of predetermined harmony. But this impression would be mistaken, I believe, not only because we find Fichte invoke this doctrine later in the *System of Ethics*,[13] but also because the concept of a 'ground of harmony' is central to his genetic model of freedom just sketched. In fact, Fichte only denies talk of harmony or a ground of harmony from a 'transcendental' perspective, that is, a perspective where we analyse the concept of a rational being in abstraction from all conditions of time, including the stages of development a rational being must undergo to attain full material freedom. From what we might call a 'developmental' perspective, it is necessary to understand how one can transition from a state of indeterminacy (or free choice) to a state of determinacy (or moral autonomy). Without this genetic story of the will's progressive self-development, Fichte thinks we would confuse a particular stage of the will for the will as a whole; and if we do that, we would produce a spurious theory of *indeterminism*, according to which the will is nothing other than liberty of indifference, or an equally spurious theory of *determinism*, according to which the will is nothing other than moral autonomy. That is why grasping the 'temporal course of the I's reflections' leading to full material freedom requires what Fichte calls a 'history of an empirical rational being' (GA I/5: 165; SL 4: 178).

8. The 'weaving of an unknown hand': Schelling in 1800

As we shall see, Fichte's appeal to the history of an empirical rational being would open the door to new possibilities in the unfolding of post-Kantian thought, the first results of which we find in Schelling's *System of Transcendental Idealism* (1800).

What is clear when we turn to Schelling's book is that he frames the problem of philosophy in terms of retracing the self-dividing activity of the absolute I into a successive series of conflicts, the resolution of which takes the form of a quest: namely, to understand how both the subjective aspect of the I (as spontaneity) and its objective aspect (as causality) can be intuited at the same time for the subject. In this way, Schelling's book unfolds as a story of the conflicts between nature and freedom whose ground of harmony progressively reveals itself to consciousness. To be sure, one finds this kind of narrative operative in Fichte's *System of Ethics*, to the extent that Fichte's theory of how we achieve full material freedom leads to a social theory of ethical life (involving the state, the church and what Fichte calls the 'learned republic'). And one could argue that a version of this framework is already present in Kant's *Religion* and perhaps even earlier in his essay 'Idea for a Universal History with a Cosmopolitan Aim' (1784). Yet there is no question, in my view, that Schelling was pushing this idea in a new direction.

To begin with, in the course of discussing the topics of choice, fate and history, Schelling raises the now-familiar question of how one's freedom of will can agree with one's actions as they appear under the laws of natural necessity. His reply, echoing earlier work, is that this connection is only possible through a 'pre-established harmony' (*prästabilierte Harmonie*). However, unlike 'Of the I', which identifies this ground in the absolute I, Schelling now tells the reader that 'we have absolutely no means of explaining at present' what this ground may be (SW I/3: 500; STI 193). By way of preparation, he observes that reflection on the nature of conflicts between individual persons eventually leads us to the study of human history. His claim is that conflicts between competing personal ends find their resolution in a legal system, just as conflicts between competing national ends find their resolution in a system of international law. And Schelling's larger point is that this interplay of choice and its limitation or restriction brings us to human history where these national and international conflicts unfold.

Accordingly, Schelling argues that we can find a 'trace' of the ground of harmony between freedom and necessity 'in the lawfulness which runs, like the weaving of an unknown hand, through the free play of choice in history' (SW I/3: 601; STI 209). That is why he claims in the *System of Transcendental Idealism* that a philosophy of history – not just a history of an empirical rational being – is a necessary step on the path to grasping the ground of a predetermined harmony. As I understand it, his point is that a social-historical perspective puts us in the right position to solve the conflict at hand, alluding to Kant's idea that history 'allows us to hope that if it considers the play of the freedom of the human will *in the large*, it can discover within it a regular course' (IaG 8:17). Why? Because at the personal level, 'choice' (*Willkür*) is nothing more than what Schelling calls the 'ever-recurring revelation' of the absolute I expressed under the constraints of finitude (SW I/3: 578; STI 191). But at a social-historical perspective level, he thinks we can see *how* the absolute I serves as a ground of harmony between freedom and necessity, since the course of history – as the collective body of free human actions – shows a trace of a plan that, if fulfilled, would *perfectly unite the two*.[14]

Looking back to the foregoing sections, it is only natural to ask if we have made headway in answering the questions pressed by Kant's early critics, especially with respect to the dilemma of reducing the will either to necessity or to chance. Much more work needs to be done to understand how Schelling's historical turn addresses this problem, and I have only provided a few hints in that direction here. But I hope to have said enough to cast light on Schelling's reasons for reframing the problem of freedom and necessity around a study of the philosophy of history. Schelling's account speaks to the problem of how freedom and necessity can coexist, except that it raises this problem to a global level (a level that would soon be taken up, in what would become another chapter of German idealism, by Hegel). Like Kant, Schelling thinks that the idea of a universal human history gives us a 'guiding thread' to discern a purposive end to the sometimes chaotic, sometimes fateful play of human freedom across the ages. And yet Schelling builds upon Kant's suggestion in a new way by applying it to the determinism/indeterminism dilemma. The task Schelling assigns to his philosophy of history is that of demonstrating how the lawfulness of necessity and the spontaneity of freedom can be harmonized, showing that the 'work of fate' was 'already the beginning of a providence imperfectly revealing itself' (SW I/3: 604; STI 212).

9. Closing remarks

Our discussion in this chapter began by following the steps leading to Kant's claim in *Groundwork* III that a free will and a will under moral laws are 'one and the same'. As we have seen, this statement would invite the first wave of sceptical reactions to Kant's theory of freedom, but it also inspired Reinhold to adopt a theory of indifferent choice. Despite his good intentions, Reinhold's account only served as grist in the mill for Creuzer, who argued (using Kant's words against him) that indifferent choice is not a power at all but a 'non-entity'. There is no question that Creuzer's book had an impact on Fichte, and his 1793 review was unique, among other things, for mentioning a 'ground' of harmony between one's noumenal freedom and one's empirical character. Yet Fichte did not return to this suggestion until the *System of Ethics* of 1798, and by that time Schelling had already taken steps in 'Of the I' under the inspiration of Fichte's doctrine of science. That Fichte was still committed to the idea of predetermination appears in his genetic model of freedom, according to which indeterminacy of choice and determinacy of will constitute two stages of the will's path to autonomy. While this was a striking claim at the time, I would not call it an unintended or *fateful* effect of Kant's theory of freedom. The year Schelling published the *System of Transcendental Idealism* in 1800 was significant for many reasons, not the least of which was that it marked the relocation of freedom in the progressive unfolding of the absolute I, making the history of freedom a novel point of departure for generations of philosophers to come.[15]

Abbreviations

A/B: *Kritik der reinen Vernunft* (*Critique of Pure Reason*), 1781/87. Translated by Paul Guyer and Allen Wood. Cambridge: Cambridge University Press, 1998.

CR: 'Creuzer Recension' ('Creuzer Review'), 1793. Translated by Daniel Breazeale. *Philosophical Forum* 32 (4) 2001: 289–96.

G: *Grundlegung zur Metaphysik der Sitten* (*Groundwork for the Metaphysics of Morals*), 1785. Translated by Mary Gregor. Cambridge: Cambridge University Press, 1998.

GA: *J. G. Fichte-Gesamtausgabe der Bayerischen Akademie der Wissenschaften.* Edited by Erich Fuchs, Hans Gliwitzky, Reinhard Lauth und Peter K. Schneider. Stuttgart-Bad Cannstatt: Frommann, 1962–2012.

IP: *Vom Ich als Princip der Philosophie oder über das Unbedingte im menschlichen Wissen* (*Of the I as the Principle of Philosophy or On the Unconditioned in Human Knowledge*), 1795. In *The Unconditional in Human Knowledge: Four Early Essays, 1794–1796*, translated by Fritz Marti. Lewisburg: Bucknell University Press, 1980.

R: *Die Religion innerhalb der Grenzen der bloßen Vernunft* (*Religion within the Boundaries of Mere Reason*), 1793. Translated by Allen Wood and George di Giovanni. Cambridge: Cambridge University Press, 1999.

SL: *Das System der Sittenlehre nach den Prinzipien der Wissenschaftslehre* (*The System of Ethics According to the Principles of the Wissenschaftslehre*), 1798. Translated by Günter Zöller and Daniel Breazeale. Cambridge: Cambridge University Press, 2005.

STI: *System des transzendentalen Idealismus* (*System of Transcendental Idealism*), 1800. Translated by Peter Heath. Charlottesville: University Press of Virginia, 1978.

SW: *Friedrich Wilhelm Joseph von Schellings sämmtliche Werke.* Edited by Karl Friedrich August Schelling. Stuttgart, Augsburg, J.G. Cotta, 1856–61.

Notes

1. While it is true that 'autonomy' and 'freedom' are related concepts, they track different concerns in the historical context that Ameriks's work serves to foreground. For instance, 'autonomy' as an Enlightenment ideal of self-determination carries ethical, social and political meanings that go past the notion of freedom as either volitional choice or uncaused causality. My concern in this chapter is mainly with the *conceptual* and *metaphysical* puzzles which arise from the idea of such causality.
2. For further discussion of Kant's theory of freedom, see Wood (1984); Allison (1990; 2020); Korsgaard (1996); Timmermann (2003); Watkins (2004); Pereboom (2006); Guyer (2017); McCarty (2009); Hogan (2009a, 2009b); Ameriks (2012); Insole (2013); Stern (2015); Kim (2015); Dunn (2015); Kohl (2015a, 2015b); Papish (2018); McClear (2020); and Schafer (forthcoming).
3. Kant had prepared the reader for this claim by defining the will in *Groundwork* II as a 'capacity ... to determine oneself according to the representation of certain laws' (G 4:427).
4. For discussion of this debate that surrounded Kant's theory of freedom, see Guyer (2017) and Ware (forthcoming).
5. See Schulze (1788: 413).
6. See Allison (1990). I discuss Kant's theory of freedom at greater length in Ware (forthcoming).
7. For further discussion, see Martin (2018).
8. In a parenthetical remark, Fichte directs the reader to an essay Kant published in 1790 where he characterizes transcendental idealism as the 'true apology' of Leibniz's philosophy.
9. Commenting on CR 16: 414–15, Wayne Martin speculates that Fichte's use of the phrase 'pre-determined' harmony instead of 'pre-established' harmony serves 'to leave open a possibility that Fichte would seek to exploit, namely that the requisite harmony is *not in fact pre-established*, indeed that it is *not yet established* at all, even if its transcendental shape is pre-delineated, and that it therefore falls to us to produce it' (2016: 29). While I agree that Fichte wishes to place emphasis on a harmony to-be-achieved, I am not convinced that his use of the phrase 'pre-determined' carries the degree of significance Martin ascribes to it. German authors during the late eighteenth century used 'pre-determined' and 'pre-established' harmony as interchangeable terms – as when Feder writes, for example, that 'the third hypothesis is the pre-established, or pre-determined, harmony (harmoniae praestabilitae)' (1793: 181).
10. See Ch. 2 of Ware (2020).
11. For further discussion of these stages, see Ware (2019) and Breazeale (2021).
12. While the moral law gives expression to a necessary manner of thinking, and hence counts as 'unbreakable', it has no reality outside of the I's self-activity. The moral law is nothing other than a necessary manner of thinking this self-activity, which is why Fichte says it counts as a genuine law of freedom.
13. I am thinking of §18, where Fichte attempts to explain how the free actions of rational beings can coexist (and thus harmonize) in community on the basis of their 'predetermination' (*Prädetermination*). Here he writes that 'all free actions are predestined [*prädestinirt*] through reason for all eternity – i.e., outside of all time – and with regard to perception every free individual is placed in harmony with these actions' (GA I/5: 207; SL 4: 228).

14 On Schelling's new account, history divides into a series of stages, with the last stage, Providence, pointing to a future reconciliation. And he is clear that the road to reconciliation can never be completed, making the revelation of the absolute I an 'infinite process'.
15 It gives me pleasure to acknowledge an intellectual debt to Karl Ameriks, whose book *Kant and the Fate of Autonomy* not only inspired the title of this chapter but also helped me work through the intricacies of Kant's concept of freedom and its enduring legacy. For constructive discussion of the ideas in this chapter, I am also grateful to Joe Saunders and to participants in my 2019 Schelling seminar at the University of Toronto.

References

Allison, H. (1990), *Kant's Theory of Freedom*, Cambridge: Cambridge University Press.
Allison, H. (2020), *Kant's Concept of Freedom*, Cambridge: Cambridge University Press.
Ameriks, K. (2000), *Kant and the Fate of Autonomy*, Cambridge: Cambridge University Press.
Ameriks, K. (2012), *Kant's Elliptical Path*, Oxford University Press.
Breazeale, D. (2021), 'Fichte and the Path from "Formal" to "Material" Freedom', in S. Bacin and O. Ware (eds), *Fichte's System of Ethics: A Critical Guide*, 85–108, Cambridge: Cambridge University Press.
Creuzer, L. (1793), *Skeptische Betrachtungen über die Freyheit des Willens mit Hinsicht auf die neuesten Theorien über dieselbe*, Jena: Croker.
Dunn, N. (2015), 'A Lawful Freedom: Kant's Practical Refutation of Noumenal Chance', *Kant Studies Online*, 1.
Feder, J. (1793), *Erklärung der Logik, Metaphysik und practischen Philosophie*, Wien: By the author.
Giovanni, Georgie di. (2005), *Freedom and Religion in Kant and His Immediate Successors: The Vocation of Humankind, 1774–1800*, Cambridge: Cambridge University Press.
Guyer, P. (2017), 'The Struggle for Freedom: Freedom of Will in Kant and Reinhold', in E. Watkins (ed.), *Kant on Persons and Agency*, 120–37, Cambridge: Cambridge University Press.
Hogan, D. (2009a), 'Noumenal Affection', *The Philosophical Review*, 118 (4): 501–32.
Hogan, D. (2009b), 'Three Kinds of Rationalism and the Non-spatiality of Things in Themselves', *Journal of the History of Philosophy*, 47 (3): 355–82.
Insole, C. (2013), *Kant and the Creation of Freedom: A Theological Problem*, Oxford: Oxford University Press.
Jacobi, F. (1785), *Über die Lehre des Spinoza in Briefen an den Herrn Moses Mendelssohn*, Breslau: Löwe.
Kim, H. (2015), *Kant and the Foundations of Morality*, New York: Rowman & Littlefield.
Kohl, M. (2015a), 'Kant on Freedom of Empirical Thought', *Journal of the History of Philosophy*, 53 (2): 301–26.
Kohl, M. (2015b), 'Kant on Determinism and the Categorical Imperative', *Ethics*, 125 (2): 331–56.
Korsgaard, C. (1996), *Creating the Kingdom of Ends*, Cambridge: Cambridge University Press.
Martin, W. (2016), 'From Kant to Fichte', in D. James and G. Zöller (eds), *The Cambridge Companion to Fichte*, 7–37, Cambridge: Cambridge University Press.

Martin, W. (2018), 'Fichte's Creuzer Review and the Transformation of the Free Will Problem', *European Journal of Philosophy*, 26 (2): 717–29.
McCarty, R. (2009), *Kant's Theory of Action*, Oxford: OUP.
McClear, C. (2020), 'On the Transcendental Freedom of the Intellect', *Ergo: An Open Access Journal of Philosophy*, 7 (2): 35–104.
Papish, L. (2018), *Kant on Evil, Self-Deception, and Moral Reform*, Oxford: Oxford University Press.
Pereboom, D. (2006), 'Kant on Transcendental Freedom', *Philosophy and Phenomenological Research*, 73 (3): 537–67.
Reinhold, K. (1789), *Versuch einer neuen Theorie des menschlichen Vorstellungsvermögens*, Jena: Croker.
Reinhold, K. (1792), *Briefe über die Kantische Philosophie*, Vol. 2, Leipzig: Goschen.
Schafer, K. (Forthcoming), 'Practical Cognition and Knowledge of Things-in-Themselves', in E. Tiffany and D. Heide (eds), *Kantian Freedom*, Oxford: Oxford University Press.
Schmid, C. (1792), *Versuch einer Moralphilosophie*, Jena: Croker.
Schulze, E. (1788), *Grundriss der philosophischen Wissenschaften*, Wittenberg: Zimmermann.
Stern, R. (2011), *Understanding Moral Obligation: Kant, Hegel, Kierkegaard*, Cambridge: Cambridge University Press.
Stern, R. (2015), *Kantian ethics: Value, agency, and obligation*, Oxford University Press.
Timmermann, J. (2003), *Sittengesetz und Freiheit: Untersuchungen zu Immanuel Kants Theorie des freien Willens*, Berlin: De Gruyter.
Ulrich, J. (1788), *Eleutheriologie oder über Freyheit und Nothwendigkeit*, Jena: Croker.
Ware, O. (2019), 'Freedom Immediately after Kant', *European Journal of Philosophy*, 27 (4): 865–81.
Ware, O. (2020), *Fichte's Moral Philosophy*, New York: Oxford University Press.
Ware, O. (Forthcoming), *Kant on Freedom*, Cambridge: Cambridge University Press.
Watkins, E. (2004), *Kant and the Metaphysics of Causality*, Cambridge: Cambridge University Press.
Wood, A. (1984), 'Kant's Compatibilism', in Allen Wood (ed.), *Self and Nature in Kant's Philosophy*, 73–101, Ithaca: Cornell University Press.

4

Fichte on self-sufficiency and teleology

Gabriel Gottlieb

1. Introduction

J. G. Fichte's normative ethics, like Kant's, is grounded in an a priori principle of morality, which he describes in *The System of Ethics* as follows: 'The principle of morality is the necessary thought of the intellect that it ought to determine its freedom in accordance with the concept of self-sufficiency, absolutely and without exception' (IV: 59).[1] Fichte's principle of morality, also like Kant's, is formal and it is sometimes said that 'nothing can be inferred from it about what we ought to do.'[2] If you desire a 'plug and play' principle that serves to test whether a certain maxim or act possesses moral worth or deserves moral praise, Fichte's principle will leave you wanting. There is no procedure, heuristic or calculative device to supplement ethical deliberation; rather, moral agency requires the hard work of reflection, examining one's convictions, acting with conscience and bringing one's entire rational and non-rational being under, what Fichte calls, the 'sway' [*Botmäßigkeit*] of self-sufficiency.

Among the interpretive difficulties Fichte's *System of Ethics* presents is identifying a clear or precise sense of the term 'self-sufficiency' [*Selbständigkeit*]. Since the concept of self-sufficiency is central to Fichte's principle of morality, the validity of any interpretation of his ethical thought hangs on how one understands it. Recent commentators have struggled to illuminate the concept, some even concluding, as in the case of Allen Wood, that the concept is 'indefinite'.[3] According to Wood, Fichte 'does not tell us clearly enough what he means by "absolute independence and self-sufficiency."'[4] Wood is responding to Michelle Kosch's consequentialist interpretation of Fichte's ethics, where self-sufficiency and independence are defined as rational mastery or control over nature, what she calls 'material independence'.[5] For Wood, if self-sufficiency were the final end that agents ought to maximize by calculative means (a view Wood rejects), then the concept of self-sufficiency would need to be relatively determinate. Provided an indeterminate end, a calculating agent will be incapable of selecting the means required for maximizing it. Kosch responds to Wood's criticism by noting that Fichte's conception of the final end of moral agency is 'no worse off than other' consequentialist-maximizing theories in this respect. On her view, Fichte only really needs to 'specify what counts as more or less independence'.[6] Kosch's response is a familiar rejoinder to ideal theorizing: as agents we do not need to worry about what the ideal looks like, only how to reform current conditions.[7] Even if the final end lacks determinacy and we are not in a position to adequately grasp what self-sufficiency as material independence looks like, as finite and dependent beings we can in each moment sufficiently grasp how to reform current conditions to remove limitations on our agency. With the removal of these limitations, the end of self-sufficiency and independence will be maximized.

There is good reason to be sceptical of Kosch's consequentialist interpretation of Fichte's normative ethics. The main objection, as Wood and Owen Ware have illustrated, is that, for Fichte, the intrinsic worth of an action resides, not in its effects or results, but in its motive.[8] However, Wood's own claim that the concept of self-sufficiency is 'indefinite' or of 'virtual unintelligibility' raises a serious worry for Fichte's ethics that commentators have not sufficiently appreciated: on what grounds can one establish that the moral principle is applicable to human beings if the concept of self-sufficiency is indefinite?[9] To more clearly see the problem, consider the following dialogue between a philosopher and a student:

> **Philosopher**: And, so, morality requires that you determine your actions in accordance with the concept of self-sufficiency, absolutely and without exception.
> **Student**: Well said, but please do tell me: what is self-sufficiency?
> **Philosopher**: I am sorry, but I can't. You see, the concept of self-sufficiency is indefinite – I just can't give you a clear enough account of it. But, be sure, morality requires that you determine your actions according to it.

I take it that this brief dialogue will leave the student justifiably sceptical. If Fichte does indeed view self-sufficiency as indefinite, then it is not clear why one should bother with his *System of Ethics*, since its central concept remains, as Wood suggests, virtually unintelligible.

To save Fichte's *System of Ethics* from this kind of objection I will aim to bring some determinacy to the concept of self-sufficiency. My primary aim, then, is to clarify the concept of self-sufficiency to avoid the kind of scepticism Wood's remarks engender. My strategy will be to determine in §2 and §3 two related senses of self-sufficiency. In §4 I will illustrate how the two senses of self-sufficiency bring determinacy to the idea of self-sufficiency as a final end. Based on the role of such a final end in his ethics, some commentators have concluded that Fichte endorses a teleological ethical theory. Just how his practical philosophy is teleological has proven to be a matter of debate. In §4 I also argue that one way in which Fichte's practical philosophy is teleological is that he endorses a teleological theory of action. I conclude the essay with §5 where I offer some brief remarks on Fichte's conception of ethical life.

2. Fichte's deduction of the moral principle

In response to Wood's claim that the concept of self-sufficiency is indefinite, I will first argue that a clear sense of self-sufficiency can be found in Fichte's deduction of the principle of morality. Fichte's deduction concludes by noting that the principle is a 'thought' that is grounded in 'an intellectual intuition of absolute activity' of the I (IV: 59). From an analysis of this intellectual intuition one can derive the principle of morality: that the intellect 'ought to determine its freedom in accordance with the concept of self-sufficiency, absolutely and without exception' (IV: 60).

Fichte's deduction is notoriously difficult to parse.[10] It is not a straightforward argument, but a series of postulates, proofs and corollaries that are meant to prompt the reader to perform the deduction as if she were constructing a geometric proposition found in Euclid's *Elements*. This is why the deduction begins with a task or postulate (*Aufgabe*), rather than premises.

The first postulate summons the reader to think of herself as separated from everything else. By doing so, she is meant to grasp that the 'essential character of the I' consists in self-activity or what Fichte calls 'a tendency to self-activity for self-activity's sake' (IV: 29). In the first postulate, one approaches oneself *objectively*, or as the object of one's reflection. Fichte's move in the second postulate is to prompt the reader to approach herself from the standpoint of the subject or *subjectively*. To do so, Fichte notes that the I is distinct from a mere thing in that a *thing* has being but not knowledge of its being, yet *the I* only has being when it has consciousness or knowledge of its being (IV: 29). What this means is that 'knowledge of the being of the I' is constitutive of the I. Fichte then leads the reader to see a necessary connection between intuiting herself as self-active and being free in the sense that she has the power to cause herself to act 'by means of mere concepts' (IV: 38). Subjectively, self-activity consists in the activity of causing oneself to act by forming concepts of an action's end.

Fichte continues to prompt the reader to notice that a free being is not determined by blind chance, external force or its own nature (IV: 33–4). A thing is not self-determining since it is either fixed in its being or it possesses determinacy in virtue of its nature or of something beyond itself. In contrast, the intellect, as self-activity or agility (*Agilität*), is not a thing or determinate; it is, thereby, capable of self-determination.[11] The intellect is 'pure activity' and as such lacks a 'any tendency, drive, or inclination' (IV: 38). For this reason, Fichte sometimes refers to the I or intellect as indeterminate – 'the I's action of self-positing is a movement of transition from indeterminacy to determinacy' (*WLnm*, 139). Fichte suggests that 'what is free is supposed to be before it is determined; it is supposed to have an existence independent of its determinacy' (IV: 36). Since the intellect lacks determinacy, it can be self-determining; however, it must first have an indeterminate existence that gains its properties and nature through itself (IV: 36). Self-determination requires that the intellect provide itself a concept of an end according to which it shapes its being. The concept must be a concept of what it is to *become*, 'a concept of its own real being' (IV: 36). The intellect's concept is a ground of its own real being since it is in virtue of the concept and by acting in conformity with it that the intellect becomes a self-sufficient I. For the intellect to be freely self-determining (to be an intellect at all), its activity must be shaped in accordance with a concept that it itself supplies.

Fichte's third postulate summons the reader to grasp *how* the I gains consciousness of its own tendency towards self-activity (IV: 39). The results of the prior two postulates are limited in an important respect: they reveal that the intellect is conscious of its tendency towards self-activity, but not how the intellect becomes conscious of it (IV: 40). To account for this, the tendency must be connected to a drive, since it is in virtue of a drive that material determination is possible. In the *System of Ethics*, Fichte defines a drive as 'a real, inner explanatory ground of an actual self-activity' (IV: 40). A drive, as he explains elsewhere, is a 'self-producing striving' that is determinate in its striving (I: 287). Drives are not determined externally; rather, a drive is part of a thing's internal being and has its causal source in it (I: 287–8). Since the original being of the I is a self-activity, this self-activity must have its explanatory ground in a drive. The intellect, then, consists in a drive through which it determines itself.

Fichte holds that anytime the intellect is determined a 'thought necessarily arises' (IV: 45). The thought that arises is neither conditioned by an object nor another thought, so it must be the case that the thought is 'determined absolutely through itself' (IV: 46). From these considerations, Fichte concludes that the thought must be 'absolute with respect to its form' (IV: 46). The thought, thereby, cannot have a conditional or hypothetical form. Consequently, the thought must be categorical in form. Regarding the thought's content, Fichte concludes that it must be the following: 'that the intellect has to give itself the unbreakable law of absolute self-activity' (IV: 48).

By prompting the reader to reflect on herself as willing, Fichte leads her to grasp a specific thought that has an absolute form and a determinate content according to which a free intellect necessarily determines itself. Here is how Fichte summarizes his results: '[W]e are required to think that we are supposed to determine ourselves consciously, purely and simply through concepts, indeed, in accordance with the concept of absolute self-activity; and this act of thinking is precisely that consciousness of our original tendency to absolute self-activity that we have been seeking' (IV: 49). The form and content of the thought are expressed as a categorical imperative that binds rational beings and constitutes their free and moral agency. Being self-active in this manner is to be self-sufficient. Fichte has established, at least in part, the meaning of self-sufficiency.

Based on Fichte's deduction we can identify a formal meaning of self-sufficiency:

Formal Meaning: formally, self-sufficiency means to legislate for oneself as the ground of one's agency the concept of absolute self-activity and to shape one's agency in accordance with this concept.

Why is this only a formal meaning of self-sufficiency? It is formal because this conception of self-sufficiency does not specify any particular action or end as self-sufficient. In fact, the entire moral law is formal as the material content of our duties must come 'from elsewhere' (IV: 166). The content of the moral law is determined by a number of factors, most importantly, the system of drives, conscience and the conditions of I-hood. However, the formal meaning of self-sufficiency offers a *definite* sense of self-sufficiency.

In response to my formal definition of self-sufficiency, Wood may object that the idea that self-sufficiency is indefinite refers not to the formal meaning of self-sufficiency but to the idea that a material meaning of self-sufficiency can be defined. Part II of the *System of Ethics* examines how the principle of morality is applicable to rational, human beings. The deduction of the applicability of the moral law offers, as I will argue, a second determination of the concept of self-sufficiency.

3. Self-sufficiency and conceptual formation

My aim is to offer an account of self-sufficiency that rejects Wood's claim that the concept of self-sufficiency is indefinite. From Fichte's deduction of the moral principle, I have argued that a formal meaning can be given to the term 'self-sufficiency'. Part of this formal meaning is that the ground of one's agency is the concept of absolute self-activity.

An important point that can be drawn from the deduction of the moral principle is that self-sufficiency involves conceptual determination. This point is expressed most clearly when Fichte states, at the deduction's conclusion, that the moral principle requires that we determine ourselves 'purely and simply through concepts, indeed, in accordance with the concept of absolute self-activity' (IV: 49). Throughout the *System of Ethics*, Fichte stresses that self-sufficiency consists in bringing one's activity under the sway of concepts, that is, the concepts of self-activity, the I or the intellect (IV: 32, 38, 74, 81, 135). Fichte's remark in §10 expresses this idea: 'a reality that has its ground in a concept is called a product of freedom' (IV: 134). The 'reality' is the efficacious exercise of one's agency in the sensible world which brings the object or world in harmony with one's concept.

To clarify his core idea, it is necessary to address Fichte's theory of action and the role of concepts in it. Fichte's theory of action is largely shaped by his theory of the drives and his contention that in acting the I shapes its drives in accordance with concepts. All actions require that the I designs (*entwerfen*) a 'concept of an end' (*Zweckbegriff*) that serves as a guide for one's acting. The concept is the formal ground of action in that the act of willing stems from the concept, and the concept materially determines the action by shaping the drives that are operative in the action and that provide the action with its content (IV: 9). The concept of an end specifies a 'product that is to be realized' through the agent's efficacious action (III: 37). The subject must 'relentlessly' (*unablässig*) keep the end in view as it orients itself towards the goal (III: 37).

Fichte provides a relatively clear sense of how he understands actions to work in §16. There he examines the process of making a choice and acting upon it. Consider a case in which you have three concepts of an end (A, B and C) where they are defined as follows:

A = buy cow milk
B = buy almond milk
C = buy soy milk

How are we to decide between these options? Making a free and rational choice depends on there being some distinguishing property that becomes normatively salient through the exercise of deliberation or reflection. Fichte refers to this property as X. Consider the following case:

X = more environmentally sustainable
C possesses X

X, as a property of C, is merely a fact that only becomes normatively salient when one has a relevant normative reason for acting. For example, one might hold the following normative requirement: whatever is most environmentally sustainable must be preferred (*ceteris paribus*) to everything else. This provides us with a normative reason for selecting C over A or B. Fichte points out that we can construct a syllogism where the major premise of the syllogism identifies what Kant calls a maxim:

1. Whatever is most environmentally sustainable must be preferred (*ceteris paribus*) to everything else (major premise).
2. Between the options of A, B and C, option C is the most environmentally sustainable (minor premise).
3. Therefore, option C is preferred.

A maxim will offer guidance by presenting a salient property under a subjective normative guise. Kant, after all, defines a maxim as a practical principle, or proposition, that contains 'a general determination of the will' and as a subjective principle that a particular subject may take as binding on her agency. Only when the principle is cognized objectively to hold for all rational wills is it determined as a practical law (5: 19). Fichte's moral theory does not rely on a set of heuristics to determine the moral worth of the maxim – instead, the determinate action (C), including one's normative reason, must be taken up in conscience.

What distinguishes Fichte's theory of action from Kant's is that free, moral agency does not require that one act independently of one's natural drive. In fact, moral freedom requires that the natural drive informs the reflective agent in acting – what matters is just how the natural drive shapes the action. Fichte identifies a system of drives that work together in shaping moral agency:

The Natural Drive: a drive the subject has as a part of the organic whole of nature. It determines itself according to its own nature (IV: 112–15). The natural drive is directed at what is material for the sake of enjoyment or satisfaction (IV: 147).[12]

The Pure Drive: a drive toward absolute self-sufficiency (not enjoyment) that arises from the capacity of the I to reflect on its consciousness of the natural drive and to restrain the I from satisfying a material end of the natural drive (IV: 139–43).

The Ethical Drive: a drive that consists in the mixing of the natural drive and the pure drive. The material of the ethical drive stems from the natural drive and it receives its form from the pure drive. Since it receives its form from the pure drive, it is aimed at self-sufficiency (IV: 152).

To see how these drives work together, let me expand on the example of purchasing milk. If I wake up hungry, I may form a particular desire for cereal. As I become conscious of my hunger, I reflect on my natural drive. I may notice that I have no milk and so form the concept of an end to buy milk for my cereal. Now,

I have three distinct ways in which I may achieve this end, A, B, and C. Like 'every possible concept of an end', each of these concepts 'is directed toward the satisfaction of a natural drive' (IV: 148). If I endorse the maxim (1) whatever is most environmentally sustainable must be preferred (*ceteris paribus*) to everything else, then I am positioned to reflect on the natural drive and to shape that drive so it corresponds to my maxim. Through reflection I am to separate myself from the natural drive and aim my action at self-sufficiency, not enjoyment (IV: 142). I reflectively determine that I must deny A and B leaving option C as the concept of an end that is grounded in my settled conviction that (1) provides a normative reason for acting that ought to shape the satisfaction of my natural drive. The conviction consists in an immediate consciousness that (1) is a duty. Conscience, as non-cognitive (or formal), is the immediate feeling and secure conviction that unites itself with a judgment about what our duty is and it is in virtue of conscience that one has a settled conviction that no longer hangs in doubt (IV: 173–5).[13] Fichte formulates the following imperative to express the view: '*always act in accordance with your best conviction concerning your duty*, or, Act according to your conscience' (IV: 156).[14] Upon determining that my conscience non-cognitively validates, my conviction that I ought to act on C for normative reason (1), the ethical drive, as the mixing of the natural and pure drive, is constituted and I am positioned to fulfil my ethical vocation by purchasing a carton of soy milk. I can obviously be distracted from realizing my goal if I see that there is a sale on almond milk, but part of achieving my end involves relentlessly keeping it in view.

Above I argued that self-sufficiency can be given a formal meaning. I now want to suggest that self-sufficiency can also be given a material meaning by tying self-sufficiency to the system of the drives and conscience. Since self-sufficiency requires that the I is determined by concepts, it must be the case that the drives and conscience are determined in the relevant sense by concepts. With this in mind, self-sufficiency has the following meaning:

Material Meaning: materially, self-sufficiency means to conceptually shape the satisfaction of the natural drive so that one's settled conviction determines the pure drive's abstention from or shaping of the natural drive.

It must be noted that the material meaning of self-sufficiency is not separate from its formal meaning. Material self-sufficiency must contain formal self-sufficiency since the natural drive is *conceptually* shaped. The conceptual shaping of the natural drive requires that an action is determined not directly by the natural drive, but by a consciousness of the natural drive as shaped by one's own conceptual powers. To provide conceptual shape to the natural drive one must reflectively separate oneself from the drive, become conscious of its aims, and provide a concept of one's action that guides the realization of the natural drive's satisfaction. However, the concept must correspond with one's settled conviction as validated by the feeling of conscience.[15] My suggestion, then, is that the formal and material meanings together constitute the meaning of self-sufficiency. If this interpretation is right, then the concept of self-sufficiency can be given a definite meaning.

There are two important points I want to draw out that help to further situate my interpretation in the text. First, Fichte contends that self-sufficiency requires that it is the I that wills, not the natural drive (IV: 148). However, all actions are 'demanded (*gefordert*) by the natural drive' (IV: 149). There is an important difference between a demand and an act of willing. The natural drive can make a demand ('satisfy my feeling of hunger!') without willing anything (eating cereal). Fichte, in fact, holds that the natural drive is incapable of willing (IV: 149). The natural drive becomes an element in the agent's willing (and its self-sufficiency) when its demand is given a conceptual form by virtue of the reflective capacities of the pure drive that allow the I to 'elevate' itself above nature and 'intervene' in the 'series of nature' (IV: 140, 141, 142). By giving conceptual form to the natural drive, the I wills, and, thus, is not simply determined by nature. By shaping the conceptual form of the natural drive so that it is identical with the conceptual form of one's settled conviction, one acts self-sufficiently (according to its formal and material meanings). In such a case, the materiality of the natural drive is left in place in that 'I find myself driven to do something that has its material ground solely within me'; however, the natural drive as the material and causal ground of the act of willing is annulled since it is one's conceptual powers in their shaping of the natural drive that are efficacious (IV: 149). When Fichte claims that '[t]he sole determining ground of the matter of our action is [the goal of] ridding ourselves of our dependence upon nature', I take him to be claiming that we only achieve independence from nature when our agency is shaped by the concept of the I, a concept which entails self-sufficiency and independence (IV: 149). As natural beings this involves ridding ourselves of sole dependence on the natural drive through our conceptual and reflective capacities and by shaping the natural world (which I take ultimately to include the social and political world) through these conceptual and reflective capacities. As a causal force, as Fichte acknowledges, 'in reality, all that remains is *formal* freedom', yet the material demand of the natural drive is present as a conceptually shaped content (IV: 149).

Second, Fichte's view is that the concept willed when the agent acts self-sufficiently could have the same result that the natural drive would have had were it to have exercised itself untouched by the pure drive. By providing conceptual shape to the natural drive, however, the end becomes one that is freely willed rather than an occurrence of some sort. Now, when one's settled conviction further shapes the form of the natural drive, even if there is an identical series of bodily movements, the content of the action and its ultimate end have changed (IV: 139). Part of the content of the action is that one is not simply formally willing a concept but willing a dutiful concept; the new end includes the content that one is willing for the sake of self-sufficiency.[16]

4. Self-sufficiency, striving and the infinite

In response to my attempt to provide a more definite meaning to the concept of self-sufficiency, one might worry that all I've done is substituted the terms 'formal meaning' and 'material meaning' for the two types of freedom Fichte identifies in the *System of Ethics*, 'formal freedom' and 'material freedom'. This is a fair response. However, I do not take it to be a flaw of my interpretation, but a strength. Fichte holds that morality and freedom are identical in that to have the thought of oneself as free is to think of oneself as moral and vice versa.[17] This means that self-sufficiency, insofar as it is a moral concept, is also a concept of freedom. On the view I've presented, if we are to ask after the meanings of formal and material freedom, what we will discover is that each type of freedom specifies an aspect of self-sufficiency. The two meanings of self-sufficiency, then, are constitutive of formal and material freedom respectively. Insofar as one is under the sway of self-sufficiency, one is formally and materially free.

There is, however, a more significant objection to my account of self-sufficiency. This objection points out that Wood's claim that self-sufficiency is indefinite refers to a third (or at least a different) sense of self-sufficiency, where self-sufficiency refers to a 'final end' that we can only strive toward, but never achieve.[18] For instance, Fichte claims:

> The ethical drive demands *freedom* – for the sake of *freedom*. Who can fail to see that the word freedom occurs in this sentence with two different meanings? In its second occurrence, we are dealing with an objective state that is supposed to be brought about – our ultimate and absolutely final end: complete independence from everything outside of us. In its first occurrence, we are dealing with an instance of acting as such with no being in the proper sense of the term, with something purely subjective. I am supposed to *act freely* in order to *become free*"
> (IV: 153)

Immediately following this passage, Fichte focuses on the first occurrence of freedom in the passage: 'the ethical drive demands *freedom*'. He notes that this instance of acting has, as of yet, no 'being' and so it is 'purely subjective'. Within the subjective sense of freedom, he draws a distinction between the *how* and the *what* of the action. The 'how' refers to how an action that is free comes about. The 'how' of the action is accounted for in terms of formal freedom where self-sufficiency has its formal meaning. The 'what' refers to what 'must come about in order to be free', what particular duties one, for instance, must perform (IV: 153). Here Fichte has in mind material freedom where self-sufficiency has its material meaning.

The phrase 'for the sake of freedom' refers to freedom in an objective sense, freedom as the final end of self-sufficient independence. If there is a third sense of freedom – and, to be clear, I will suggest that there is not – it would be freedom in its objective sense. Objective freedom is characterized as 'our ultimate and absolutely final end'; it is the final end of our striving as moral beings: 'the [free] action must be part of a series, the infinite continuation of which would render the I absolutely independent' (IV: 153). Relatedly, Fichte states, '[T]he final end of a rational being necessarily lies in infinity; it is certainly not an end that can ever be achieved, but it is one to which a rational being ... is supposed to draw ceaselessly nearer and nearer' (IV: 149).

The interpretation of Fichte's conception of the final end is a matter of controversy. Kosch views these and related passages as outlining a neo-Baconian consequentialism where the constitutive and final end of rational agency is material independence understood as a rational mastery over nature.[19] Ware is sceptical of the consequentialist reading; instead, he argues that Fichte is defending a social perfectionism in which the final end consists in the perfection of individual and social harmony.[20] The sense of harmony Ware has in mind appears in Fichte's following claim: 'absolute agreement or harmony with himself; he ought to produce such harmony in everything that is present for him, for he himself is free and independent only on the condition of such harmony' (IV: 234). As might be evident, both Kosch and Ware attribute to Fichte a teleological ethical theory.[21]

We have to be careful not to conflate two senses of the term 'teleology' in discussing Fichte's concept of the final end. The first sense of teleology has to do with the structure of an ethical theory. John Rawls provides a classic statement of teleology in the ethical sense. For teleological theories, 'the good is defined independently from the right, and then the right is defined as that which maximizes the good'.[22] Rawls's conception of teleological ethics, however, is too narrow, since a teleological ethical theory may define the good independently of the right, allow that the right receives its character due to its relation to the good, but reject the principle of maximization. What, then, distinguishes teleological ethical theories is (1) their conception of the good and (2) whether they endorse a maximizing principle. Classical utilitarianism is teleological in that it defines the good as happiness and views right action as that which maximizes the good. Kosch views Fichte's normative ethics as a consequentialist teleological theory since, on her view, it defines the good as material independence and right action is defined in terms of the maximization of material independence.[23] Ware's picture of Fichte's social perfectionism is, however, a non-maximizing teleological ethical theory. In fact, Ware explicitly acknowledges that his interpretation of Fichte's teleological ethics does not hold that 'the goodness of an action is a maximizing property (in the sense of furthering the end of material independence)'.[24]

I think, however, Ware's qualification leaves open an objection. He does not entirely exclude the goodness of an action from having some relation to the maximizing of a good; instead of the good consisting in material independence from nature, the good could be the maximization of individual and social harmony. However, I do not see how harmony and maximization are compatible. There is a sense in which the maximization of harmony is unintelligible since harmony is an absolute; there is no more or less of harmony, even if we sometimes casually speak this way. You are either in harmony or out of it. One can approximate harmony or come closer to it, but to call that 'maximization' is an abuse of language. Once one has harmony, there is no more of it to be had, and if one falls out of harmony, then the task at hand is not to get more harmony but to rather place oneself into the set of relations in which harmony is achieved. There is also good reason to think that harmony is not a consequence, if by a consequence what is meant is something discrete from the act itself.[25] If harmony is a state of being that requires for its achievement and maintenance a certain type of activity, such that the state of being and activity are one and the same, then the achievement of harmony is not a discrete consequence of any action's activity. The activity is constitutive of the harmony. On Ware's perfectionist reading, it appears that the sense of harmony that Fichte has in mind is viewed as a harmonious activity in just this sense. This entails that the perfectionist reading is teleological, even though it disavows consequentialism and the principle of maximizing. The reason the perfectionist reading is teleological is because it views harmony as a conception of the good and right action as receiving its character from the good.

The second sense of teleology has to do with the structure of action. This conception of teleology is not unrelated to the first, but it is worth distinguishing it to clarify the distinct teleological aspect of Fichte's theory of moral agency. All actions have an end or goal towards which the agent is oriented. Actions also have a means or a way – what Fichte calls a series – according to which the goal is realized. We can describe an action as teleological when the motive of the action – the reason for the sake of which one acts – bends the action towards a goal to which one is, by virtue of the kind of being one is, disposed.[26] The thought here is that actions are teleological in that one's agency has a particular dispositional shape or tendency to it, an orientation towards an end, you might say, built into the structure of the action.[27] The end of the action is the completion or achievement point after which the agent strives. Reaching the achievement point is the realization of the kind of being one is or the kind of being one posits oneself to be. For Fichte, the end is not a discrete state of affairs, as required by consequentialism, but the *activity of being an I*, the kind of being one posits oneself to be.[28] It must be noted that a teleological ethical theory need not endorse a teleological theory of action, since one's preferred theory of action may reject talk of dispositions.

On my view, Fichte defends a teleological theory of action, a point that commentators have failed to appreciate. While I do not think Fichte endorses a consequentialist ethics (*pace* Kosch), I am sympathetic with Ware's reconstruction of Fichte's *System of Ethics* as a teleological ethical theory. However, I think his interpretation fails to adequately centre the concept of the I, or I-hood, as the final end, preferring instead to highlight harmony as a state of being any I would actualize in virtue of being an I. What I have to say below might be seen as an attempt to clarify an aspect of Fichte's conception of the final end in a way that is largely compatible with the teleological interpretation offered by Ware.

What I want to highlight is that Fichte's moral principle is formulated within the context of a teleological theory of action; it provides a concept of self-sufficiency that operates as an end of action that constrains all moral agency, while the I consists in a disposition to strive to realize the end of self-sufficient independence, not because that is a valued state of affairs one seeks to maximize, but rather because striving to achieve the end is to realize one's being as I-hood. On this view, self-sufficient independence is the dispositional end posited as a necessary feature of the concept of the I; the I is under the sway of the concept of self-sufficiency, since the concept of self-sufficiency is a constitutive concept of the I. The concept of self-sufficiency, as specified in the moral principle, serves as a concept of an action's achievement point (or end), and at this point lies an I that has conceptually shaped itself into a formally and materially self-sufficient and independent I.

Now, my talk of disposition might strike some as un-Fichtean. I think, however, this impression is misguided. In the deduction of the principle of morality Fichte employs dispositional language when he claims that the 'ESSENTIAL CHARACTER OF THE I … CONSISTS IN A TENDENCY (*Tendenz*) TO SELF-ACTIVITY FOR SELF-ACTIVITY'S SAKE' (IV: 29).[29] He also refers to '*the absolute tendency toward the absolute*' (IV: 28). Fichte is clear that the tendency of the I should not be conflated with the concept of a drive, since a drive is 'a real, inner explanatory ground' of the I's 'actual self-activity' which operates 'necessarily in a materially determined manner' (IV: 40, 29). The difference between a tendency and a drive is that a tendency to self-activity belongs to the I as an essential property whereas the drive belongs to the I as explanatory material ground of the I's self-activity.[30] This means that the tendency of the I is not unrelated to the concept of a drive, for the tendency 'NECESSARILY EXPRESSES ITSELF (äussert sich Nothwendig) IN RELATION TO THE ENTIRE I AS DRIVE' (IV: 40). What is important, for my purposes, is that the tendency of the I to self-activity constitutes an essential character of the I. Nevertheless, to describe the I's consciousness of its tendency, a drive is posited as that through which the tendency is expressed and through which consciousness of it is possible. Fichte also describes drives in dispositional terms when he compares the concept of a drive to the image of the steel spring he employs throughout Part I: 'Just in the case of the steel spring, the drive will result in a self-activity as soon as the external conditions are present' (IV: 41).

The real worry one might have about interpreting the tendency of the I in dispositional terms is that it appears as if what is attributed to the I is a natural or contingent disposition that undermines the freedom of the I. While the natural drive should be understood in naturalistic terms, the I's tendency towards self-activity should not. First, the I as such is not a part of nature, and since the disposition or tendency is an essential feature of the I, it cannot be a part of nature. As Fichte remarks, 'The I is originally supposed to be a tendency' (IV: 39). Fichte's thought must be that in its self-positing, the I constitutes itself as a tendency towards absolute self-activity. The I's tendency, in other words, is not dependent on or based in nature; instead, it is original to the I as such. Furthermore, the disposition or tendency is the I's own self-activity, not an external cause of the I's moral agency.

It is helpful to draw on Fichte's distinction between the I as a self-reverting activity (intellectual intuition) on the one hand, and the I as an idea on the other. If the I is originally a tendency towards self-activity, then it is the I as a self-reverting activity that Fichte has in mind. However, this conception of the I's tendency is related to the conception of the I as an idea. The self-reverting activity expresses the form of I-hood whereas the 'entire content of I-hood is included in the thought of the I as an idea' (I: 516). While the entire *Wissenschaftslehre* proceeds from the I as self-reverting (or self-positing), practical philosophy proceeds from the self-reverting I to the I as idea, and it exhibits the content of I-hood in the form of a system of ethics that identifies the actions and duties required for achieving the idea of the I, for becoming a pure I.

What it means, then, to say that the I possesses a tendency in regard to the agency of the I is that the orientation of the I's action is shaped by its self-active being, which, due to its finitude, is always in the process of becoming what it, in a sense, posits itself to be, a pure I or complete and thorough rational being. I suggested above that an action can be described as teleological when the motive of the action bends the action towards a goal to which one is, by virtue of the kind of being one is, disposed. My thought is that the act of self-positing involves constituting oneself as the kind of being whose essence is I-hood and that this involves likewise positing a goal towards which one, as an I, is disposed. From a formal standpoint, this means one's being consists in self-reverting activity. However, the motive for which one acts bends one's action towards the goal of realizing the idea of the I by actualizing through one's agency the concept of the I fully in its content. Our actions, then, are for the sake of realizing the end of I-hood (as an idea). In virtue of being a self-reverting activity, one immediately has the concept of the I as an idea to be realized. What exactly does it mean to actualize the concept of the I fully in its content? If, as Wood suggests, the final end is indefinite, we should discover that Fichte cannot specify what the end consists in. Here, however, is what Fichte says:

> The I as an idea is identical with a rational being. On the one hand, it is the latter insofar as this being has completely [*vollkommen*] exhibited universal reason within itself, has actually become rational through and through [*durchaus*], and is nothing but rational. As such, it has ceased to be an individual, which it was only because of the limitations of sensibility. On the other hand, the I as an idea is the rational being insofar as this being has also succeeded in completely realizing reason outside of itself in the world, and which thus also remains posited within this idea.
>
> (I: 515–16)

To fully actualize the content of the I as an idea is to become a rational being that is rational 'through and through' in all of its activity. This is what it means to achieve self-sufficiency and independence, to be, as I've put it, formally and materially self-sufficient.

Now that I've made the distinction between teleological ethical theories and teleological action theories, it will be useful to return to the objective sense of freedom Fichte identifies when he claims that 'the ethical drive demands *freedom* – for the sake of *freedom*'. Fichte is clear that the two senses of freedom are subjective and objective. Subjective freedom consists in the conceptual shaping of one's natural drive under the sway of the concept of self-sufficiency. The formal and material conceptual shaping of the natural drive is done for the sake of objective freedom or the state of being through and through a rational, pure I. Objective freedom is not a third sense of freedom but is simply the realization of subjective freedom such that one is a perfect instantiation of I-hood.

5. Conclusion

I want to conclude by addressing how my interpretation offers a way of understanding the shape of ethical life. For Fichte, ethical life is shaped by the concept of the I, where the I's content specifies an idea to be realized. This goal is internal to the concept of the I, and by positing oneself as an I, one constitutes oneself as the kind of being disposed towards realizing the idea of I-hood. I-hood as an idea is *a* concept of an action's end.

According to Fichte's philosophy of striving, we are always working to become an I, both in the relatively discrete actions we take up (e.g., buying soy milk) and in the actions that we carry out over months, years or an entire life. When I act to purchase milk, buying the milk is a concept of an end. However, there is a second-order concept of an end I'm striving to achieve at the same time, the concept of being or becoming an I; and, it is this second-order concept that serves as a constraint on how I work to carry out the first-order concept. I think the distinction between first-order and second-order concepts of an end is implicit in the following passage:

> The final end of the moral law is absolute independence and self-sufficiency, not merely with respect to our will, for the latter is always independent, but also with respect to our entire being. This goal is unachievable, but there is still a constant and uninterrupted process of approximation to this goal. Accordingly, there must be a constant, uninterrupted series of actions by means of which one draws nearer and nearer to this goal, a series that starts from the initial standpoint occupied by each person. In each case, conscience can approve only of those actions that lie in this series. One can think of this with the help of the image of a straight line. Only the points lying along this line can be approved, and absolutely nothing that lies outside it.
>
> (IV: 209)

The final end (the second-order concept) the moral law prescribes is the end of I-hood, a pure and absolutely free I. The end is unachievable because we are finite beings or beings of limited power and knowledge. The immediate end, the first-order end, is the end approved by conscience. Throughout our lives we work to realize a finite number of first-order ends along a series of actions in our attempt to realize our final concept of an action's end, the end of being a pure, self-sufficient I. Throughout our striving we develop through reflection, experience and education greater insight into what it means to be an I – that certain convictions are, for instance, inconsistent with the norms of self-sufficiently.[31] As we do this, we can get closer to this end, nearer and nearer, even as it remains out of reach. The concept of the I demands that we self-sufficiently build a life by conceptually shaping the natural drive to achieve self-sufficiency and independence as an I. An entire life, on this view, constitutes a complex action guided by the end of I-hood. Or, put differently, ethical life just is the unfinished project of becoming a self-sufficient I.[32]

Notes

1. All citations of Fichte follow the format of volume and then page number as in Fichte 1971. I've relied on the following English translations: Fichte 2005, 2000, 1994.
2. Wood 2016: 102.
3. Wood 2016: 179–80.
4. Wood 2016: 176.
5. Kosch 2018, especially Ch. 3.
6. Kosch 2018: 44.
7. See Anderson 2010, for an example.
8. Wood 2016: 103 and 150 and Ware 2020: 177. Fichte notes: 'It is claimed that the human mind finds itself to be absolutely compelled to do certain things entirely apart

from any extrinsic ends, but purely and simply for the sake of doing them. [...] In so far as such a compulsion is supposed to manifest itself necessarily in human beings [it] constitutes what is called *the moral or ethical* nature of human beings.' (IV: 13).

9   Wood 2016: 179 and 148. Ware 2020: Ch. 8 helpfully addresses Wood's view that self-sufficiency is 'indefinite.' His approach is distinct from my own in that he does not directly specify the meaning of self-sufficiency in his response to Wood. Additionally, Ware's interpretation of the final end highlights the I's 'agreement' or 'harmony' with itself, rather than the concept of the I, which is the focus of my interpretation.

10 Guyer 2015 reconstruct Fichte's argument as a regressive transcendental argument, while Ware 2020 stresses, in contrast, its dialectical structure. Neither have sufficiently highlighted the performative dimension of the argument – that recognition of its soundness hangs on one's actual constructive performance of the steps involved.

11 Fichte defines 'agility' as 'the transition to acting' that is involved in moving from an indeterminate, 'passive state of repose ... to one of determinacy' (*WLnm*, 141, 133).

12 See also IV: 121 for Fichte's remarks on the formative drive (*Bildungstrieb*), an aspect of the natural drive (IV: 121).

13 This formulation draws on Kosch's interpretation of Fichte's theory of conscience. See Kosch 2018: Ch. 4.

14 Just how to understand Fichte's theory of conscience is a matter of debate. Some commentators, including Hegel 1977: 150–1 and Neuhouser 1990, claim that his theory of conscience is too subjective and arbitrary. See Breazeale 2014 for a response to Hegel and Neuhouser, and Wood 2016: Ch. 5, Kosch 2018: Ch. 4 and Ware 2020: Ch. 5 for responses to this criticism and competing interpretations of conscience in Fichte.

15 See Brownlee 2022 for a helpful discussion of the distinction between conscience and conviction in Fichte.

16 Kosch views this new end in terms of 'mastery of the outside world' (Kosch 2018: 27).

17 Fichte writes, '[T]hese are not two thought, one of which can depend upon the other; rather this is one and the same thought' (IV: 53). In contrast to what Allison 1986 calls the 'reciprocity thesis', Ware 2020 argues that Fichte endorses an 'identity thesis'. See also Wood 2016: 121–3.

18 A related objection is that Fichte's theory of moral agency endorses a form of Hegel's 'bad infinity'. I am not able to address this concern here, but Martin 2007 examines the issue.

19 Kosch 2018. See 36ff for her interpretation of these passages. Kosch writes, on the 'more modern, Baconian ... vision of the path to greater independence, technical mastery is not held fixed and the scope of plans and projects is allowed to expand with and beyond it [...] it is this ... model that Fichte has in mind' (Kosch 2018: 49).

20 Ware 2020. See especially Chs. 7 and 8. The harmony Ware has in mind refers to what Fichte calls 'absolute agreement or harmony with himself; he ought to produce such harmony in everything that is present for him, for he himself is free and independent only on the condition of such harmony' (IV: 234). Ware also cites the following passage: 'If all human beings could become perfect, and reach their highest and final goal, then they would be fully equal to one another; they would be only one; a single subject' (6: 310). However, Ware could be more forthcoming about the meaning of harmony. There is reason to think there are numerous (though related) notions of harmony at work in Fichte's philosophy. For instance, the following

passages identify a specific sense of the term: never contradicting oneself (VI: 297), lacking in diversity (VI: 297), representing things so they harmonize with the pure I (VI: 298), the harmony of external things with practical concepts (VI: 299, IV: 70), harmony between the original I and the actual I (IV: 143), the feeling of harmony (IV: 144), certainty as a form of epistemic harmony (IV: 169), harmony with oneself (IV: 234).

21 In contrast to Kosch, but in agreement with Wood, Ware holds that Fichte's ethics is deontological (Ware 2020: 175–80.). Ware argues Fichte's ethics is deontological at the level of moral deliberation, but at the level of philosophical reflection, it is teleological (177).

22 Rawls 1971/1999: 21.

23 Kosch 2018: 52.

24 Ware 2020: 228, n. 30.

25 Kosch's consequentialism appears to view the consequence promoted as 'some end beyond the act itself' (Kosch 2018: 52, n. 13).

26 This formulation is influenced by Charles Taylor remark that 'central to teleological explanation is the notion that the subject whose behaviour is to be explained is bent in a certain direction or towards a certain consummation' (Taylor 1970: 84).

27 For my purposes, 'disposition' and 'tendency' are interchangeable.

28 Williams 1973 makes this point about consequentialism.

29 Fichte employs in the *System of Ethics* the term 'disposition' (*Gesinnung*) when speaking about a moral or dutiful disposition. I do think that there is a connection between the tendency (*Tendenz*) of the I, the drives (*Triebe*) of the I, and the moral disposition (*Gesinnung*) of dutiful persons; exploring this connection is not possible here. While Breazeale and Zöller translate *Tendenz* as 'tendency' in their translation of the *System of Ethics*, Breazeale selects 'disposition' for the translation of *Tendenz* in his translation of the *Wissehschaftslehre nova methodo*.

30 Wood 2016: 115 examines the difference between a tendency and drive.

31 I cannot comment here on the social dimension of Fichte's view of ethical life, though I am sensitive to the fact that a fuller account of self-sufficiency must do so. Ware 2020, Kosch 2018 and Wood 2016 have more to say about this aspect of Fichte's moral theory.

32 I'm grateful to the following people for their comments on the essay: Tim Brownlee, Anthony Bruno, James Clarke, Ben Crowe, Penelope Haulotte, Joe Saunders and Owen Ware.

References

Allison, Henry (1986), 'Morality and Freedom: Kant's Reciprocity Thesis', *Philosophical Review*, 95 (3): 393–425.

Anderson, Elizabeth (2010), *The Imperative of Integration*, Princeton: Princeton University Press.

Breazeale, Daniel (2014), 'In Defense of Fichte's Account of Ethical Deliberation', *Archiv für Geschichte der Philosophie*, 94 (2): 178–207.

Brownlee, Timothy (2022), 'Conscience, Conviction, and Moral Autonomy in Fichte's Ethics', *British Journal for the History of Philosophy*, 1–20. https://doi.org/10.1080/09608788.2022.2077301.

Fichte, J. G. (1971), *Fichtes Werke*, ed. I. H. Fichte, Berlin: de Gruyter.
Fichte, J. G. (1994), *Introductions to the Wissenschaftslehre and Other Writings (1797–1800)*, trans. Daniel Breazeale, Indianapolis: Hackett.
Fichte, J. G. (2000), *Foundations of Natural Right*, trans. Michael Baur and ed. Frederick Neuhouser, Cambridge: Cambridge University Press.
Fichte, J. G. (2005), *The System of Ethics*, trans. Daniel Breazeale and Günter Zöller, Cambridge: Cambridge University Press.
Guyer, Paul (2015), 'Fichte's Transcendental Ethics', in Sebastian Gardner and Matthew Grist (eds), *The Transcendental Turn*, 135–58, Oxford: Oxford University Press.
Hegel, G. W. F. (1977), *The Difference between Fichte's and Schelling's System of Philosophy*, trans. Walter Cerf and H. S. Harris, Albany: SUNY Press.
Kosch, Michelle (2018), *Fichte's Ethics*, Oxford: Oxford University Press.
Martin, Wayne (2007), 'In Defense of Bad Infinity: A Fichtean Response to Hegel's *Differenzschrift*', *Hegel Bulletin*, 28 (1–2): 168–87.
Neuhouser, Frederick (1990), *Fichte's Theory of Subjectivity*, Cambridge: Cambridge University Press.
Rawls, John (1971/1999), *A Theory of Justice*, Cambridge: Harvard University Press.
Taylor, Charles (1970), 'Explaining Action', *Inquiry: An Interdisciplinary Journal of Philosophy*, 13 (1–4): 54–89.
Ware, Owen (2020), *Fichte's Moral Philosophy*, Oxford: Oxford University Press.
Williams, Bernard (1973), 'A Critique of Utilitarianism', in *Utilitarianism: For and against*, 77–135, Cambridge: Cambridge University Press.
Wood, Allen (2016), *Fichte's Ethical Thought*, Oxford: Oxford University Press.

Part Two

The nineteenth century: The post-Kantians, idealists and pragmatists; nature, politics and experience

5

The feeling of freedom: Schelling on the role of freedom in grasping nature

Dalia Nassar

'The free person alone knows *that there is a world outside him.'*
– Schelling, *Ideas for a Philosophy of Nature*

One of the most widespread views about Schelling concerns the relation between his early and late works. It is commonly assumed that there are fundamental differences between Schelling's early idealistic writings and his later proto-existentialist work, and it is often his 1809 essay on human freedom that marks the point of transition – from a rationalist idealism inspired by Fichte and Spinoza, to a position that emphasizes experience and freedom over against reason and necessity. The pervasiveness of this view can be seen in the fact that Schelling interpreters are themselves often divided: between those who focus on the early (rational) Schelling, who contributed to the Kantian and Fichtean legacies, and those who focus on the later Schelling, who is much closer to Kierkegaard, Nietzsche and Heidegger.

Schelling's early emphasis on necessity and rational construction goes hand in hand with what we identify with idealism. In this sense, idealism is taken to mean that nature (or reality) is determined by a fundamental idea, which realizes itself in time and space. A 'subjective idealist', to use Frederick Beiser's terminology, regards the human mind (or the categories, in Kant's case), to be the origin or source of the rational idea.[1] By contrast, an 'objective idealist', to invoke Beiser again, regards the idea as inherent in nature, in the world. The idea is thus not specifically human; in fact, the human being is a moment within the idea's self-realization – a more complex manifestation of the same rules that underlie the rest of the natural world. Schelling (according to Beiser) is in the latter camp, although his very early writings are sometimes (mistakenly) regarded as Fichtean.

But what does this idealism mean for Schelling's understanding of freedom? Although freedom is not clearly at the centre of Schelling's early writings, it is never denied or even questioned. In fact, at times freedom surprises the reader in its appearance at various points in Schelling's early corpus. Schelling's February 1795 letter to Hegel, in which he writes that '[t]he alpha and omega of all philosophy is *freedom*', is perhaps the most well-known example of his view that philosophy is essentially concerned with freedom. What then does his idealism, and his emphasis on necessity, imply for his account of freedom? Does it imply that for the early Schelling human freedom is nothing other than rational self-legislation?[2] In other words, does it mean that Schelling, in his early writings, has no real conception of freedom, insofar as freedom is understood as rational necessity – self-realization according to the *idea*?

On a number of levels, this seems to be the case. Schelling emphasizes necessity both in his earliest philosophical writings and in his philosophy of nature and identifies it with rationality and idealism. As he writes in the 1797 *Ideas for a Philosophy of Nature*, the aim is to grasp the *necessity* of nature, which means both the subjective necessity of my mind's representation of nature and the objective necessity within nature (HKA 1/5, 83; *Ideas*, 23).[3] There is, in other words, no place for freedom as something distinct from natural/rational necessity.

This account, furthermore, makes sense when we consider Schelling's claims about the relation between transcendental philosophy and *Naturphilosophie*: transcendental philosophy begins with the mind, and from there seeks to derive nature, while *Naturphilosophie* begins with nature, and from there seeks to derive mind. The two directions assume a fundamental unity – or compatibility – between nature and freedom (see *STI*, 7). Schelling's famous statement at the conclusion of the Introduction to the *Ideas* can be regarded as consolidating this view: 'nature should be mind made visible, mind the invisible nature. Here then is the absolute identity of mind *in us* and nature *outside us*' (HKA 1/5, 107; *Ideas*, 42).

These various claims imply that for the early Schelling, there is no opposition between the laws of the mind and those of nature, between human freedom and natural necessity. They are ultimately grounded in a fundamental rational unity.

But is it that straightforward? Is it really the case that nature and freedom are originally grounded in a rational unity, and if so, what exactly do we mean by 'rational unity'? What is this unity and on what is *it* grounded?

A look at Schelling's first work in the philosophy of nature – the *Ideas* – reveals a more complex and intriguing story, one in which freedom and nature are indeed coextensive, but not reducible to a rational idea, or to any conception of rational necessity. To get at Schelling's distinctive account of freedom and its relation to nature, we must begin by considering the goals of this first work in the philosophy of nature, first by understanding its historical context and Schelling's critique of his contemporaries and predecessors writing on the nature of nature, and then moving on to consider Schelling's own philosophy of nature, and the way in which Schelling seeks to account for both consciousness and embodiment – and in so doing, comes to regard them as mutually dependent. In other words, Schelling came to the compelling and largely overlooked view that mind and body, freedom and nature, can only emerge in relation to one another – even though they are not reducible to one another.

1. Background

To begin with, it is important to offer a brief discussion of what the *Ideas* is about and what it aims to achieve. The work concerns matter theory, the foundations of chemistry and the concept of nature in general. Throughout Schelling considers the latest theories on combustion, light, electricity and magnetism and attempts to make sense of these various natural phenomena from a philosophical perspective. Schelling's references, in turn, are largely to natural philosophers, including Le Sage, Buffon, Herschel, La Mettrie, Euler and Lichtenberg, although he also makes reference to philosophers, above all Kant, who had published on matter theory eleven years earlier, in the *Metaphysical Foundations of Natural Science* (1786). Conspicuously, there is not one mention of Fichte in the 1797 edition of the text (and in the 1806 edition, the two mentions are critical). Spinoza and Leibniz are two other philosophers who are mentioned but play a less significant role than Kant.

Schelling demonstrates a solid understanding of eighteenth-century matter theory and of the ways in which philosophy can and must contribute to its theoretical underpinnings. Thus while the book is deeply engaged with natural philosophy, it is also (and fundamentally) a philosophical work, in that it considers questions that remain largely undiscussed or under-theorized in natural-philosophical writings. One of Schelling's primary aims in the book is to offer a critique of mechanical philosophy and furnish an alternative to mechanical conceptions of matter. The trouble with mechanical philosophy and its variations (including Newtonianism and Kant's adaption of Newtonianism) is that it is 'a purely rational system [*ein rein spekulatives System*]', whose aim is to develop a coherent account of matter based on a fundamental principle. It simply applies its account of nature onto reality, without any concern for whether its concepts are in fact applicable to experience: 'it does not ask what *is*, and what can be determined from experience'; rather, it 'makes assumptions of its own, and then asks: if this or that were the case, as I take it to be, what would follow from that?' (HKA 1/5, 105; *Ideas*, 167). Why does Schelling regard mechanical philosophy in this way?

Mechanical philosophy in the eighteenth century can be distinguished into two main camps, both of which seek to provide a general account of matter. The first, Cartesian, view regards matter as inert and only capable of being affected by the external forces of motion, while the second, Newtonian, view seeks to make sense of phenomena such as action at a distance and gravity, both of which imply that material forces are not reducible to the physical impact forces of the Cartesians. In fact, gravity implies an internal force that is not based on the external laws of motion.

Schelling criticizes both accounts on similar grounds: neither, he argues, furnishes what it purports to furnish, namely an 'explanation' of matter. The Cartesian picture does not ask: what makes matter possible. Rather, it begins with the simple assertion that matter exists, and without further elucidating this assertion, moves to make claims *about* matter (HKA 1/5, 196; *Ideas*, 157). Such a procedure does not offer an *explanation* of matter because it presupposes matter. What it goes on to call an 'explanation' (such as a mechanical-causal account of matter's activity in space) is not concerned with matter as such – with what makes matter possible – but with its action in space (with the laws of motion). For this reason, Schelling argues, it is not an explanation at all, but a description or a 'very precise expression of the phenomenon [*sehr präciser Ausdruck des Phänomens*]' (HKA 1/5, 229n; *Ideas*, 194n1).[4] Matter is left unexplained. This leads to a fundamental blindness with regard to matter. By simply beginning with matter, this account does not ask *how* a body in space, how embodiment, is possible in the first place.

The Newtonian view of matter as possessing original forces is equally problematic (HKA 1/5, 193; *Ideas*, 154). On the one hand, the notion that matter *has* forces presupposes that matter exists independently of these forces and is not reducible to them: thus it *has* forces. Yet, if matter is essentially in space, it cannot exist independently of its spatial location and the forces that this implies. On the other hand, forces such as attraction and repulsion presuppose occupied space – they do not act in empty space. In other words, they *presuppose* matter. This means that neither matter nor forces can exist independently of one another, such that it is meaningless to speak of matter as *having* forces. This is how he puts it:

> When Newton himself said of the force of attraction that it was *materiae vis insita, innata*, etc., he was mentally attributing to matter an existence independent of the attractive force. Matter could thus also be *real*, without any attractive forces; that it has them (that, as some of Newton's disciples said, a higher hand has impressed this tendency upon it, so to speak) is a *contingent* thing, as regards the existence of matter itself. But if attractive and repulsive forces are themselves conditions of the *possibility* of matter – or rather, if matter itself is nothing else but these forces, conceived in conflict, then these principles stand at the apex of all natural science, either as lemmas from a higher science, or as axioms that must be presupposed before all else, if physical explanation is to be otherwise possible at all.
>
> (HKA 1/5, 192; *Ideas*, 154)

Ultimately the trouble with the Newtonian picture is that it seeks to *use* forces to *explain* matter; in so doing, however, it regards forces as separable from matter – when, in fact, matter cannot be thought of at all without forces. Or, as Schelling puts it, 'you cannot think [*denken*] matter at all without force' (HKA 1/5, 79; *Ideas*, 18). Thus, although it purports to explain matter, the Newtonian view provides no explanation at all – rather, it defers explanation, by seeking to explain matter through occult forces, not otherwise explicable.

Kant, in the *Metaphysical Foundations of Natural Science*, sought to offer a third alternative. In contrast to the Cartesians who regarded matter as pure extension in space, and the Newtonians who regarded matter as possessing only one internal force (gravity or attraction), Kant argues that matter is dynamic in that it is the outcome of two opposing forces: extension and limitation, or repulsion and attraction. These forces, he explains, can be *inferred* from the empirical *concept* of matter (AA 4: 509). As that which exists in space, matter must be extended (this is the meaning of impenetrability) and limited. For it is only insofar as extension is limited, Kant maintains, that we can have a *body* in the first place.

Importantly, Kant's account is based on *inferences* from the *concept* of matter and has nothing to do with presentation in intuition. The fundamental forces, he writes, 'can be assumed only if they unavoidably belong to the *concept* that is demonstrably fundamental and not further derivable from any other (like that of the filling of space), and then, in general are repulsive and attractive forces that counteract them'. This means, however, that we can never be certain of these forces; for insofar as they are merely conceptually inferred, Kant explains, we cannot 'presume to suppose them as actual,' and 'their possibility,' he adds, 'can never be comprehended' (AA 4: 524).

Both the Newtonians and Kant argued that matter is inseparable from its forces. Neither however grasped the implications of this claim. For if matter and its forces are inseparable, then these forces cannot be regarded as causes of material phenomena (as the Newtonians maintained). Causes are separable from that which they cause, while these forces cannot be. Furthermore, and contra Kant, if attraction and repulsion are inseparable from matter, then they cannot be merely conceptually attached to or inferred from the concept of matter. Insofar as they are conditions for the possibility of matter, and for our presentation of matter in space, Schelling contends, attraction and repulsion must be *real* as opposed to merely *logical* concepts.[5] Merely logical concepts offer a coherent account of the natural world, proceeding analytically from a first premise or a concept, without having to be applicable to experience. The value of such concepts lies in their logical coherence. But there is no *necessary* connection between the concept and what *is*, i.e., experience. Schelling's aim is to provide precisely this connection.

2. Schelling's alternative

If matter and its forces are inseparable, the question arises with regard to the status of these forces. As Kant had argued, they are not objects of experience – given that they cannot be actually exhibited in intuition. But they are also not physical causes of objects insofar as they are inseparable from these objects and thus cannot stand outside of them as a 'cause' does to an 'effect'. This implies, Schelling concludes, that they must lie beyond experience. More specifically, it implies that they lie outside of the purview of the physical sciences. Or, as Schelling puts it, we must alert 'natural science to the fact that it is here employing a concept which, not having grown up on its own soil, must seek its credentials elsewhere, in a higher science' (HKA 1/5, 208; *Ideas*, 171). The foundations or origins of matter, in other words, are not to be found in the empirical study of nature. This means that insofar as they 'precede all experience, the universal forces are considered absolutely necessary' (HKA 1/5, 189; *Ideas*, 148). Their necessity is based on the fact that they are conditions for the possibility of the experience of matter.

In this way, Schelling sets up the framework through which he wants to pursue the problem that Kant had left unresolved: if the dynamic forces of matter are necessary for the possibility of our experience, they are neither objects of empirical knowledge (physical causes) nor logical concepts that are (to quote Kant) merely hypothetical.[6] Thus Schelling's task is to demonstrate where their necessity *comes from*, i.e., to determine the *origins* of these *real* concepts and to show how these concepts can be used with *validity*. In other words, Schelling must pose and respond to two questions. The first is: how do we come to conceive of these forces in the first place, given that they are not directly experienced (HKA 1/5, 195; *Ideas*, 156)? And second, where does their necessity come from? Schelling's framework and the questions that he poses lead in one clear direction: he must offer a kind of *transcendental account* of matter and its forces.

Chapter 4 of Book 2 in the *Ideas* is titled 'First origin of the concept of matter, from the nature of intuition and the human mind [*Erster Ursprung des Begriffs der Materie aus der Natur der Anschauung und des menschlichen Geistes]*'. This title indicates not only the claim that matter is a concept that is inherently connected to the mind but also that the task is to determine the 'origin' of this concept – and, on that basis, demonstrate its validity.

The confusion about the forces of matter, Schelling begins, is a result of a general forgetfulness regarding our active participation in experience. For, he notes, the forces of matter are inextricably connected to *our* experience, to the way in which *we* perceive and structure what we intuit. He writes,

> People forget that these forces are the primary conditions of *our knowledge*, which we attempt in vain to account for from out of our knowledge (either physical or mechanical); that by nature they already lie beyond all knowledge; that as soon as we ask for the reason for them they already lie beyond the realm of experience, which *presupposes* those forces; and that only in the nature of our cognition *as such*, in the first and most primal possibility of our knowledge, can we find a justification for setting them ahead of all natural science, as principles that are utterly indemonstrable in science itself.
>
> (HKA 1/5, 195; *Ideas*, 156)

Attraction and repulsion, he continues, cannot be presented in intuition, yet they are '*conditions* for the possibility of all objective knowledge [Bedingungen *der Möglichkeit aller objektiven Erkenntniß*]' (HKA 1/5, 208; *Ideas*, 171). This requires us to pursue a 'transcendental discussion' of these forces. Or, as he puts it,

> We are therefore set out upon a search for the *birthplace [Geburtsstätte]* of these principles, and the *locale [Ort]* where they are truly and originally at home [*eigentlich und ursprünglich zu Hause*]. And since we know that they necessarily precede everything that we can claim or assert about the things of experience, we must surmise from the outset that their *origin* is to be sought among the conditions of human knowledge as such, and to that extent our inquiry will be a *transcendental discussion [transscendentale Erörterung]* of the concept of matter in general.
>
> (HKA 1/5, 208; *Ideas*, 171; emphasis added)[7]

Schelling's language is striking: the use of the term 'birthplace' and the repeated employment of its synonyms ('locale' and 'origin') mirror Kant's claim in the *Critique of Pure Reason* that the transcendental analytic does not seek to analyse concepts, but to investigate their possibility a priori, by searching for their 'birthplace [*Geburtsorte*]' (A66/B90). This linguistic parallel continues in the next paragraph, where Schelling's language approaches Kant's in the B-Deduction.

In the *Metaphysical Foundations*, Kant analysed the dynamic concept of matter without asking, what are the conditions for the possibility of its presentation? Or, why does matter – as an *object of intuition* – *necessitate* the forces of attraction and repulsion?[8] This was, however, precisely the question which he sought to answer in the Deduction in relation to the categories. For, as Kant of course knew, analysis cannot furnish actual knowledge.⁹ A deduction is necessary. He did not carry out this deduction in relation to matter, however, because matter, unlike the categories, is an 'empirical concept' (AA 4, 469 – 70). It does not carry a priori necessity, and thus its necessity cannot be achieved through a deduction. (We require other foundations – such as mathematics – to furnish this necessity.)

Schelling's contention is that although matter is an empirical concept, it is necessary, and his goal is to demonstrate this empirical necessity through a transcendental account of matter. In other words, he must demonstrate how matter (and its forces) *necessarily* appears as an object of *intuition* – and not as a mere concept.¹⁰ As Schelling puts it, the aim is to allow 'the concept to rise, as it were, before our eyes, and thus to find the ground of its necessity in its own origin' (HKA 1/5, 209; *Ideas*, 172).

Given that matter is not an a priori concept, Schelling's starting point and his task must differ from Kant's. He cannot, in other words, begin with an a priori concept of matter and demonstrate its necessity in that way. But he also cannot begin with the empirical concept of matter. For, Schelling explains, it is not the origin of the concept of matter *as a concept* that he is after, but the origin of the concept in that which grants it reality in the first place, i.e., in intuition. Thus he writes: '[A]ll reality that can accrue to it [i.e., the concept] is lent to it **solely** by the *intuition* that preceded it [*leiht ihm doch **nur** die* Anschauung, *die ihm vorangieng*]. And hence, in the human mind, concept and intuition, thought and image, can and should never be separated' (HKA 1/5, 210; *Ideas*, 173; bold added).

The source of the reality of the concept of matter, then, is intuition. Accordingly, the aim must be to show how intuition delivers the necessary concept of matter. Thus Schelling's 'transcendental discussion' is not a 'deduction' of categories but an account of the reality that *inheres in intuition*. His aim is to demonstrate how intuition and thereby the objects of intuition are real.

He offers a clue as to how he will proceed. There is an *original* unity between intuition and concept, a unity that *precedes* the *application* of the concept onto intuition. The aim, then, is to discover this original unity and discern how, in intuition itself, there is a structure of necessity. What then is intuition?

3. Freedom and compulsion

Intuition, according to Schelling, 'must be produced by an external impression' (HKA 1/5, 211; *Ideas*, 174). But in order for such an impression to occur, it must impress something that will recognize it as external. It must be an impression not on a passive being but on an active, receptive being, a being that will recognize the impression as external to itself.

This means that the impression must be impressed upon an 'original activity in me', an activity, Schelling writes, 'that must also continue to remain free, after the impression in order that it may be able to raise the latter to consciousness' (HKA 1/5, 210; *Ideas*, 173). What Schelling is pointing to here is the fact that my experience of an external world is dependent on my experience of myself in contrast to this externality and vice versa. It is only if I recognize myself as a self, as having an interiority, that I am able to recognize the external impression *as external*.

The external impression originates as a feeling of constraint; as such, however, it must be accompanied by a feeling of non-constraint, a feeling of freedom – a feeling of myself as not being *merely* constrained. Schelling writes: 'It [my activity] *feels its confinement* only insofar as it feels at the same time its original *lack of confinement*' (HKA 1/5, 212; *Ideas*, 175). It is only insofar as I sense myself as free that I sense the constraint *as a constraint*, that I recognize the external *as external*. Accordingly, Schelling explains,

> [W]ith the first consciousness of an external world, the consciousness of myself is also present, and conversely, with the first moments of my self-consciousness, the real world appears before me. The belief in the reality outside me arises and grows with the belief in my own self; one is as necessary as the other; both – not speculatively separated, but in their fullest, *most intimate* co-operation – are the element of my life and all my activity.
>
> (HKA 1/5, 211; *Ideas*, 174)

The feeling of necessity, of being compelled to represent the world as external to myself, is thus always accompanied by a feeling of myself. I become aware of myself *as myself* in contrast to some external object, acting against me. Through this encounter, I at once experience being constrained (by the object) and being free (my independence of the object). Accordingly, with my experience of necessity also comes my experience of freedom. The two emerge simultaneously. To feel necessity at all, I must also and simultaneously feel that which is non-necessary (HKA 1/5, 212; *Ideas*, 175).

The origin of matter, then, is to be found in my experience of constraint and freedom, of something pressing itself upon me, and of myself, as I press against this something. It is important to emphasize that the constraint that this impression exercises upon me has a spatial character and is not an intellectual constraint – as is the case with, for instance, the principle of non-contradiction, which constrains me to think in a particular way. This is not Schelling's starting point. Rather, the starting point is in the *sensation* of constraint, in the *feeling* of something *external to me* pressing upon me. Or, as he puts it, '*here* we are talking of opposing activities in us, insofar as they are *felt* and *sensed*. And it is from this felt and originally sensed conflict in ourselves that we want the *actual* to come forth' (SW 1/2, 220, n.1; *Ideas*, 176, n. 5).

What Schelling's explication suggests is that my experience of myself – and, more specifically, of my sense of myself *as a self* – depends on my embodiment. After all, it is only insofar as I am embodied that I feel constrained (I suffer something other than myself) and, in turn, experience myself as free; i.e., I recognize myself as capable of suffering but not merely suffering. The fact of matter, the *fact* of something existing in space, thus cannot be divorced from my experience of myself and vice versa: my self-consciousness, my experience of myself, cannot be divorced from matter or embodiment. As Schelling puts it, '[t]he free person alone *knows* that there *is* a world outside him' (HKA 1/5, 211; *Ideas*, 174; translation altered).

Accordingly, matter cannot be divorced from its presentation in intuition. It is not merely a concept but something felt and sensed. It is that which presses itself upon me and enables me to sense myself as a self. Thus the question of what matter is and what kind of conceptual determination adequately represents matter must be connected to its presentation in intuition – to the fact that it is something felt and sensed.

But how does this simultaneous *feeling* of constraint and freedom become an *object* of experience – become matter? To answer this question, we have to look at intuition more closely. In the first instance, it is *in* intuition that the conflict between internal and external, between my sense of myself as free and my sense of myself as constrained, emerges. As such, however, the two factors are not mutually exclusive, as they are from a logical or conceptual perspective, in which freedom implies the opposite of necessity and vice versa. Rather, the two must coexist, and indeed it is only in and through their opposition that intuition is possible. In other words, it is only because I experience necessity that I also experience freedom and thus become an intuiting being. In intuition, then, opposition is not a problem and does not result in mutual exclusion. It is necessary. Or, as Schelling puts it, '*[t]he nature of intuition, that which makes it intuition, is that in it absolutely opposite, mutually restricting activities are united*' (HKA 1/5, 215; *Ideas*, 177). It is only through this opposition that I experience myself as both free and constrained – and thus experience myself as a self and the world outside of me. And it is only through this experience that matter, corporeality in space, emerges.

This means that self-consciousness and matter are both products of this opposition. My materiality and my sense of self are, in me, inherently connected. Matter is not external to my consciousness, and in fact, it is only because I am embodied – have feeling and sensation – that I am able to experience myself as free. There is not a fundamental separation between myself as free and myself as natural or embodied; I am free insofar as I am embodied.

I want to pause here and think about the implication of this claim. There is no opposition between freedom and nature; my freedom is not something that requires the *negation* of nature, as the concepts of freedom and necessity negate one another. Rather, freedom depends on nature, on necessity, on embodiment. But this does not mean that freedom is reducible to nature, nor does it mean that nature is equivalent to human freedom. The relation is not one of identity. Schelling makes this clear when he describes matter as the 'visible analogue' of spirit (HKA 1/5, 215; *Ideas,* 177). Analogy does not imply identity, but both similarity and difference, such that the relation between human freedom and nature is one of inextricable connection and likeness, that does not involve identity. Much more needs to be said about this analogical relation between freedom and nature, but for now, I will only make two further remarks.

First, Schelling's claim is that in me, as a human being, freedom and nature are co-determining. The origin of freedom, of my ability to determine myself, is fundamentally connected to my embodiment, my interaction with bodies in space. This means that reason or rationality is not the ground or basis of this original co-determination of nature and freedom. Rather, reason is a product of this reciprocal determination – it is the *outcome* of a self-conscious mind. Accordingly, experience does not come about or is not made possible through rational a priori constraints (as provided by the categories of the understanding, for instance), but through a pre-rational encounter, whose exact character has yet to be fully comprehended (and Schelling's project in the *System of Transcendental Idealism* can be understood as an attempt to grasp precisely this non-rational original unity of freedom and nature).

Second, Schelling's claim is that the internal conflict of intuition is realized in both matter and consciousness. Thus, because matter emerges out of this conflict, it is not made up of parts (an infinity of parts), nor is it a simple particle (as the anatomists argue). Rather, matter is a unity that emerges through difference or opposition; it is an internally differentiated whole – *like* the unity of consciousness. Accordingly, Schelling contends that just as the latest philosophy has taught us that thinking is inseparable from the forms of thought (i.e., the categories), so it is the case with matter. Matter is inseparable from its forces. It is only after intuition has exhibited matter as an internally differentiated unity that it becomes an object for the understanding at all. By reflecting on this unity, the understanding divides. Thus, Schelling concludes:

> That matter is *made up* of parts, is a mere judgment of the understanding. It consists of parts, *if* and *for so long as* I wish to divide it. But that in itself it originally consists of parts is false, for originally – in productive intuition – it arises as a *whole* from opposing forces, and only through this *whole in intuition* do parts become possible for the *understanding*.
>
> (HKA 1/5, 227; *Ideas*, 190)

4. Conclusion

In this first work on the philosophy of nature, Schelling delivers a compelling account of human freedom that sheds important light on his conceptions of the relationship between freedom, necessity, the human being and nature. Rather than developing a rationalist-deterministic account of freedom, in which freedom is the realization of an idea that is either in nature or in the human mind, Schelling articulates an account of freedom that is inextricably connected to embodiment, to being in the world, with others, and to sensing, feeling, experiencing what *is*. This emphasis on the 'real' as opposed to the rational and conceptual is also evident in Schelling's critique of purely speculative accounts of matter and in his locating of matter in intuition: in the experience of being compelled. In both of these ways, the early Schelling does not appear at all distant from his later emphasis on freedom and critical response to rationalism and idealism. Rather, in both instances, Schelling is rejecting the reduction of freedom to rational necessity, to logical constraints.[11] In so doing, he also offers a compelling way by which to think of human freedom and nature. Schelling does not deny our naturalness; in fact, he emphasizes it – but not at the expense of freedom. Schelling is from this perspective quite distinctive and, I think, can offer important insights to contemporary questions regarding the relation between the human and the natural and the ethical role of the human in the natural world.

Notes

1 See Beiser 2002.
2 See for instance Kosch 2006 and more recently, Kosch 2014.
3 All references to Schelling's and Kant's texts will be made in the body of the text. I will refer to the *Historisch-kritische Ausgabe* (HKA) and the English translations when available. For Kant I will refer to the *Akademie Ausgabe* (AA), with the exception of the *Critique of Pure Reason*, where I will provide the A/B pagination.
4 Kant came to a similar conclusion in the 1790s, writing in the *Opus postumum* that 'the mathematical foundations of natural science do not form a part of the system of the moving forces of matter' (AA 21: 286).
5 'Either we analyse the concept of matter itself, and show, *maybe* that it absolutely has to be thought of as something that occupies space, albeit within certain bounds, and that therefore we have to presuppose as a condition of its possibility a force, which occupies space, and another force, opposed to this, which sets bounds and limits to that space. But in this analytical procedure, as in all such, it happens only too readily that *the necessity originally attaching to the concept vanishes from our grasp*, and that we are misled, by the ease of resolving the concept into its components, into considering it as itself an *arbitrary self-created concept*, so that in the end it is left with nothing more than a merely *logical significance*' (HKA 1/5, 209; *Ideas*, 171–2; emphasis added).
6 Kant writes: 'But who pretends to comprehend the possibility of the fundamental forces? They can be assumed only if they unavoidably belong to the *concept* that is demonstrably fundamental and not further derivable from any other (like that of the filling of space), and then, in general are repulsive and attractive forces that counteract them. We can indeed certainly judge *a priori* about the connection and consequences of these forces, whatever relations among them one can think without contradiction, but cannot yet presume to suppose them as actual. For to be authorized in erecting an hypothesis, it is unavoidably required that the *possibility* of what we suppose be completely *certain*, but with fundamental forces their possibility can never be comprehended' (AA 4: 524).
7 It is interesting that Schelling uses the term 'Erörterung' to describe what he is about to undertake. The term can be translated into English as discussion (as Harris and Heath have done), but it can also be translated as debate, argument or consideration. Importantly, it is in contrast to *explanation*, which Schelling takes to be *either* physical or mathematical. In the case of the *fundamental* forces of matter, no explanation [*Erklärung*] is possible.
8 As Kant writes, 'if the material itself is transformed into fundamental forces … we lack all means of *constructing* this concept of matter, and presenting what we thought universally as possible in intuition' (AA 4: 525).
9 Thus Schelling explains that the mere analysis of the concept of matter can only deliver a probable but not a necessary account of matter: 'Either we analyse the concept of matter itself, and show, *maybe* that it absolutely has to be thought of as something that occupies space, albeit within certain bounds, and that therefore we have to presuppose as a condition of its possibility a force, which occupies space, and another force, opposed to this, which sets bounds and limits to that space. But in this analytical procedure, as in all such, it happens only too readily that *the necessity originally attaching to the concept vanishes from our grasp*, and that we are misled,

by the ease of resolving the concept into its components, into considering it as itself an *arbitrary self-created concept*, so that in the end it is left with nothing more than a merely *logical significance*' (HKA 1/5, 209; *Ideas*, 171–2; emphasis added).
10 Concepts, Schelling notes, have 'no reality'. 'The mere *concept* is a word without significance, a sound to the ear without meaning' (HKA 1/5, 209–10).
11 In his late lectures, Schelling describes negative philosophy as mere logicism because it is only concerned with what can be derived a priori or determined through logical derivation. Thus he writes in his 1842 Berlin lectures: 'In this philosophy, every consequence was justified by what preceded it, but it was justified only as a mere concept. It was from beginning to end an *immanent* philosophy, that is, it progressed in mere thought and was by no means a *transcendent* philosophy' (SW 2/3, 138). He contrasts this to positive philosophy which 'enters into experience and grows, as it were, together with it'. As a science, positive philosophy is not concerned with what is 'before all experience', but above all with experience, which means that there is no 'transition into experience' from the a priori construction to what appears before us (180).

References

Beiser, Frederick C. (2002), *German Idealism: The Struggle against Subjectivism*, Cambridge, MA: Harvard University Press.

Kosch, Michelle (2006), *Freedom and Reason in Kant, Schelling and Kierkegaard*, Cambridge: Cambridge University Press.

Kosch, Michelle (2014), 'Idealism and Freedom in Schelling's *Freiheitschrift*', in Lara Ostaric (ed.), *Schelling: Critical Essays* 145–59, Cambridge: Cambridge University Press.

6

Is autonomy sufficient for freedom?

Charlotte Alderwick

In this chapter I show that the Kantian notion of autonomy, understood as rational self-determination, collapses when it is taken up in a system which posits nature as rationally structured, such as those we find in the early post-Kantian idealists.[1] This notion of autonomy, within the Kantian system, is a key element of human freedom: rational agents are free in that their determination originates in reason. This ability of agents to self-determine is unique, on Kant's account, as natural causality is heteronomous – beings in sensible nature are determined externally, rather than internally by the self-imposed moral law. The early post-Kantians took this conception of freedom as autonomy seriously, and it forms the basis for their conceptions of human freedom. However, the dualism between freedom and nature was not preserved in these post-Kantian systems. The dualisms in Kant's philosophy were seen as deeply problematic, for reasons that are well known:[2] the divide characteristic of transcendental idealism between the natural world and the intelligible world also entails a divide between the normative and the natural; the rational and the natural; and renders problematic the ability of agents to act freely *within* the world of nature.

The early post-Kantian systems are therefore characterized by the attempt to retain Kant's conception of freedom as autonomy (rational self-determination), but to combine this with a conception of nature as itself rationally structured. Rather than placing rational self-determining agents outside of a nature which is fundamentally opposed to their mode of activity, these views place the agent within a nature that is of the same kind – thereby seeking to unite the rational and the natural, the necessary and the free, the normative and the natural.

Or, at least, this was the aim. However, I want to show that when coupled with the claim that nature is rationally structured, attributing rational self-determination to agents does *not* entail freedom, but rather a particular form of determination by the whole. On an account of nature such as the early Schelling's, where nature exhibits a rational structure, *all* natural products are engaged in rational self-determination, therefore the ability to rationally self-determine is no longer unique to human agency. Further, as the rational principles which are present in the agent also structure nature as a whole, the claim that by being self-determining agents are thereby autonomous also comes under threat: the distinction between autonomy and heteronomy is itself called into question. As I will argue, Kant's conception of freedom is made possible by his transcendental idealism: the account of freedom as autonomy ceases to be effective as a way of thinking about human freedom when it is removed from the transcendental idealist framework.

In this chapter I focus on making clear this problem: on demonstrating why, when removed from a Kantian system and coupled with a conception of nature as rationally structured, autonomy is no longer sufficient for freedom. I begin by outlining Kant's conception of human freedom, as constituted by autonomy: the ability to self-determine through reason rather than being determined by external causes. I highlight in particular the second part of that ability – while the early post-Kantians focus on the first part (the ability to rationally self-determine), they tend to overlook the fact that this is tied to the second part (freedom from external determination). I want to show that Kant's separation between rational agency and deterministic nature is central to his conception of freedom: the separation of the agent from nature is part of what *enables* the agent to be autonomous.

I then sketch the consequences of attempting to use Kant's conception of freedom as autonomy outside of a transcendental idealist framework, within a system which claims that nature is rationally structured. I use Schelling's *Naturphilosophie* to do this, as the implications are most clear in these texts. As I will argue, in the *Naturphilosophie* the ability of agents to rationally self-determine ends up being just one form of determination by the whole; thus it stops looking like freedom. On this picture, nature as a whole and all natural products are rationally structured and inherently active, and all are engaged in a process of rational self-determination. The agent therefore ceases to be unique (as its form of agency is shared by all of nature) and further ceases to be autonomous in the sense required to secure transcendental freedom.

1. Negative freedom and laws of nature: Freedom in the *Critique of Pure Reason*

Although his positive conception of freedom is not found in his first *Critique*, this text is a necessary starting point for understanding Kant's theory of freedom. In this text the space for what Kant will later refer to in the *Groundwork* as a negative conception of freedom is carved out: Kant shows here that the rational agent can be thought of as free from determination by sensible causes when we consider her to be a member of the intelligible world rather than a member of the natural world. This conceptual space which allows us to think of the agent as free in the negative sense forms the basis for the *Groundwork*'s argument that we must therefore also consider the agent to be free in the positive sense.

Specifically, the metaphysical/conceptual[3] separation between the intelligible world and the world of nature is emphasized and argued for in the first *Critique* in a way that it is not in the *Groundwork* – in the latter, Kant sometimes writes as if the division between the two is merely that they serve as useful comparison points to one another. However, as I argue below, the distinction between the two, and the claim that they form two separate metaphysical/conceptual realms which are governed by fundamentally different structuring principles, is the cornerstone of Kant's theory of freedom as autonomy: without this claim, autonomy fails to do the work which Kant needs it to in order to secure the freedom of the rational subject. A further aspect of the first *Critique* which is key to understanding this claim is Kant's account of laws of nature in the second analogy, which are further discussed in relation to spontaneous causality in the third antinomy. In the *Groundwork* Kant frequently compares the moral law to natural laws: I argue that we need to understand the moral law (as it would operate in the kingdom of ends) in the same way as we understand natural laws in the world of nature.

1.1 The second analogy and natural laws

Kant's aim in the analogies is to demonstrate the necessity of certain of the categories of the understanding for the existence of the world of appearances. The arguments aim to show that without these categories playing a structuring role, the objects of appearance would not be able to appear as they do: the existence of nature is dependent on the structure which the categories provide. Note the strength of the claim here: Kant is not claiming that the external world would exist but in a different form or that the external world would exist but agents would be unable to make sense of it; he is claiming that the world of external objects would not exist *at all* in the absence of these structures.[4] The second analogy aims to demonstrate the necessity of the category of causality: the claim is that it is only by virtue of the efficient causal structure which underlies the behaviour of the external world that agents are able to distinguish between objective sequences of events and subjective experience. In short, it is only because the external world is causally structured that we are able to identify it *as* the external world, in contrast to our inner experience. In the absence of this distinction between the inner and the outer, Kant argues that the representation of the external world would be impossible:

> Experience – in other words the empirical knowledge of appearances – is thus only possible in so far as we subject the succession of appearances, and thus all alteration, to the laws of causality; and, as likewise follows, the appearances, as objects of experience, are themselves possible only in accordance with this law.
> (KrV, B234)

For the purposes of this chapter it is not necessary to rehearse the argument of the second analogy in detail. Instead I want to draw attention to the implications of this section for how we should understand the operation of laws of nature (laws of efficient causality) on Kant's view. Firstly, laws of nature are prescriptive rather than descriptive: the law of causality does not merely describe how objects behave; it determines how they must behave. All objects in nature are necessarily subjected to these laws because to be an object *is* to be constituted in this way.[5] This highlights that laws do not have the same mode of existence as objects – they are not *part of* the world of nature in the way that objects are – they rather are a *structuring element*; they are part of the fabric which makes the world possible. Laws of nature are structuring principles, and this is why they necessitate the behaviour of objects in the way that they do: they legislate universally within their domain because they are an element of the fundamental structure of all the objects for which they legislate.

It is these features of the laws of nature – that they are prescriptive, and legislate universally by virtue of being part of the structure of the objects for which they legislate – that makes them fundamentally incompatible with spontaneous causality. This incompatibility is brought out clearly by Kant's discussions in the third antinomy. Although the solution to this antinomy enables Kant to open up the conceptual space for the existence of spontaneous causality (and, therefore, to secure the possibility of transcendental freedom), it also becomes clear here that if this kind of causality is to exist, it must necessarily do so outside the world of nature.

1.2 The third antinomy and the possibility for autonomy

The third antinomy deals with a contradiction that reason encounters when trying to apply the category of causality to the phenomenal world understood as a whole: although the category of causality applies universally and unproblematically within our experience, when reason attempts to use this category to think about the causal origins of the world of experience, it encounters the kind of insoluble contradiction characteristic of the antinomies. As the thesis argues, when attempting to explain *all* appearances, the principle of universal causality falls short: as the principle states that every event has a prior cause, it entails an infinite regress of causes, leaving us unable to account for a beginning to the system. This inability to account for a beginning leaves the system ungrounded and thus contradicts the principle of universal causality as the system of causes itself lacks a causal explanation. Therefore, in order to account for the beginning of the system, and thereby provide causal completeness to the series, the thesis argues that it is necessary to 'assume a [cause] which is not itself determined, in accordance with necessary laws, by another cause antecedent to it, that is to say, an *absolute spontaneity*' (A446/B474). This kind of cause would have the character of transcendental freedom: 'a power of absolutely beginning a state' (A445/B473). Therefore by assuming the existence of this cause the thesis secures both the explanation needed to account for the beginnings of phenomenal nature and the possibility of the existence of the kind of causality which constitutes transcendental freedom.

The antithesis responds by drawing attention to the structuring role that the law of causality plays: it is a necessary condition for the existence of phenomenal nature:

> Transcendental freedom thus stands opposed to the law of causality; and the kind of connection which it assumes as holding between the successive states of the active causes renders all unity of experience impossible.
>
> (A446–7/B474–5)

As Kant argued in the second analogy, the law of causality necessarily applies universally within appearances because it is part of the underlying structure which makes appearances possible. Without that structure this world would simply fail to exist. Therefore, the antithesis argues, the existence of spontaneous causality (and therefore transcendental freedom) must be ruled out, as it would entail the non-existence of the world of nature.

The issue with both of these arguments, Kant claims, is the assumption of transcendental realism: they take the world of nature to be an object and therefore as subject to the categories in the same way that objects within nature are. In fact, the categories are structuring principles which constitute the world of nature, and therefore they only apply within this system – the error of the antinomies is the attempt to apply these necessary structures to the system as a whole. Therefore, the antithesis argument is correct when it claims that any exceptions to the principle of universal causality would destroy the very existence of nature: within the world of nature, if any one of its structuring principles were violated, the system would break down. Further, given Kant's transcendental idealism, this violation (as the antithesis points out) would be impossible: because these principles are prescriptive it is only possible for objects to appear at all because they are structured in this way. This is why Kant must argue that spontaneous causality would only be possible if it were part of an intelligible world – the necessary and universal structures of the natural world make its existence within that world impossible. However, as transcendental idealism allows the possibility of an intelligible world, we are justified in assuming that spontaneous causality exists in that world.

The third antinomy therefore indicates the centrality of transcendental idealism to Kant's theory of freedom: if spontaneous causality and natural causality are fundamentally opposed in the way that the third antinomy demonstrates that they are, then it is only on the basis of an ontology which can make sense of them as operative independently of one another that we can posit the existence of both. Note that this separation from nature is *necessary* to enable this way of thinking about freedom – already it should be clear that this is not an incidental claim but at the heart of the way that Kant thinks about autonomy.

I now turn to the *Groundwork*, where Kant makes the move from the possibility of freedom to its actuality, and I want to emphasize that the separation from nature plays a central role in his arguments here too: what it is to be autonomous is defined in opposition to natural causality; Kant's conception of rational agents entails their absolute separation from lawful nature; and again the intelligible and the natural are shown to be fundamentally incompatible by virtue of the principles which structure them.

2. The *Groundwork*: Autonomy, rational self-determination and transcendental freedom

The *Groundwork* is a complex work which poses a number of interpretive issues I do not have space to cover here.[6] Instead I focus on key features of Kant's account of autonomy in this text. In particular I highlight that autonomy (the ability of rational agents to self-legislate) is understood through a contrast to natural causality, which is Kant's exemplar of heteronomy (determination by 'alien'[7] or external causes). This lack of determination by external causes (negative freedom) is then used by Kant in *Groundwork* III to argue for the existence of transcendental freedom. The *Groundwork* therefore reiterates the claim I highlighted in my discussion of the first *Critique* – autonomy is only possible for a being which stands outside the world of nature – as well as extending this to make the argument that this kind of autonomous being would therefore be transcendentally free.

2.1 Freedom as autonomy in the *Groundwork*

My focus here will be on two of Kant's key claims about autonomy: firstly, that autonomy is necessarily *self*-determination; secondly, that this determination can only come from reason.[8] As I will argue, the separation of the rational being from nature is necessary for both of these claims about the nature of autonomy to hold.

It is striking throughout the text that this conception of the autonomous will as self-legislating is frequently cashed out in contrast with laws of nature, for example, at 4:452–3 Kant writes:

> With the idea of freedom the concept of *autonomy* is inseparably bound up, and with it the universal principle of morality, which in the idea lies at the foundations of all actions of *rational* beings, just as the law of nature lies at the foundation of all appearances.

There are a number of features of the moral law which it has in common with natural laws: both legislate *universally* (within their own domain); and both are *foundational*, in that their existence is *constitutive* of that domain. Kant's discussion of the Formula of Universal Law is instructive here – particularly the two different ways that Kant claims this formula can be stated:

> There is therefore only a single categorical imperative, and it is this: *act only according to that maxim through which you can at the same time will that it become a universal law*. [...] Since the universality of the law according to which effects happen constitutes that which is actually called *nature* in the most general sense (according to its form), i.e. the existence of things only in so far as it is determined according to universal laws, the universal imperative of duty could also be expressed as follows: *so act as if the maxim of your action were to become by your will a* **universal law of nature**.
>
> (4:421)

2.2 The formula of universal law

Kant is claiming here that acting by a maxim which the agent at the same time wills as universal is *the same as* acting by a maxim which the agent at the same time wills to become a law of nature. And, as Kant states, this is because the universality of the law according to which effects happen constitutes that which is actually called nature in the most general sense (according to its form), i.e. the existence of things only in so far as it is determined according to universal laws.

(ibid.)

The fact that Kant draws our attention to this feature of natural laws – they determine universally, and *they make objects possible* by virtue of this determination – is instructive for how we should view the workings of the moral law as it would be manifested in the kingdom of ends. It is central to the way that natural laws work that they legislate necessarily and universally: they apply, without exception, for the whole of nature. In fact, as we know from Kant's arguments in the second analogy, that they do legislate in this way is the condition of possibility for the existence of objects in nature at all. If we consider the moral law in its operation in the intelligible kingdom of ends in the same way (as Kant's formula of universal law invites us to do) then we get the following picture: in the kingdom of ends, the moral law legislates universally; it determines every object*[9] which exists within that kingdom and does so necessarily, as this determination is the condition for the possibility that those object*s exist at all. The central feature of both laws of nature and laws of practical reason that I am aiming to emphasize here is that they both necessarily legislate universally. This becomes especially important when we recall that these laws are prescriptive – they necessitate the way that all objects (or object*s) must behave and in doing so create a structural framework which is the condition of possibility that those objects (or object*s) exist at all. This is the basis for the claim in the third antinomy that the existence of any spontaneous cause would invalidate the existence of nature: if this kind of cause existed then the unity of nature would be destroyed because natural laws would fail to legislate universally.

Therefore the objects made possible by this universal structure would cease to exist. I want to argue that this same story will apply to the moral law, if we understand it in terms of how it would legislate within, and therefore structure the existence of, the kingdom of ends. In the kingdom of ends the moral law would legislate universally: the existence of this kingdom would be made possible by virtue of the necessary structure provided by the universality of the law. Therefore, a version of the third antinomy claim would also hold for the intelligible world – any exception to the moral law would, by invalidating its universality, entail the destruction of the entire kingdom of ends. The destruction of these systems is avoided, both in the case of nature and in the case of the kingdom of ends, by Kant's distinction between the two realms. Spontaneous causality does not invalidate the existence of nature as a system because (if it exists) it exists as external to the system; the kingdom of ends contains no distinction between 'ought to be the case' and 'is the case'[10] because there is nothing within it which is not determined by the moral law. The distinctive feature of both of these domains is that the law which governs them is sovereign – the law acts as a structuring principle which determines the fundamental nature of the domain which it governs; therefore within these domains no deviation from the law is possible. The separation of these domains is therefore crucial to their existence – bringing the domains together is necessarily impossible as it would require invalidating the sovereignty of one, or both, of the governing principles:

> [A] kingdom of ends is possible only according to the analogy with a kingdom of nature – but the former just according to maxims, i.e. self-imposed rules, the latter just according to the laws of externally necessitated causes.
>
> (4:438)

2.3 Summary

I have been arguing that the separation of the intelligible agent from nature is a central, rather than incidental, part of Kant's conception of autonomy, and therefore his conception of freedom. As well as the contrast between natural laws and the moral law being a key aspect of many of the arguments in the *Groundwork*, there is also the element of universality and necessity which must attach to both types of law, on this view: as each must legislate absolutely, the existence of the two laws in the same domain would entail the destruction of both, as neither would meet this criterion. Thus, the dualism between the world of nature and the intelligible world is crucial for Kant's arguments for the autonomy of rational agents: if we are to posit transcendental freedom, this *must* exist as external to the world of nature.

Note also that, on this account, two criteria need to be satisfied in order for the will to be transcendentally free (though in *Groundwork* 3 Kant argues that the first entails the second): firstly, the absence of heteronomy, or determination by alien causes; secondly, absolute spontaneity, the will must give itself its own law.

I now want to show that on post-Kantian accounts of nature as rationally structured, there may be a way to secure the second criterion, however, as I will argue, the first cannot be satisfied: on these accounts, the crucial distinction between heteronomy and autonomy vanishes. Therefore, although the agent could be characterized as autonomous in the sense of being rationally self-determining, this self-determination becomes equivalent to determination by rational nature. This means that two central elements of the Kantian conception of freedom are lost: the absolute spontaneity of the agent and the difference in structure between rational agency and other natural products. In the rest of this chapter, I use Schelling's *Naturphilosophie*, and the conception of freedom which it entails, to demonstrate why this conclusion is necessitated: why, on this kind of system, autonomy is no longer sufficient for freedom.

3. Rational self-determination in Schelling's *Naturphilosophie*

3.1 The *Naturphilosophie* and the *Critique of Judgement*

Schelling's *Naturphilosophie* is heavily influenced by the latter part of Kant's third *Critique*, where Kant discusses the possibility of teleological causation in nature. The *Naturphilosophie* follows some of Kant's positive claims here: firstly, that there are some entities in nature (natural organisms) which judgement is compelled to recognize as purposive. Secondly, that these entities must be understood by judgement as having a causality of the same kind as rational agency (not merely efficient, but characterized by ends or purposes, and by self-organization in accordance with these ends). Finally, that the coexistence in nature of this kind of causality with mechanistic causality can only be possible if both are united in a common ground – and, as mechanism cannot be used to explain teleology, but teleology can be used to explain mechanism, this ground must have the structure of teleological causation.[11] However, Schelling and Kant part ways over the ontological status of this ground, as Kant's conception of nature necessitates that the ground which could unite mechanism and teleology cannot exist as part of the system of nature. The third antinomy explicitly entails this conclusion – as this kind of causality would be an exception to the mechanistic causality which characterizes phenomenal nature, the laws of nature would fail to legislate absolutely, and therefore the very existence of nature would be impossible.[12] Therefore, for Kant, whatever grounds the unity of teleology and mechanism can only be supersensible: it can only exist as external to the world of nature. This would place the ground squarely in the realm of things-in-themselves, rendering us unable to make any positive claims about its existence. Kant therefore argues that it must remain a regulative principle[13] – in our judgements of certain aspects of nature and in our actions we must act *as if* this supersensible ground has a real existence, although we will never be able to have knowledge as to the veracity of this claim.

For Schelling, this positing of the ground of unity of teleology and mechanism as supersensible is untenable, for a number of reasons.[14] Thus, for Schelling, if we are to make sense of the commonality which exists between the causality of agents and the causality characteristic of organisms; of the ability of agents to perform actions within nature; and of the life and dynamism which characterizes nature as a whole, we must take Kant's arguments in the third *Critique* to their logical conclusion: we must take seriously the claim that nature is a system which is fundamentally teleological, rather than mechanistic, in its structure. Schelling accepts Kant's argument that teleology can explain mechanism but mechanism cannot explain teleology and therefore concludes that our model for understanding nature as a whole must be teleological – we must view nature as evolving according to a rational concept, an end which also structures its parts and their relationship to the whole. If nature as a whole did not exhibit this form of causality, then it would be impossible for it to exist in any of its parts: therefore entailing the denial of the purposive nature of organisms and the ethical activities of human agents. Therefore, for Schelling, if we are to take seriously the existence of entities of this sort within nature (and, in the absence of the distinction between nature and the intelligible world, it is only within nature that these entities could exist), we must take nature as a whole to be characterized by this same sort of ends-based causality structured by rational principles.

3.2 The *Naturphilosophie*

Schelling's *Naturphilosophie* has at its basis a rejection of the mechanistic conception of nature. As well as being motivated by concerns about specific elements of the mechanistic account,[15] for Schelling this way of thinking about nature has problematic consequences for agency: it entails either the reduction of freedom and subjectivity to mechanistic nature, or we are forced to take the Kantian position which claims that these aspects of the being of agents exist as separate from the natural order. For

Schelling, neither of these claims are tenable – therefore we must rethink our conception of nature in such a way that enables us to claim both that agents are fundamentally natural beings which can be explained in the same terms as other natural products and that subjectivity and freedom are real and irreducible aspects of agency. In order to do justice to both claims, we must reconceive nature as the kind of system that contains some elements of subjectivity, reason and freedom, as only this kind of system could be capable of giving rise to products which have these qualities. This is one reason that Schelling takes Kant's posited supersensible ground as his starting point in the *Naturphilosophie* – in order to account for both the free and the mechanistic in nature, we must build up our conception of nature from the starting point of a single universal principle which grounds nature and which manifests itself in both the subjective and the objective, the mechanistic and the free. This principle is taken to be operative in all natural products – in the language I have been using above, it legislates absolutely for all of nature because its operation is constitutive of nature.

Therefore the first maxim of *Naturphilosophie* is that nature must be taken as an autonomous, mind-independent, self-sufficient and self-legislating realm:

> [S]ince nature gives itself its own sphere of activity, no foreign power can interfere with it; all of its laws are immanent, or *nature is its own legislator* (autonomy of Nature). Whatever happens in nature must also be explained from the active and motive principles which lie in it, or *nature suffices for itself* (autarchy of Nature).
>
> (*Outline*, 17)

Rejecting Kant's claim in the *Critique of Judgement* that purposive causation in nature is only possible if the concept is added externally, the *Naturphilosophie* locates the conceptual structure which makes teleology possible *within* nature – nature is governed by a fundamental principle which grounds its existence and structures each of its individual manifestations. For Schelling, as well as being led to posit the existence of this principle through the conceptual considerations I outlined in the previous section, our empirical investigations of nature also entail that we posit a unifying whole which synthesizes and gives meaning to the various natural products that we observe in the world:

> [We are led to] a common principle in which, fluctuating between organic and inorganic nature, is contained the first cause of all change in the former and the final ground of all activity in the latter. Because this principle is everywhere present, it is nowhere; because it is everything, it cannot be anything determinate or particular.
>
> (*World-Soul*, 89)

This principle, which is at the basis of nature but is not separate to nature (as a nature grounded in an external principle would not be autonomous and self-legislating), is what Schelling refers to as the absolute. The absolute is the first principle which grounds all natural products; it is neither subjective nor objective but is the indifference point which grounds both subjectivity and objectivity, the organic and the inorganic, the mechanistic and the free in nature. The absolute is both the totality of nature and is present as a structuring principle within each individual being in nature. Thinking of the absolute as a structuring principle is useful in the context of this chapter: the absolute is the structure which legislates for all nature, and therefore as well as being the ground of nature, it is operative in all natural products: being structured in this way is constitutive of each particular part of nature as well as for nature as a whole. As Schelling puts it:

> These two conflicting forces conceived at the same time in conflict and unity, lead to the idea of an *organising principle*, forming the world into a system. Perhaps the ancients wished to intimate this with the *world-soul*.
>
> (*World-Soul*, 96)

The particular structure which the absolute exhibits through its products can be derived from considerations about its nature – as ground of nature the absolute is pure productivity, an infinitely productive force that is capable of giving rise to all possible natural forms. However, as pure undifferentiated productivity, the absolute could not concretely exist: productivity can only be actualized through the existence of products. Therefore the absolute must self-limit; it must inhibit its own productivity such that it can give rise to distinct entities, to concretely manifest its productivity in individual natural products.[16] This limiting tendency which makes the concrete manifestation of productivity possible comes from within the absolute: the absolute has two fundamental but opposed tendencies, its drive for absolute productivity or universality, and its drive for limitation or particularity which inhibits the productive drive thereby enabling it to manifest itself in concrete products. This makes explicit both the relationship of dependence between the absolute principle and the system of nature (the system of nature depends on the absolute as its ground; the absolute depends on the system of nature as without natural products it would be unable to manifest its productive nature), and the sense in which this principle is internal to rather than outside of nature (the self-organization of natural beings is due to the structure provided by the absolute principle which is internal to each natural product). Thus product and productivity, the absolute and nature, never exist as separate from one another, and all natural products are constituted by this combination of productivity and limitation:

> There is no such thing in nature as the merely produced: there is no pure product [...] Similarly, there is no pure productivity. Productivity must be made determinate; it must be limited by the fixity and permanence of product.
>
> (Fischer 2020: 4)

This begins to indicate the nature of the products which the absolute gives rise to: all natural products reflect the nature of the whole which provides their ground and structure. Therefore *all* natural beings contain a combination of an active productive drive, as well as a limiting drive to particularity. Further, all natural products are self-legislating, as they all contain the principles for their growth and development within themselves.

Although natural products are in a sense self-determining, there is also a sense in which they depend on the absolute as a whole for their determination – the absolute provides the basic structure which organizes (i.e., legislates for) the whole of nature, from the inorganic to the organic to the human subject. As Stone notes:

> [For Schelling] nature is composed of one single fundamental structure – the interdependence of opposed forces [of productivity and limitation] – that elaborates itself at different levels of realisation.
>
> (2018: 129)

Therefore there is an important sense in which, for Schelling, natural products form one single product, nature as a whole: 'all these various products = *one product that is inhibited in sundry stages*' (*Outline*, 6). The rational structure which constitutes the absolute is manifested in different ways throughout nature in the natural products that we experience as distinct and determinate particulars; however there is an important sense in which, from the perspective of the whole, these are all different aspects of one single product: nature as a whole.

3.3 The breakdown of autonomy in the *Naturphilosophie*

From this brief summary of Schelling's *Naturphilosophie* I hope it is already becoming clear that, given this ontology, the distinction between autonomy and heteronomy – between self-legislation and external determination – which is so central to Kant's conception of freedom, breaks down completely. There is a sense in which all natural products are autonomous, as they are rationally self-determining: all natural products contain their own legislative principles within themselves, and all are self-determining in that their existence and action are structured by these internal principles. However, there is also a sense in which these principles do not originate in the individual, but in nature as a whole: the internal principles which enable natural products to self-legislate are principles which are derived from nature as a whole. Therefore the distinction between autonomy and heteronomy loses its meaning – as the lines between the individual and nature are blurred, to be a natural product is to be both autonomous (as all natural products are structured by internal principles) and heteronomous (as these principles originate in nature as a whole).

One key criterion of Kant's conception of freedom as autonomy is therefore erased on this account: for Kant, what constitutes the freedom of agents is their ability to legislate for themselves, to self-determine through rational principles. On Kant's account, this marks agents out from the rest of nature: firstly from nature itself as nature's legislative principles come from an external source; and secondly from natural products, as they are determined by the external principles which constitute them and therefore they lack the ability to self-legislate. However, on the ontology of the *Naturphilosophie*, nature itself self-legislates through rational principles which are internal to it, and this rational self-determination is exhibited in all of its products: everything from stones to waterfalls to mice to human agents is autonomous, in the sense of self-legislating through rational principles. These beings all self-legislate, but the laws they give to themselves are nature's laws at the same time as being their own.

Further, the second of Kant's criteria for transcendental freedom that I identified above (absolute spontaneity) also loses its bite in the same way. Firstly, in the sense that we can argue from one perspective that all natural products exhibit absolute spontaneity (as they act according to a law which is internal to them, undetermined by efficient causal antecedents), however from another perspective the spontaneity they exhibit expresses the agency of nature as a whole, rather than their own agency.[17] Secondly, this demonstrates again that the form of causality which Kant took to be distinctive of rational agency, and the hallmark of human freedom, is now the form of causality which characterizes *all* nature. Even the particular capacity for reason which agents exhibit is no longer sufficient to mark them out as different from other natural products in terms of their ability for free action – Schelling holds that the difference is only that human agents have an awareness of the rational principles which guide their action, but rather than affording them a different kind of freedom from other natural products, it in fact produces the illusion of freedom: 'because [the] understanding does everything it does with consciousness, hence the illusion [arises] of its freedom' (*Ideas*, 172). Thus the distinctive form of causality which Kant attributes to only free rational agents is now the form of causality which characterizes the workings of nature as a whole – autonomy has become insufficient for freedom.

3.4 Schelling's new directions

Though I do not have the space to cover Schelling's philosophical development following the *Naturphilosophie* here, I want to briefly argue that one way that this development can be read is as an attempt to find another way to think about human freedom. As the Kantian notion of autonomy is unable to secure the unique freedom and moral status of agents, when coupled with a conception of nature as rationally structured and containing an agency of its own, something more is required in order to account for human freedom.

However, what this additional element which secures freedom could be proves elusive: in his *System of Transcendental Idealism* Schelling attempts to argue that there is a pre-established harmony which entails that the volitions of agents coincide with their actions in nature;[18] however this 'solution' is short-lived, as in his texts which outline what is known as the System of Identity Schelling now argues that individual freedom is illusory – going so far as to argue that individuality itself is an illusion which arises from the perspective of the finite, when in fact all apparent individuals are merely aspects of the whole.[19] This, arguably, is entailed by the ontology of the *Naturphilosophie* outlined above when taken to its logical conclusion.

It is only when Schelling writes his 1809 *Freedom* essay that a new solution to the question of the possibility of human freedom emerges – again, I do not have the space to do justice to this account here; however what is central is that it entails the positing of an irrational element *within* the system of nature. In this text, Schelling argues that nature contains *both* rational and irrational elements and gives equal priority to nature's drive for unity and drive for particularity, so that which one is sovereign can be determined by the choice of the agent. This choice, to prioritize selfhood over harmony with the whole, which is only able to arise in human agents, is what constitutes evil and therefore freedom.[20] Freedom, for Schelling, must entail the ability to choose *against* as well as in line with the rational order – this is one reason why a being who self-determines in accordance with rational nature can never be free in the full sense. This account of human freedom in the *Freedom* essay therefore looks very different from the Kantian conception of freedom as autonomy, but it demonstrates that in order to make sense of human freedom within rather than separate to nature, something additional, and very different to autonomy, is required.

Notes

1. I am focusing on Schelling's *Naturphilosophie* here for reasons of space, and because I argue that it shows this collapse of autonomy entailing freedom most clearly. However, I take my conclusions here to apply to other systems of this kind – for example Hegel's philosophy of nature, and systems such as McDowell's which aim to derive human spontaneity from a rationally structured nature. These systems all attempt to do the same thing – to retain the Kantian conception of freedom as rational self-determination, but to place this within a nature which is also engaged in rational self-determination. As I show below, Kant's separation of free causality from natural causality is central to his conception of freedom as autonomy; therefore these systems which try to retain the Kantian conception within rather than outside of nature will necessarily fail. This is not to say that there is no prospect for a meaningful conception of human freedom within nature but to stress that this cannot be achieved through utilizing the Kantian understanding of autonomy – more work needs to be done in these systems to specify exactly what constitutes human freedom and how this kind of causality is able to be distinct from as well as produced by nature.
2. There are a number of worries which motivate the elimination of dualisms from the systems of the early post-Kantian idealists – see Beiser 1987 and 2002 and Franks 2005 for good accounts of these motivations.
3. For the purposes of this chapter I want to remain neutral on the issue of the ontological status of the intelligible world for Kant. I take my claims to apply regardless of this issue, as however Kant intended this distinction to be read, it is clear that these are fundamentally different domains which are structured by different legislating principles.
4. It is worth making clear that when I use the term 'external world' I take this to be equivalent with the world of experience or what Kant sometimes terms 'appearances'. This is because, for Kant, the external world *is* the world of experience. Although we must posit the possibility that something exists beyond this world, terms such as 'the external world' and 'the world of nature' for Kant *always* refer to the world of our experience: nature, for Kant, *is* the world as it is structured through the forms of inner and outer intuition, and the categories of the understanding.
5. It's useful to reiterate here the point I drew attention to above: for Kant, to be an object is equivalent to being an object of possible experience; to be an object *is* to be partially constituted by the forms of intuition, and the categories of the

understanding. Therefore when I discuss objects here, this is equivalent to objects *for us* – which, for Kant, are the only kind of object possible.

6. For good accounts of the text and the debates arising from it, see for example Henrich (1975); Allison (2011); Schonecker (2015).
7. GMM 3 4:446.
8. I agree with Kosch that this conception of freedom as rational self-determination 'has no unproblematic name in Kant's texts. Nor is it unambiguously explained in any of them. Instead it underlies much of Kant's thinking about freedom without being sufficiently separated out from other concepts at crucial junctures' (2006: 23). However I think it is clear from the *Groundwork* that this conception of freedom is what Kant takes to be at stake, even if it is not explicitly named as such.
9. As, for Kant, objects only exist within appearances, we cannot posit the existence of objects in the intelligible world. However, Kant seems to posit the existence of *something* in the intelligible world, therefore here I refer to these something as object*s. One worry might be that, on some readings, all objects in nature, not just agents, would have some kind of intelligible character; however presumably they would not be determined by the moral law in the way that intelligible agents are. I think that Kant is ambiguous on this point – in discussions of the nature of the noumenal which are not related to morality, he sometimes suggests that any object in nature would have a noumenal character (e.g., KrV A249) despite warning that to posit any positive existents in the noumenal is problematic (e.g., KrV B309). However when discussing morality Kant claims that we must act as if the intelligible world as a whole is structured by the moral law. Therefore I take this to be an issue for Kant's theory more generally rather than an issue for my argument here.
10. KdU 403.
11. Kant argues for these claims in KdU S63–S68.
12. Kant also restates this conclusion in his discussion of the 'Antinomy of Teleological Judgement' in the third *Critique* (KdU 387).
13. KdU S71.
14. Schelling's main discussion of and response to Kant's arguments in the third *Critique* are found in the introduction to his *Ideas* – to my mind it is one of Schelling's most clear pieces of sustained argument and a completely beautiful piece of philosophy.
15. See, for example, Schelling's arguments against the Newtonian account of matter in *Ideas* 153–60.
16. *Ideas* 150.
17. See Alderwick 2021, chapter 3 for an extended discussion of this claim.
18. See, for example, *System* 192.
19. See, for example, *Presentation*, 352–3.
20. *Freedom* 28–32.

References

Alderwick, C. (2021), *Schelling's Ontology of Powers,* London: Edinburgh University Press.
Allison, H. E. (1990), *Kant's Theory of Freedom,* Cambridge: Cambridge University Press.
Allison, H. E. (2011), *Kant's Groundwork for the Metaphysics of Morals: A Commentary,* Oxford: Oxford University Press.

Beiser, F. C. (1987), *The Fate of Reason: German Philosophy from Kant to Fichte*, Cambridge, MA: Harvard University Press.

Beiser, F. C. (2002), *German Idealism: The Struggle against Subjectivism 1781–1801*, Massachusetts: Harvard University Press.

Esposito, J. L. (1977), *Schelling's Idealism and Philosophy of Nature Associated*, London: University Presses Inc.

Fischer, N. (2020), 'Freedom as Productivity in Schelling's Philosophy of Nature', in G. A. Bruno (ed.), *Schelling's Philosophy: Freedom, Nature and Systematicity*, 53–70, Oxford: Oxford University Press.

Franks, P. W. (2005), *All or Nothing: Systematicity, Transcendental Arguments, and Scepticism in German Idealism*, Cambridge: Harvard University Press.

Henrich, D. (1975). 'Die Deduktion des Sittengesetzes: über die Gründe der Dunkelheit des letzten Abschnittes von Kants "Grundlegung zur Metaphysik der Sitten"', *Wissenschaft Buchgesellschaft*: 55–112.

Henrich, D. (2008), *Between Kant and Hegel: Lectures on German Idealism*, London: Harvard University Press.

Kabeshkin, A. (2017), 'Schelling on Understanding Organisms', *British Journal for the History of Philosophy*, 25 (6): 1180–201.

Kant, I. (1987), *Critique of Judgment*, trans. W. S. Pluhar, Hackett: Indianapolis.

Kant, I. (2002), *Groundwork for the Metaphysics of Morals*, ed. T. E. Hill and trans. and ed. A. Zweig, Oxford: Oxford University Press.

Kant, I. (2007), *Critique of Pure Reason*, trans. N. Kemp Smith, Hampshire: Palgrave Macmillan.

Kosch, M. (2006), *Freedom and Reason in Kant, Schelling, and Kierkegaard*, Oxford: Oxford University Press.

Nassar, D. (2014), *The Romantic Absolute: Being and Knowing in Early German Romantic Philosophy 1795–1804*, London: University of Chicago Press.

Schelling, F. W. J. (1978), *System of Transcendental Idealism*, trans. P. Heath, Charlottesville: University Press of Virginia.

Schelling, F. W. J. (1995), *Ideas for a Philosophy of Nature,* trans. E. E. Harris and P. Heath, Cambridge: Cambridge University Press.

Schelling, F. W. J. (2001), (Vater, M.G. trans.) 'Presentation of My System of Philosophy (1801)', *The Philosophical Forum*, 32 (4): 339–71.

Schelling, F. W. J. (2002), *Philosophical Investigations into the Nature of Human Freedom*, trans. J. Gutman, Shrewsbury: Living Time Press.

Schelling, F. W. J. (2004a), *First Outline of a System of the Philosophy of Nature*, trans. K. R. Peterson, New York: SUNY Press.

Schelling, F. W. J. (2004b), 'Introduction to the Outline of a System of the Philosophy of Nature, or, on the Concept of Speculative Physics and the Internal Organization of a System of This Science', in K. R. Peterson (trans.), *First Outline of a System of the Philosophy of Nature*, 193–232, New York: SUNY Press.

Schelling, F. W. J. (2010), *On the World Soul*, trans. I. H. Grant, Collapse Vol. VI: Geo/Philosophy, pp. 58–95, Falmouth: Urbanomic.

Schonecker, D. and Wood, A. W. (2015), *Immanuel Kant's Groundwork for the Metaphysics of Morals: A Commentary*.

Stone, A. (2018), *Nature, Ethics, and Gender in German Romanticism and Idealism*, London: Rowman and Littlefield International.

Whistler, D. (2016), 'Schelling on Individuation', *Comparative and Continental Philosophy*, 6 (3): 329–44.
White, A. (1983), *Schelling: An Introduction to the System of Freedom,* New Haven: Yale University Press.

7

Freedom and Hegel's theory of the state

Christoph Schuringa

1. Introduction

Hegel's conception of freedom, as has been frequently noted, is closely related to that of Kant in that it takes freedom – in the fullest, most proper sense – to be rational self-determination. As such, freedom is, for Hegel, something like the highest actualization of the human will. At the same time, as is also widely noted, Hegel takes Kant to task for an 'empty formalism' that allegedly vitiates his version of this conception. In order to have content, Hegel insists, freedom must be filled out in terms of its instantiation in the array of concrete social relations embodied in what he calls *Sittlichkeit*, standardly translated 'ethical life' (i.e., the triad of family, civil society, and the state – with the state as its apex and with the function of fully consummating freedom).

In this chapter I will avoid entering into a general discussion of the relation of Hegel's conception of freedom to Kant's, not least since the topic of freedom is so pervasive in Hegel's philosophy that it might reasonably be taken to be *the* topic of his thought.[1] This is brought out, for one thing, by the identification of freedom with reason that is at the root of the notion of freedom as rational self-determination. Again, Hegel's conception of history is aptly characterized, in Benedetto Croce's phrase, as 'the story of freedom'. Here I want to concentrate on a specific issue through which we can bring the larger issues concerning Hegel's conception of freedom into focus.

The more specific topic I propose to focus on is the following. It involves the conception of freedom set out in certain of Hegel's early writings and its relation to his claim that the state is the 'actualization of concrete freedom' in his *Philosophy of Right* (1821).[2] In the early writings in question (his 'The German Constitution' of 1798–1802,[3] his *System of Ethical Life* of 1802–3, and his essay on the 'Scientific Ways of Treating Natural Law' of 1802–3) Hegel distinguishes sharply between 'empirical freedom' and true freedom.[4] It is only the latter that is conceived as rational self-determination. Already in 'The German Constitution' we get the idea that true freedom will be actualized in the state. It is in the *Philosophy of Right* that Hegel gives full expression to the idea that true freedom will be secured by the state, as part of the triad of 'ethical life'. However, it is also crucial to this mature account of the way in which the state secures freedom that it must do so by means of mediation with freedom as it appears in the family and civil society. As Hegel presents such mediation, the fully fledged, self-standing freedom (or, in more properly Hegelian terms, freedom 'actualized') secured by the state latching onto a 'subjective' freedom present in the family and civil society. While Hegel's presentation of the family and civil society as home to such subjective freedom may be plausible on its own terms, however, his appealing to such a notion of freedom in the service of his theory of the state is problematic. He had, after all, presented compelling arguments in the earlier writings to the effect that such freedom is not just different in kind from 'true freedom' but illusory. Hegel lacks an argument why such freedom should now no longer be regarded as illusory, and so he lacks an argument as to how the relevant subjective freedom can be a candidate for participation in the mediation he requires at all. Furthermore this mediation is supposed to be part of Hegel's story about how he can provide the 'content' that eludes Kant's 'formalism'. It threatens, however, to situate at the centre of Hegel's philosophy of spirit a dualism that he cannot, despite his best intentions, find the means to mediate. On the one side, it would appear, is 'true freedom'; on the other, a void conception of freedom.[5]

In what follows I begin (in § 2) with a sketch of the *Philosophy of Right* as concerned with the topic of freedom and introduce the crucial claim made in this text that the state is the actualization of 'concrete freedom'. I then (in § 3) retrace Hegel's distinction between true and empirical freedom in his earlier writings. I show in § 4 how the need to reconcile 'universal' and 'particular' (and to demonstrate their unity in the 'individual') in PR leads Hegel to import the notion that true freedom must be mediated by a kind of empirical freedom (or, equivalently, that universal will must be mediated by particular subjective wills). In § 5, I raise difficulties for the dualism that returns to haunt Hegel's account of freedom in §§260ff. of the *Philosophy of Right* in particular. Finally (in § 6), I broach the question in what direction a solution to these difficulties might lie.

2. Freedom as the topic of the *Philosophy of Right*

The topic of Hegel's *Philosophy of Right* is freedom. 'The Idea of right is freedom' (PR §1A, 25/30) and 'right is [...] in general freedom, as Idea' (PR §29, 58/80).[6] Or equivalently, he assures us, the topic is the will. These formulations are equivalent because, for him, freedom is the essence of the will, and so to grasp what freedom is is to grasp what the will is in its fullest sense. 'The *freedom* of the will [...] constitutes the concept or substantiality of the will, its gravity, just as gravity constitutes the substantiality of a body' (PR §7, 41/54–55). Freedom is, as it were, the principal attribute of the will: knowing what freedom is is knowing what the nature of the will is.

Hegel's Introduction to PR is in large part devoted to laying out the way in which the work deals with that part of science concerned with the will or with freedom. A signal passage is §4 (35/46):

> The basis [*Boden*] of right is the *realm of spirit* [*das* Geistige] in general and its precise location and point of departure is the *will*; the will is *free*, so that freedom

constitutes its substance and destination [*Bestimmung*] and the system of right is the realm of actualized freedom, the world of spirit produced from within itself as a second nature [*als eine zweite Natur*].

The freedom that Hegel has in mind is '*self-determining universality*' (PR §21, 52/71). As he notes, '[h]ere is the *point at which it becomes clear* that it is only as *thinking* intelligence that the will is truly itself and free' (PR §21R, 53/72). Freedom, allowing in nothing arbitrary or external, is utter self-determination. Such self-determination *is* reason. Reason has two sides: the intellect and the will (which one must not think of, Hegel insists, as if each was carried in a different pocket, but as aspects or sides of *one* reason; PR §4A, 35/46). To be free is, thus, for reason's self-determination to be at work. Although this same idea is present in Kant (and ultimately has roots in Rousseau), it remains strange to our ears.[7] It sounds at its strangest if we put it by saying that freedom is absolute necessity – a consequence that Hegel is notoriously keen to embrace. For me to be free is for me to determine my will utterly through reason and leave nothing to chance.

Hegel strenuously resists a Kantian understanding of right[8] as he understands it, and of the associated concept of freedom. He rejects, he says, a 'definition of right' that 'embodies the view, especially prevalent since Rousseau, according to which the substantial basis and primary factor is supposed to be not the will as rational will which has being in and for itself or the spirit as *true* spirit, but will and spirit as the *particular* individual, as the will of the single person in his distinctive arbitrariness' (PR §29R, 58/80–81). Once such a view is accepted, Hegel continues, 'the rational can of course appear only as a limitation on the freedom in question'. Such a view is 'devoid of any speculative thought and is refuted by the philosophical concept'. Hegel's strenuous rejection of a conception of right, or of freedom, that takes 'arbitrary' particular subjects to be their bearers will be crucial in what follows: a conception that ties right or freedom to such arbitrary subjects, each with its idiosyncratic characteristics, will issue in (purported) freedom that is itself 'capricious' and arbitrary. For freedom to be thus capricious is for it to remain limited by idiosyncrasies of the subject. But the idea of freedom's being subject to limitation is that of a freedom not fully realized and hence something falling short of true freedom.

The *Philosophy of Right* progresses through a series of stages, and Hegel specifies that it does so, in one of his relatively few uses of this term, by means of 'dialectic' (PR §31R, 60/84). These are stages in a logical sense: they are not historical stages. (Of course, as is well known, Hegel seeks, in addition, to vindicate a thoroughgoing integration of logic with history, an integration exhibited in other reaches of his system.) As we progress, true freedom comes ever more fully into view. We begin with the most abstract (that is, most impoverished, or deficient in content) conception of the will or, equivalently, of freedom. Each conception, as per 'dialectic', turns out, in exhibiting its defects, to turn over into the next, so as to remedy the defects of the previous. We begin with 'abstract right', in which the freedom in play is that of mere appropriation. We are here in the realm of property. Appropriation involves my agency being bound up in something external, so that my agency remains precarious (as Hegel makes clear in his helpful recapitulation at PR §104R, 132/199). It is shored up through the forming of contracts, but such contracts are easily broken – I can be left with nothing and my agency turns out to be, after all, no agency at all. 'Abstract right' requires what Hegel calls 'morality' (*Moralität*) to supply its defects. Here the stability lacking in abstract right is assured by the establishment of an enduring *subjectivity*. This makes me the author of my actions in such a way that I can (as it were) stand behind them and take responsibility for them. The demands of 'morality', however, in turn require a totality constituted by universal subjective wills, or, in other words, 'morality' requires 'ethical life' (*Sittlichkeit*). As we progress into *Sittlichkeit*, the alleged emptiness of Kant's concept of the will, or equivalently of freedom, gets filled in. Having got to *Sittlichkeit*, we are now in a position to say that, looking back, it had been the case all along that in order for there to be as much as abstract right, and in order for there to be as much as morality, ethical life had needed to be in the picture (if, at the beginning, in the background). It is only in *Sittlichkeit* that freedom 'exists as Idea' (§141R, 185/287; cf. §142, 189/292).

It is only in *Sittlichkeit* that freedom will get to be concrete and actual. 'Ethical life is the *Idea of freedom* as the living good which has its knowledge and volition in self-consciousness, and its actuality through self-conscious action. [...] Ethical life is accordingly the *concept of freedom which has become the existing* [vorhandenen] *world and the nature of self-consciousness*' (PR §142, 189/292). It will, however, be in the state, and only in the state, that 'freedom, as the *substance*, exists no less as *actuality* and *necessity* than as *subjective* will' (PR §33, 62/87). In the substantial unity of the state, 'freedom enters into its highest right' (PR §258, 275/399). It is here that freedom first appears as 'concrete freedom'. As will become important in what follows, 'concrete freedom' is the unification of 'subjective' and 'objective' freedom (PR §260, 282/406).

Hegel's theory of the state has attracted a great deal of controversy. It has often been insisted, for example, that Hegel requires an unacceptable submission to the authority of the state. This criticism is misplaced, however – whether or not one finds authoritarian tendencies in specific aspects of Hegel's detailed account of the state. As Z. A. Pelczynski has pointed out, Hegel's 'definition of the state is [...] highly stipulative, and quite removed from the conventional meaning of the term' (Pelczynski 1984: 55). Hegel's conception of the state is self-consciously a revival of the ancient Greek idea of the *polis*: as the highest and most integrated collectivity in which a nation lives (higher and more integrated than, say, trade associations). Hegel therefore does not intend to set up the state as an external authority. It is not *submission to* but *membership of* the state that, according to Hegel, will secure human freedom. And it is *only* such membership that secures true freedom. The state does not merely safeguard or preserve freedom that human beings have anyway, in abstraction from the state. Through his membership in the state a human being will 'not be "as free as before", but *more* free; he will have achieved a higher, more adequate and more satisfying type of freedom – true, real or actual freedom' (Pelczynski 1984: 62–3).

I will not here provide an argument that for Hegel in the *Philosophy of Right* true freedom (whatever else he may say about freedom in this text) means self-determination, but take this for granted.[9] It may, however, be worth briefly considering the concern, often mooted, that there is something paradoxical about the idea of self-determination or, in the phrase Kant often uses, 'giving oneself the law'.[10] Whatever else one may want to say about this notion of self-legislation, it is important that there is nothing paradoxical about it: what it means is the will's being subject to its own principle – namely, reason.

3. Empirical and true freedom in Hegel's early texts

I have already signalled what Hegel's conception of true freedom will be in PR: rational self-determination. I have also already hinted that such true freedom will involve a negotiation between 'subjective' and 'objective' freedom (to employ Hegel's terminology in that text).

I now want to rewind to an earlier period in Hegel's thinking. In 1802–3 (and probably beginning somewhat earlier, in the case of 'The German Constitution') Hegel composed a series of texts in which the issue of freedom looms large. These texts also already begin to insist that freedom must be fleshed out in terms of the state (or, sometimes, the *Volk*). What I want to dwell on is the clear way in which, at this period, Hegel distinguishes between two conceptions of freedom. One of these conceptions lines up with rational self-determination and is, according to Hegel, to be endorsed; the other is that of an 'empirical freedom' and is to be rejected. As I will argue in § 4, however, a dualism between just these two conceptions of freedom is one that Hegel struggles to overcome in his account of freedom in the section on the state in PR.

The clearest exposition of the distinction is in Hegel's essay 'On the Scientific Ways of Treating Natural Law, on Its Place in Practical Philosophy, and Its Relation to the Positive Sciences of Right'.[11] The text consists of four sections, the first of which deals with an empirical way of treating natural law. A second section considers a Kantian way of treating natural law, in the course of which discussion Hegel raises the 'empty formalism' objection against Kant (NL 123/460). That section ends with a discussion of freedom in which Hegel rejects an empirical conception of freedom and emphasizes the need to reconcile universality and particularity if there is to be true freedom. As Hegel elaborates in the third section, such universality must be manifested in a *Volk* (an ancestor of what will, in PR and other later writings, become the state), and it must do so by means of a division into different *Stände* (estates). It is through a division of society into different sectors, each having an assigned function in the whole, that the issue of how universality can get into individual persons is to be settled. In the final section, in which Hegel returns to the topic of what a science of natural law should look like and offers his own account of such a science, he importantly praises Montesquieu (NL 175/524) and Aristotle (NL 159/505) for realizing that the ethical totality is prior to the individuals who make it up and rejects Fichte's suggestion for how universality – and thereby the self-determining freedom marked by such universality – might get into the individuals (NL 171/518). I will return to the last issue in § 4.

It is on Hegel's rejection of 'empirical freedom' as 'null' that I want to concentrate here. He writes:

> That view of freedom must be utterly rejected which regards it as a choice between opposite determinacies (so that if + A and − A are given, freedom consists in determining oneself either as + A or as − A, and is completely tied to this either-or). Anything resembling this possibility of choice is purely and simply an empirical freedom, which is the same thing as ordinary empirical necessity and is completely inseparable from it. Freedom is rather the negation or ideality of the opposites, of + A as well as − A, the abstraction of the possibility that neither of the two exists; something external would exist for it only if freedom were determined solely as + A or solely as − A. But freedom is the direct opposite of this: nothing is external to it, so that no coercion [*Zwang*] is possible for it.
>
> (NL 136–37/476–77)

Empirical freedom is illusory, since all it can amount to is being determined this way or that – falling into one determination or its opposite. But freedom is precisely, Hegel thinks, the overcoming of external determination. This can be seen by considering that something arbitrary impinging on me constitutes coercion (*Zwang*). For me to be free is to be raised above the very opposition + A / − A.

As Hegel goes on to explain:

> Every determinacy [*jede Bestimmtheit*] is in essence either + A or − A, and the − A is indissolubly joined to the + A, just as the + A is to the − A. Thus, whenever an individual has adopted determinacy + A, he is also tied to − A, and − A is for him an external [element] over which he has no control. In fact, because of the absolute link between + A and − A, he would be brought, by the determinacy + A, directly under the alien power of − A, and the freedom which supposedly resides in determining itself either as + A or − A would never escape from necessity. If it determines itself as + A, it has not nullified − A; on the contrary, − A subsists absolutely necessarily for it as an external [element], and the converse applies if it determines itself as − A. Freedom is freedom only in so far as, either positively or negatively, it unites − A with + A and thereby ceases to occupy the determinacy + A. In the union of the two determinacies, both are nullified: + A − A = 0. If this nought is thought of only in relation to + A and − A, and the indifferent A itself is thought of as a determinacy and as a plus or minus in opposition to another minus or plus, absolute freedom stands above this opposition, and above any opposition or externality; it is utterly incapable of any coercion, and coercion has no reality whatsoever.
>
> (NL 137/477)

Empirical freedom, then, is no freedom at all. It merely resolves itself (or disappears) into empirical necessity, since empirical determinacies here limit (coerce) the subject. And so the very idea of doing + A or − A (or, in other language, of doing or forbearing in respect of some potential action in some situation) shows itself to be inadequate to the idea of freedom itself. True freedom must be able to, so to speak, hold its own in the face of these determinacies. And so, Hegel thinks, true freedom cannot be confined to the individual – *this* idiosyncratic subject here, formed and pulled hither and thither by specific circumstances. 'For the individual is a single entity [*eine Einzelheit*], and freedom is the nullification of singularity [*Einzelheit*]' (NL 137/478). Nevertheless a 'concept of the universal freedom of all, supposedly distinct from the freedom of individuals' is a 'hollow [*nichtige*] abstraction', just as much as the 'freedom of the individual, equally isolated' (NL 136/476). As Hegel writes later in the essay,

> [A]bsolute ethical life is so essentially the ethical life of everyone that one cannot describe it as reflected, as such, in the individual; for it is as much the essence of the individual as the aether which permeates nature is the inseparable essence of natural forms [...]. Just as those lines and angles of the crystal in which it expresses the external form of its nature are negations, so likewise is ethical life, in so far as it expresses itself in the individual as such, negative in character. For first of all, it cannot express itself in the individual unless it is his soul, and it is his soul only in so far as it is a universal, and the pure spirit of a people.
>
> (NL 159/504–5)

The problem with empirical freedom was not, or not merely, that it resolves itself into necessity. True freedom, too, turns into necessity – since true freedom will turn out to be utter self-determination. The problem was that it remains subject to coercion (*Zwang*) and is thereby subject to something arbitrary and external to it. We thus, Hegel urges, need to overcome the empirical conception. We saw also, however, that the empirical conception brings with it something that we do not want to lose: the idea that it is the *individual* who gets determined.

Crucially, Hegel has insisted that true freedom is not that of *mere* empirical individuals. Instead, it is a universal freedom that realizes itself *in* individuals. The issue of how the universality he is after can be realized in individuals is one that will continue to be key as Hegel spells out what 'concrete freedom' comes to in later writings, and in particular the *Philosophy of Right*.

4. Universality and individuality

So far we have seen that Hegel has marked off true freedom from an illusory empirical freedom by emphasizing the universal character of the former, in contrast to the subjective, particular character of the latter; or the unlimited character of the former in contrast to the limited character of the latter. We have also seen Hegel's recognition, in the earlier writings, that this leaves a need to flesh out a conception of true freedom that allows it at the same time to figure as the freedom of individuals – a universal freedom that does not hover over individuals as an abstraction but that can be theirs *as individuals*. This will require, in some form, a mediation of universality by particularity, so as to deliver such (as we might put it) individuality.

In the Natural Law essay, Hegel already decisively rejects Fichte's proposal for how universal freedom is to find its way into individuals. There he suggests, making direct reference to Fichte, that 'constitutional law as such could also seek to apply itself entirely to individual matters and, as a perfect police-force, to permeate the being of each individual completely'. But, he says, this would have the consequence of 'destroying civic freedom – and this would be the harshest despotism; in this way, Fichte wishes to see the entire activity and being of the individual as such supervised, known, and determined by the universal and the abstraction to which he stands opposed' (NL 171/518). It is no good, Hegel insists, if freedom merely exists at some higher level (that of the state as a whole), as if *this* could constitute civic freedom.

The reconciliation of individuality with universality became a central theme for Hegel, and it animates the entirety of the *Sittlichkeit* section of PR. This reflects Hegel's wish to reconcile what he found valuable in Plato's political philosophy with what he found valuable in Rousseau. In Plato's *Republic*, a work to which he devoted a great deal of attention and on which he lavished fulsome praise in his Lectures on the History of Philosophy, he found a case, as Pelczynski puts it, for the 'absolute priority of the community over the individual', whereas Rousseau insisted on the 'absolute primacy of the individual over the community' (Pelczynski 1984: 57–8). Plato was right insofar as the individual is what she is only in light of her participation in the community, but this missed the importance of subjectivity that Rousseau's radical emphasis on the individual was seeking to secure. Hegel now aspired to give both the priority of the community over the individual *and* the individuality of the individual their due.

Here a programmatic point can be made about Hegel's approach to this issue. He insists at length in his *Logic*[12] that there is a special kind of universality, 'concrete universality', in which the opposition between universal and particular is overcome. By contrast with particulars, *individuals* are concretely universal. This would seem to provide, in Hegel's mind, the resources for the kind of mediation between subjects and their communal being that he needs for his account of freedom. In another context, he equates human beings with spirit and spirit with concrete universality (across the juncture between the second and third parts of the *Encyclopaedia of the Philosophical Sciences*, §377, §376; PM 3/9, PN 443/537). The difficulty here, however, consists in advancing beyond this programmatic point. It is evident that Hegel seeks the solution to the issue in this direction (and in the next section I will look more closely at how he tries to resolve it in PR). But there is a gap. It may be true that Hegel's *Logic* provides a framework for resolving the issue, if its claims in favour of the concrete universal are to be accepted. But it is another thing to demonstrate that the required mediation between particulars (in this case, subjects) and a universal (the state) can in fact be shown to materialize. I will suggest that Hegel fails to show this in a manner that does not involve falling back on ascribing a kind of freedom to the subjects that ends up sounding just like the 'empirical freedom' which he had argued in his early writings was void and for whose reinstatement he had in the meantime offered no argument.

5. A dualism in the *Philosophy of Right*

In the *Philosophy of Right*, the state figures as the 'actuality of the ethical Idea' (PR §257, 275/398). As such, the state resolves the issue of how individuals can be universally free. Hegel is explicit that the freedom realized in the state allows the reconciliation of what he calls 'subjective' and 'objective' freedom:

> The state is the actuality [*Wirklichkeit*] of concrete freedom. But *concrete freedom* requires that personal individuality [*Einzelheit*] and its particular interests should reach their full *development* and gain *recognition of their right* for itself (within the system of the family and of civil society), and also that they should, on the one hand, *pass over* of their own accord into the interest of the universal, and on the other, knowingly and willingly acknowledge this universal interest even as their own *substantial spirit*, and *actively pursue it* as their *ultimate end*. The effect of this is that the universal does not attain validity or fulfilment without the interest, knowledge, and volition of the particular, and that individuals do not live as private persons merely for these particular interests without at the same time directing their will to a universal end [*in und für das Allgemeine wollen*] and acting in conscious awareness of this end. The principle of modern states has enormous strength and depth because it allows the principle of subjectivity to attain fulfilment in the *self-sufficient extreme* of personal particularity, while at the same time bringing it back to *substantial unity* and so preserving this unity in the principle of subjectivity itself.
>
> (PR §260, 282/406–7)

This passage displays Hegel's problem very clearly. The problem it lays bare is that of showing how 'concrete freedom' offers a unification of 'subjective' and 'objective' freedom (see PR §258R, 276/399). It also exposes, however, the difficulty Hegel encounters in attempting a coherent solution. He is clear that the solution will require 'mediation' between two kinds of freedom. But there are two difficulties. First, there is the difficulty of progressing beyond the *assertion* that such mediation occurs, to showing *how* the mediation occurs. Second, and more seriously, there is the issue that it is not clear how Hegel can count both kinds as, properly, kinds of freedom.

The passage is particularly helpful in that it gives a lucid gloss on what is meant by the distinction between subjective and objective freedom. While there are numerous subtleties to this distinction as deployed across Hegel's writings,[13] in the present case there is little doubt as to what he has in mind. Subjective freedom corresponds to 'particular interests', whereas objective freedom corresponds to the 'interest of the universal'.

To come now to the two difficulties. First, how can the individual 'pass over into' the universal? Hegel is at risk of merely stipulating this. Second, how could there be anything at the level of civil society (or 'lower' still than that in Hegel's system of right) that could play the role of mediation? It certainly cannot be *true* freedom, belonging to members of civil society (or reaching even 'lower' down), that is in question: for only with the state does *true* freedom come on the scene. But Hegel seems to suggest precisely that the mediation is to occur by means of the distinctive ('subjective') freedom that such subjects possess.

To turn first to the issue of Hegel's apparently dogmatic assertion that the required mediation is operative. We saw already that the talk of 'passing over' in §260 appears untethered to any story about how the passing over happens: Hegel even says 'of their own accord', without any explanation of how *that* can be so. Similar difficulties are detectable at §258, when Hegel writes: 'The state is the actuality of the substantial *will*, an actuality which it possesses in the particular *self-consciousness* when this has been raised to its universality' (275/399). But, again, we are bound to ask: *how* is the particular self-consciousness 'raised to' universality? We may indeed go along with Hegel's point that 'if the state is confused with civil society and its determination is equated with the security and protection of property and personal freedom' (§258R, 276/399), we will go astray. But having accepted that there should be no *equation* between freedom in the state and freedom in civil society, how are we to make sense of the *connection* between them? It cannot be that the universality – and the universal freedom – secured in the state can be shown to latch onto what is present in civil society, lacking an account of how civil society has the required features.

We are told that the state is 'objective spirit' and so it is 'only through being a member of the state that the individual himself has objectivity, truth, and ethical life. *Union* as such is itself the true content and end, and the destiny [*Bestimmung*] of individuals is to lead a universal life'. Rationality will consist in 'the unity of objective freedom (i.e., of the universal substantial will) and subjective freedom (as the freedom of individual knowledge and of the will in its pursuit of particular ends)' (PR §258R). Perhaps it helps to say, as Hegel does in an Addition recorded by Griesheim, that 'the essence of self-consciousness [...] realizes itself as a self-sufficient power of which single individuals [*die einzelnen Individuen*] are only moments' (PR §258A, 279/403). But this restates the problem that in the state (or 'the march of God in the world', as the Griesheim Addition goes on to specify) we are mere moments of a universal substance; our individuality is not in the picture.

At first glance, Hegel's complex account of civil society portrays it as a realm of caprice and subjective conflict. It is 'the field of conflict in which the private interest of each individual comes up against that of everyone else' (PR §289R, 329/458). It would seem that, strictly, the only conception of freedom that can apply here is that of *empirical freedom*. Indeed, such is what Hegel seems to have in mind when he writes that 'this personal [*eigene*] sphere may be seen as belonging to the moment of *formal freedom*, which provides an arena in which personal cognition and personal decisions and their execution, as well as petty passions and imaginings, may indulge themselves' (PR §289R, 330/459).

One might have imagined that Hegel's strategy would be to insist that it is only in the *state* that true freedom is secured, with any conception of freedom appearing 'lower down' the *Sittlichkeit* stretch of the system turning out, after all, not to have been freedom. But this is not the route he takes. Instead, he insists that subjects 'already' have something that can be called freedom on those lower rungs of *Sittlichkeit*.

Again, in one of the more shocking features of Hegel's account of the state, subjective freedom reappears at its very apex: his account of the monarch. The ultimate decision-making power must be vested in a particular subject, namely the monarch. Here the subjectivity of abstract right reappears as 'the *personality of the state*' (PR §279R, 317/445).[14]

Subjective freedom reappears in yet another place within Hegel's account of the state, in the form of public opinion and freedom of the press. Here, however, there is little indication of an attempted mediation with 'true', concrete freedom. Hegel writes that '[f]ormal subjective freedom, whereby individuals [*die Einzelnen*] as such entertain and express their *own* judgements, opinions, and counsels on matters of universal concern, makes its collective appearance in what is known as *public opinion*' (PR §316, 353/483). As M. B. Foster rightly notes, the institutions of freedom of the press, public opinion, parliament and associated machinery 'are for Hegel the conditions within the political sphere of the freedom of the subject class, and their whole *raison d'être* is that they secure a realization within the political sphere for those freedoms of the subject which are characteristic of the sphere of "bürgerliche Gesellschaft"' (Foster 1935: 168). Crucially, for Hegel the value of freedom of the press is that it remains ineffective, 'confined to empty malice and to the self-condemnation which is implicit within it' (§319R, 358/489).

It is difficult not to conclude from the evidence adduced above that there is a profound dualism to be found running through Hegel's account of the state and that this dualism reflects the distinction between empirical (null) freedom and true freedom in the Natural Law essay. After all, Hegel has given us grounds to question the earlier argument that served to sharply distinguish them. He continues to maintain that *true freedom* is the very antithesis of *Willkür* or 'caprice', as enshrined in subjective freedom. Such a dualism threatens Hegel's account of the state as the locus of true freedom not just in that it appears to underlie this account: it permeates it, as is manifested in his return to subjective freedom in the monarch and in the freedom of the press.

There has been extensive discussion of Hegel's apparent attempts to reconcile a classical liberalism (the native home of 'subjective freedom') with what has been seen as a more 'communitarian' outlook, thought to be manifested in his overtly organicist conception of the state. Many have supposed that the direction Hegel himself would have been most liable to turn in to soften the apparent contrast is an authoritarian one that would simply do away with subjective freedom, although it is highly debatable whether this is close to Hegel's intentions. For Hegel, after all, it is vital to his conception of the state as organism that it should have proper members, not mere parts akin to cogs in a machine. I will resist here any attempt to resolve the matter by weighing down more heavily on one of Hegel's conceptions of freedom rather than the other. Instead I turn now in the direction of a solution that seeks to overcome the dualism entirely.

6. In the direction of a solution

Hegel's quest for an account of freedom that recognizes freedom to be at once universal and the possession of individuals marks a fundamental contribution to post-Kantian thinking about freedom, even if, as we have seen, he struggles to bring that quest to a successful conclusion. How might it be more successfully prosecuted?

This question can be seen as one of the central questions occupying Karl Marx in his writings of 1843 and 1844 (in particular his *On the Jewish Question* and the so-called *Economic and Philosophical Manuscripts*). In *On the Jewish Question*, Marx fleshes out the problem in terms of a bifurcation in the subject between *citoyen* and *bourgeois*. The *citoyen* is a member of the state and subject to its universal demands. The *bourgeois* is the atomistic, private individual pursuing her own particular ends. This internal bifurcation is disturbing because the individual's identity as *citoyen* has to confront her as something alien, hovering above her as abstract and alien.[15]

Marx insists that this bifurcation can be overcome only through communism, whereby each exists mutually for each. There is now no private interest; each acts for the sake of each. This is an image of true concrete universality.

It is no accident that Marx offers to secure the wanted concrete universality by appealing to human reality. As he insists throughout his *Critique of Hegel's Doctrine of the State*, the project of imposing mediations on reality externally, however good your logic is, will not work. If Marx is right, however, Hegel's fundamental aspiration – to demonstrate that the true freedom of individuals is rational self-determination – will have been brought in touch with the means of its own vindication.[16]

Notes

1. For an enumeration of passages bearing this out, see Schacht 1972: 289.
2. The work was published in 1820 but bears the date 1821 on its title page.
3. I am following here the dating proposed by Laurence Dickey and H. B. Nisbet in their edition of *Political Writings*.
4. I will focus in this essay on the first of these texts. For its connections with the other two, see Foster 1929.
5. For an account of such a dualism, to which this essay is indebted, see Foster 1929.
6. Hegel's text will be cited by paragraph number (with 'R' indicating a written Remark by Hegel, 'A' indicating an oral Addition recorded by Hegel's students), followed by a page reference to the English translation used/page reference to the German text.
7. For an excellent presentation of this idea in Kant, see Engstrom 2009.
8. I fall in line with the practice of pretending as if 'right' can function in English as a translation of the German *Recht*, as in translations of *Philosophie des Rechts* as 'philosophy of right'. In reality, this is not a normal usage in English: *Recht* has the connotation of 'law' in the most general sense of that term not captured by ordinary English usage (as opposed to English usage specially tailored for speaking about German philosophy) of 'right'.
9. For an argument that this conception of freedom, rooted in Kant, is *the* conception of freedom Hegel is operating with, see Patten 1999.
10. Robert Pippin dwells on the supposedly paradoxical nature of this conception in Pippin 2008. For a response to Pippin, see McDowell 2017.
11. For a useful account which connects this text to Hegel's later political philosophy, see Riedel 1984, chapters 3–4.
12. In its parallel treatments, his magnum opus *The Science of Logic*, and Part One of his *Encyclopaedia of the Philosophical Sciences*, likewise entitled *The Science of Logic*.
13. See especially the useful discussion in Patten 1999.
14. For a helpful account, see Rosenzweig 2010: 411ff.
15. For a fuller account, see Schuringa (forthcoming).
16. I am grateful to Alec Hinshelwood and Joe Saunders for comments that have helped to improve this chapter.

References

Primary texts

NL: Hegel, 'On the Scientific Ways of Treating Natural Law, on Its Place in Practical Philosophy, and Its Relation to the Positive Sciences of Right', in *Political Writings*, trans. H. B. Nisbet, ed. Laurence Dickey and H. B. Nisbet. Cambridge: Cambridge University Press, 1999/'Über die wissenschaftlichen Behandlungsarten des Naturrechts, seine Stelle in der praktischen Philosophie und sein Verhältnis zu den positiven Rechtswissenschaften', in TWA 2.

PM: Hegel, *Philosophy of Mind*, trans. William Wallace and A. V. Miller, rev. and ed. Michael Inwood. Oxford: Oxford University Press, 2007/*Enzyklopädie der philosophischen Wissenschaften* II, TWA 10.

PN: Hegel, *Philosophy of Nature*, trans. A. V. Miller. Oxford: Clarendon, 1970/*Enzyklopädie der philosophischen Wissenschaften* II, TWA 9.

PR: Hegel, *Elements of the Philosophy of Right*, trans. H. B. Nisbet and ed. Allen Wood. Cambridge: Cambridge University Press, 1991/*Grundlinien der Philosophie des Rechts*, TWA 7.

TWA: Hegel, *Werke*, ed. Eva Moldenhauer and Karl Markus Michel. Frankfurt: Suhrkamp, 1986.

Secondary texts

Engstrom, Stephen (2009), *The Form of Practical Knowledge: A Study of the Categorical Imperative*, Cambridge, MA: Harvard University Press.
Foster, Michael B. (1929), *Die Geschichte als Schicksal des Geistes in der Hegelschen Philosophie*, Tübingen: Mohr.
Foster, Michael B. (1935), *The Political Philosophies of Plato and Hegel*, Oxford: Clarendon.
McDowell, John (2017), 'Why Does It Matter to Hegel That Geist Has a History?', in Rachel Zuckert and James Kreines (eds), *Hegel on Philosophy in History*, 15–32, Cambridge: Cambridge University Press.
Ng, Karen (2020), *Hegel's Concept of Life: Self-Consciousness, Freedom, Logic*, New York: Oxford University Press.
Patten, Alan (1999), *Hegel's Idea of Freedom*, Oxford: Oxford University Press.
Pelczynski, Z. A. (1984), 'Political Community and Individual Freedom in Hegel's Philosophy of State', in Z. A. Pelczynski (ed.), *The State and Civil Society: Studies in Hegel's Political Philosophy*, 55–76, Cambridge: Cambridge University Press.
Pippin, Robert B. (2008), *Hegel's Practical Philosophy*, Cambridge: Cambridge University Press.
Riedel, Manfred (1984), *Between Tradition and Revolution: The Hegelian Transformation of Political Philosophy*, trans. Walter Wright, Cambridge: Cambridge University Press.
Rosenzweig, Franz (2010 [1920]), *Hegel und der Staat*, ed. Frank Lachmann, Berlin: Suhrkamp.
Schacht, Richard L. (1972), 'Hegel on Freedom', in Alasdair MacIntyre (ed.), *Hegel: A Collection of Critical Essays*, pp. 289–328, Notre Dame, IN: University of Notre Dame Press.
Schuringa, Christoph (forthcoming), 'Gattungswesen and Universality', in Luca Corti and Johannes Georg Schülein (eds), *Life, Organism and Cognition in Classical German Philosophy*, Berlin: Springer.

8

'In and through their association': Freedom and communism in Marx

Andrew Chitty and Jan Kandiyali

1. Introduction

In Kant's 'positive' conception of freedom, freedom consists not simply in acting independently of alien laws but in acting in accord with the 'autonomy of the will', that is, on laws that are prescribed by the nature of the will as such (*Groundwork*, 446–7, 450, 453–4). This claim about freedom is plausible insofar as the will is my own essence – at one point Kant identifies it with my 'proper self' – so that when I act on laws prescribed by its nature my actions are the expression of my essence (457–8). Kant goes further to argue that acting on such laws requires treating all other persons in a certain positive way, specifically so as to respect their wills or, in his terminology, so as to treat them as 'ends in themselves' (428–31). In short, for Kant genuine freedom involves at once expressing my own essence and treating others in a certain positive way.

In this chapter we argue that Karl Marx's thought on freedom incorporates both of these Kantian ideas. For Marx, I achieve what at one point he calls 'real freedom' by engaging in a certain kind of labour through which I express my essence: both my 'individual' and my 'communal' essence. This labour expresses my individual essence in that it involves the development of my essential powers and capacities. It expresses my communal essence in that it is motivated by the desire to satisfy the needs of other human beings.[1]

So, we argue that, for Marx, as for Kant, genuine freedom involves at once expressing my own essence and treating others in a certain positive way. However, the conception of 'essence' and the kind of treatment involved are different. And Marx differs further from Kant in arguing that genuine freedom is only possible in a certain type of society, namely a future communist society.

In what follows we aim to spell out these broad claims. We proceed as follows. In § 2 we consider a canonical passage where Marx asserts that genuine freedom can only be achieved in a communist society. We consider two basic accounts of how this happens. We favour the second account but argue that in its initial form this relies on attributing to Marx too simple a conception of freedom. In § 3 we argue for attributing to him a more complex conception of freedom, as voluntary self-realization. In § 4 we show why for Marx capitalism prevents rather than enables this conception of freedom and why by contrast a future communist society enables it. Finally in § 5 we compare this conception of freedom to Kant's.

2. Freedom 'in and through' association

In a number of passages Marx implies that humans can become genuinely free only in a communist society. The most extensive one is this:

> The transformation, through the division of labour, of personal powers (relationships) into material [*sachliche*] powers, cannot be dispelled by dismissing the general idea of it from one's mind, but can only be abolished by the individuals again subjecting these material powers to themselves and abolishing the division of labour. This is not possible without the community. Only in community [with others has each] individual the means of cultivating his gifts in all directions; only in the community, therefore, is personal freedom possible. In the previous substitutes for the community, in the State, etc. personal freedom has existed only for the individuals who developed within the relationships of the ruling class, and only insofar as they were individuals of this class. The illusory community, in which individuals have up till now combined, always took on an independent existence [*verselbständigte sich*] in relation to them, and since it was the combination of one class over against another, it was the same time for the oppressed class not only a completely illusory community, but a new fetter as well. In the real [*wirklichen*] community the individuals obtain their freedom in and through their association.
> (*The German Ideology*, CW5: 78)²

The idea that humans can achieve freedom only in a specific type of society is not original to Marx. Such a claim is, for instance, present in Rousseau's assertion that in the civil state the human being acquires 'moral freedom, which alone makes him truly master of himself' (*Social Contract* 1.8). It is also, of course, central to Hegel's political philosophy and his view that the modern state is the 'actualisation of freedom' (*Philosophy of Right*, §258A).

However, while it is clear that Marx follows Rousseau and Hegel in this respect, it is less clear *why* he thinks that genuine freedom is only possible in a communist society. Indeed, the literature on Marx suggests different answers to this question, corresponding to different accounts of how it is that, in the words of the above passage, individuals in a communist society will 'obtain their freedom in and through their association'. In this section, we consider two accounts of the connection between freedom and communism in Marx.

The first is a 'collective control' account. According to it, in a communist society individuals exert collective control over the organization of their own society. Unlike pre-communist societies in which human beings have been dominated by the social relations within which they produce, a communist society will be characterized, as

Marx says in the first volume of *Capital*, by 'conscious and planned control' over the production process (Marx 1976: 173). On this view, the genuine freedom that individuals acquire in a communist society consists simply in exercising this collective control. As Allen Wood puts it, 'true self-determination must consist in the imposition of human control on the social conditions of human production' (Wood 2004: 51).[3]

Although Marx, both in the above passage and elsewhere, clearly associates collective control with communism, it is far from clear that he sees the freedom that is attained in communist society as *consisting* in this control. Indeed, this interpretation is at odds with Marx's focus in the above passage on individual (or as he puts it there 'personal') freedom: he says that in the real community it is simply 'individuals', and not individuals acting as part of a group, that obtain their freedom 'in and through their association'.

This suggests a second account, which we call a 'conditions of individual freedom' account. According to this view, in communist society social relations are such that they provide conditions that enable each member to act freely. Marx seems to have this in mind in the above passage when he says that '[o]nly in community [with others has each] individual the means of cultivating his gifts in all directions; only in the community, therefore, is personal freedom possible'. Here, a particular community (that provided by a future community society) is seen as an enabling condition of the freedom of individuals.

However, the 'conditions of individual freedom' account admits of multiple variants, depending on what individual freedom is taken to consist in and how a future communist society is said to enable it. One variant of this account that is commonly attributed to Marx is what we can call a 'material abundance' interpretation. According to this view, communism brings about a high level of material abundance, which ensures that my actions are free in that I am not compelled to act in any particular way to meet my needs. In these conditions of material plenty, my actions are also free in that I have the material means available to do whatever I wish; I can 'do one thing today and another tomorrow [...] just as I have a mind' (*The German Ideology*, CW5: 47).[4]

However, the 'material abundance' account does not seem to us the best interpretation of Marx's view. Its limits can be seen by reflecting on the fact that, on this view, free action does not require treating others in any particular way: it might be true that a communist society, and only such a society, can provide the abundance required for free action, but this is compatible with my free action involving a purely instrumental and self-interested attitude towards others in that society. Yet, as we shall argue, in the account of communist production in the 1844 *Comments on James Mill* Marx sees individuals as achieving their freedom through intentionally providing others with the goods and services they need. Furthermore, we shall also argue that some of Marx's other remarks about freedom in a future communist society – such as his description of communism as a society in which 'the free development of each is the condition for the free development of all' – are only plausible if we attribute to Marx a view of free action as involving a similarly other-regarding motivation.

Following this clue, in the next section we argue that Marx was committed to an alternative variant of the 'conditions of individual freedom' account, which goes beyond the 'material abundance' interpretation in that it sees free action as requiring individuals to treat each other in a certain positive way.

3. Free activity as voluntary self-realization

The conception of free action that we propose to attribute to Marx is that it consists in the 'self-realization' of the individual performing it. We can cite two kinds of textual evidence to support this attribution. First, in some places Marx directly connects freedom with self-realization. For example, in a passage in the *Grundrisse* (1857–8) he speaks of 'self-realisation, objectification of the subject, hence real freedom, whose action is, precisely, labour' (Marx 1973: 611).

Second, in a number of writings from the 1840s Marx describes communist society as a society in which humans become free for the first time. For example, in *On the Jewish Question* (1843) he describes it as 'human emancipation' and intimates that in it each individual will see in others 'the realisation of his own freedom' (CW3: 234, 230). In the *Communist Manifesto* (1847) he says it will be a society in which 'the free development of each is the condition for the free development of all'. And in the long passage we have quoted above from *The German Ideology* he strongly implies that genuine freedom can only be attained in a communist society. Yet at the same time in his description of communism in the *Comments on James Mill*, he says that this will be a society in which individuals achieve self-realization (CW3: 227–8). Taken together, these passages suggest that Marx identifies genuine freedom with self-realization, though of course they are compatible with a weaker connection between the two concepts.

Finally, the view that freedom consists in self-realization has some inherent plausibility, at least if we combine it with an understanding of the 'self-realization' of an individual as the expression of that individual's essence in their activities. For, insofar as we identify an individual's essence with their 'true self', when their activities express their essence they express their true self. Thereby they are self-determining, and self-determination is one widely used conception of freedom.[5]

If we turn to the *Comments on James Mill* passage just mentioned, we can read it as describing communist production as being a matter of self-realization in just this sense of the expression of each individual's essence in their activities. There, Marx thinks of my essence as having both 'individual' and 'communal' aspects. He associates the expression of the individual aspect with activity through which I exercise and develop my powers and capacities and also objectify those powers and capacities in the product of my labour:

> In my *production* I would have objectified my *individuality, its specific character*, and therefore enjoyed not only an individual *manifestation of my life* during the activity, but also when looking at the object I would have the individual pleasure of knowing my personality to be *objective, visible to the senses* and hence a power beyond all doubt.
>
> (CW3: 227)

By contrast he associates the expression of the communal aspect of my essence with my production of goods and services in order to satisfy the needs of others (where we take it that for Marx 'a need' means 'something required for self-realisation').

> In the individual expression of my life I would have directly created your expression of your life, and therefore in my individual activity I would have directly *confirmed* and *realised* my true nature, my *human* nature, my *communal nature*.
>
> (CW3: 227)[6]

It is worth noting several features of this account of self-realization. First, although we have described the expression of the individual and the communal aspects of my essence as separate aspects of self-realization, it is clear that Marx does not take them to be in tension with one another but, on the contrary, complementary. Indeed, his view is that in a future communist society individuals will be able to realize both aspects of their essence in one and the same activity. That is, in a communist society individuals will exercise and develop their own powers and capacities *through* activities that are done in order to satisfy the needs of others. It could even be said that the powers and capacities whose exercise and development constitute the realization of the individual aspect of my essence are just those powers and capacities that can be used to satisfy others' needs, thus suggesting that the two aspects of my self-realization are deeply interlinked.[7]

Second, although we have described the second aspect of self-realization as 'communal', this should not be taken to mean that what is expressed is the essence of some supra-individual collective agent, such as the nation or state. This aspect of my self-realization is communal, not in the sense that what is realized is a collective agent, but in the sense that my self-realization has a communal focus: individuals each express their essence through providing others with the goods and services they need in order to flourish. But it is individuals, and not a collective agent, that each express their essence through such activity.

Third, although the early Marx's account of self-realization has this communal aspect, it is important to note that Marx does not think of individuals in communist society as sacrificing their own interests so as to help others. His vision of a communist society is rather one of individuals inseparably serving their own and each other's interests. For this reason, it would be a mistake to equate the communal aspect of self-realization with altruistic action, understood as action motivated by a selfless concern for others' well-being. As Marx himself later puts it, communism will not be the 'love-imbued opposite of selfishness' (*Circular Against Kriege*, CW6: 41).

Finally, to say that for Marx real freedom consists in self-realization as we have defined it above is insufficient, for this would be compatible with individuals being coerced – whether by others or by circumstances – to exercise and develop their powers and capacities so as to satisfy others' needs. However, it is clear that Marx would not consider action performed under such coercion to be free. After all, one of the evils that Marx identifies in alienated labour is that it is 'not voluntary [*freiwillig*], but coerced', and this carries the clear implication that its opposite, the unalienated labour of communist society, will not be coerced. Thus, we propose, in addition to the individual and communal aspects of self-realization described above, another component of Marx's conception of freedom is that such self-realization is undertaken voluntarily, by which we mean, in the absence of coercion.[8]

That the conception of freedom we attribute to Marx includes voluntariness is important because it challenges a surprisingly resilient misinterpretation of Marx – found most famously in Isaiah Berlin's essay 'Two Concepts of Liberty' – according to which Marx is a proponent of positive freedom (in Berlin's sense of freedom as self-determination) who rejects negative freedom (in Berlin's sense of freedom as non-interference). It is true that the notion of self-realization we have attributed to Marx can be seen as a version of Berlin's positive freedom, as well as of Kant's. It is also true that Marx criticizes Berlin's negative freedom, arguing that 'it makes every man see in other men not the realization of his own freedom, but the barrier to it' (*On the Jewish Question*, CW3: 230). But in our view this criticism only shows that he does not think that this freedom is sufficient for genuine freedom. Rather than rejecting it, he incorporates the core idea in Berlin's negative freedom – that people cannot be said to be free if their actions are done in the presence of coercion – along with a version of Berlin's positive freedom into his account of freedom. To act in a genuinely free way, for Marx, is to *voluntarily* engage in self-realizing activity.[9]

4. Communism and the enablement of freedom

In this section we shall ask how a communist society provides enabling conditions for freedom in Marx's sense of voluntary individual and communal self-realization. We approach this question indirectly, by first of all considering why Marx takes it that capitalism fails to enable such freedom and instead systematically tends to prevent it.

For Marx, capitalism can be defined as a society in which the means of production are owned by private companies; workers own no means with which to produce other than their own labour power; companies pay workers a wage to produce; companies compete with each other to sell the resulting goods and service on the market for profit; and the state coercively enforces companies' ownership over the means of production. How does capitalism so conceived fail to enable the three aspects of Marx's freedom that we have considered?

It is relatively easy to see why Marx thinks that capitalism prevents the individual aspect of self-realization. As we have seen, Marx associates the individual aspect of my self-realization with the exercise and development of my powers and capacities, and the objectification of those powers and capacities in the product of my labour. Simply put, capitalism generates forms of work that are not conducive to the individual aspect of self-realization. This is because, for Marx, competition between capitalist companies forces each company to strive to maximize its profits. Therefore companies must generate the maximum output from their workers at the lowest cost. This constraint typically leads to the worker engaging in labour that 'does not develop freely his physical and mental energy but mortifies his body and ruins his mind' (*Economic and Philosophical Manuscripts* CW3: 274). The point here is not that capitalist employers deliberately engender non self-realizatory forms of labour. Rather, it is that under capitalism it is 'quite accidental and inessential [...] whether the act of labour itself, is for [the worker] the enjoyment of his personality and the realisation of his natural abilities and spiritual aims' (*Comments on James Mill*, CW3: 220).

If it is reasonably clear why Marx thinks that capitalism prevents the individual aspect of my self-realization, it is less obvious why Marx should think that it prevents the communal aspect. After all, if the communal aspect involves the satisfaction of others' needs, then it might be argued that this also happens under capitalism. So what is it about capitalism that prevents the communal aspect of self-realization?

One answer that is often attributed to Marx, or to a broadly Marxian view, is that work under capitalism does not satisfy the *genuine* needs of others. Capitalism creates 'inhuman, sophisticated, unnatural and imaginary appetites' (*Economic and Philosophical Manuscript*s CW3: 307). Production is then geared towards the satisfaction of these 'false needs' rather than genuine needs – needs required for self-realization – at the satisfaction of which communist production will be aimed.

However, this argument is not very plausible. Much might be said against capitalism, but it is hard to deny that workers under capitalism produce many things that other people genuinely need. A more plausible answer, and arguably one that is more authentically Marx's, is that although workers under capitalism produce things that other people need, they do not produce for others *in order to* satisfy others' needs. That is, because a capitalist society in which workers have to sell their labour power to survive, workers are typically motivated to labour 'out of egoistic need and necessity', only as a means of satisfying their own 'dire need' (*Comments on James Mill*, CW3: 220). Thus, while work under capitalism may satisfy others' needs, in Marx's view, it is generally performed out of a self-regarding motivation rather than a concern for others as such.[10] By contrast, the communal aspect of my self-realization is a matter of me producing for others *in order to* satisfy their needs.

Finally, Marx thinks that capitalism excludes from productive activity the other aspect of freedom that we identified above – voluntariness. As we have seen, Marx describes wage-labour under capitalism as 'forced labour'. Of course, Marx is aware that workers under capitalism are not forced to work in the manner of slaves and serfs. Unlike pre-capitalist labourers, wage labourers have full ownership over their labour power. However, since a capitalist society is one in which capitalists have full ownership over the means of production, and workers cannot produce the means of satisfying their basic needs without using these means of production, it follows that they are still ultimately forced to sell their labour power, in that they have no reasonable alternative.[11] For this reason, Marx argues that capitalism is less different from slavery and feudalism than its defenders would have us believe. It is a system of 'forced labour, however much it might appear as the result of free contractual agreement' (Marx 1981: 958).[12]

In short, for Marx both individual and communal self-realization are, though not impossible to achieve, systematically prevented by capitalism, while *voluntary* self-realization is impossible to achieve under capitalism.

We are now in a position to answer the question of how a communist society, by contrast with a capitalist one, would provide the enabling conditions of Marx's freedom. Let us define a communist society as a society in which there is no private property in the means of production; members collectively organize their own production; and goods and services are distributed according to individuals' needs. Let us also assume that we are talking about a society in which there is no coercive state – such a state has 'died out' (Engels, *Socialism Utopian and Scientific*, CW24: 321).

Consider the three aspects of voluntary individual and communal self-realization in turn. First, the individual aspect of self-realization: the exercise and development of my essential powers, and the objectification of those powers in the product of my labour. Now a communist society is one in which members collectively organize their productive activity. Let us suppose, as Marx does, that human beings, once their basic needs are met, are motivated to express their own essence.[13] Then members would try to organize production in such a way that the productive activity of each member involves the exercise and development of their essential powers and capacities. The degree to which they are able to do this will depend on various factors, such as the society's level of technology. However, it would not be 'accidental and inessential' whether through my labour I exercise and develop my essential powers and capacities, for this would be the aim of communist production.

Second, a communist society would also enable the communal aspect of self-realization: the intentional satisfaction of others' needs. In a capitalist society whether someone's needs are met is contingent on their labour contribution: those who do not work do not eat. As we have seen, Marx argues that this encourages people to produce for self-regarding motives: agents under capitalism typically produce out of 'egoistic need and necessity'. In a communist society, by contrast, people's needs are met irrespective of their labour contribution. Since their own needs are met independently of their labour contribution, people will be able to focus on the needs of others.

Thirdly, production in a communist society would be voluntary. Since, as we have said, in a communist society people's needs are met irrespective of their labour contribution, they are not coerced into producing by the threat of loss of their livelihood. Nor are they coerced to work by the state. Therefore, insofar as they do produce their productive activity is not done in the presence of any coercion but is rather voluntary.[14]

Furthermore, if we make the same motivational assumption stated above, namely that once their basic needs are met people are motivated to express their own essence, we can *also* see that in a communist society my voluntary self-realization would be enabled by the voluntary self-realization of all other members. For the self-realization of those others includes intentionally producing to satisfy the needs of others apart from themselves, including myself. Insofar as they understand my 'needs' to include my requirements to be able to engage in voluntary self-realization, this means that the voluntary self-realization of all others provides the enabling condition for my voluntary self-realization. The same will be true for every member of the society. This, we suggest, is what Marx had in mind when he said that communism would be 'an association in which the free development of each is the condition of the free development of all' (*Communist Manifesto* CW6: 506). In a communist society, my self-realization centrally involves intentionally providing others with the conditions of their self-realization.

Here it is helpful to compare our account of this mutual enablement of self-realization with that given by G.A. Cohen with his analogy of a jazz band. Cohen writes:

> One way of picturing life under communism, as Marx conceived it, is to imagine a jazz band each player in which seeks his own fulfilment as a musician. Though basically interested in his own fulfilment, and not in that of the band as a whole, or of his fellow musicians taken severally, he nevertheless fulfils himself only to the extent that each of the others also does so, and the same holds for each of them.

He concludes:

> So, as I understand Marx's communism, it is a concert of mutually supporting self-fulfilments, in which no one takes promoting the fulfilment of others as any kind of obligation. I am not, of course, denying that each delights in the fulfilment of the others [...] But no such delight is required: it is not something in the dimension of affect which is supposed to make communism possible. Instead, a lofty material endowment ensures that 'the free development of each is the condition for the free development of all'.
>
> (Cohen 1990: 32)

In our view, as in that of Cohen, the self-realization (or what he calls 'self-fulfilment') of all others provides the enabling condition for the self-realization of each. However, Cohen explicitly defines an individual's self-realizatory activity as not necessarily motivated by any desire to satisfy the needs of others: the members of his Jazz band are interested in their 'own fulfilment'. By contrast, for our Marx self-realization intrinsically includes what we have called a 'communal' aspect; it necessarily involves activity done in order to satisfy the needs of others. Cohen's view is compatible with the 'free development of each' phrase in *The Communist Manifesto*, in which concern for others is not mentioned. However, we suggest that it is only if self-realization is understood as having this communal aspect that the whole picture that this phrase describes is plausible. With the motivational assumption that people want to produce for others, we can see how the voluntary self-realization of each contributes to providing the enabling conditions for the voluntary self-realization of all others – how 'the free development of each is the condition of the free development of all'. Without this assumption, whether or not this happens becomes a matter of pure chance.[15]

This, then, is our account of how for Marx in a communist society individuals achieve their freedom 'in and through their association'. It is similar to the 'material abundance' account that we introduced in § 2, in that for both accounts communist society provides the enabling conditions of individual freedom. However, it differs from that account, first by construing the freedom in question as consisting specifically in voluntary self-realization, where self-realization has both individual and communal aspects, and second by specifying that the enabling conditions for this voluntary self-realization on the part of each are intentionally brought about as part of the voluntary self-realization of all others.[16]

In concluding this section, it is worth noting two limitations of our argument, on behalf of Marx, that a communist society would enable voluntary self-realization on the part of its members.

First, the argument does not conclude that all individuals in a communist society would *necessarily* engage in voluntary self-realization, since given the absence of coercion in that society some individuals might choose not to. It concludes only that this society provides enabling conditions for every individual to engage in such activity. However, with the elimination of the capitalist barriers to voluntary self-realization, Marx expects individuals to spontaneously engage in it. This is obviously a contestable claim, though Marx could argue that the contrary claim, that people will only produce for others when they are compelled to as a means of satisfying their own needs, is equally contestable, not least because it appears to generalize motivation under capitalism to human motivation as such.

Second, even if we grant Marx's claim that a communist society would enable freedom understood as voluntary self-realization, it is a further step to conclude that *only* a communist society would do so. In reply, Marx could argue that, given that a capitalist society cannot enable such freedom, the onus is on others to describe an alternative to communism that would. Until they do so he is entitled to conclude that only a communist society would enable freedom in this sense.

5. Marx and Kant on freedom

For Kant genuine freedom involves both expressing my own essence and treating others in a positive way. The resulting connection between my freedom and my treatment of others is perhaps his greatest innovation in the theory of freedom. Based on the account we have given above, it is clear that this connection is preserved in Marx's conception of freedom. However we can discern several key differences between Marx's way of making out the connection and Kant's.

First, Marx 'socializes' Kant. For Kant, freedom involves first of all acting in accord with the laws that are prescribed by the nature of the will as such, and only second and consequently, treating others as ends in themselves. By contrast for Marx the connection between genuine freedom and treating others in a positive way is much closer, for this freedom is a matter of expressing an essence that is both individual and communal, where both the individual and the communal aspect are defined in terms of the needs of others. Marx moves away from Kant's essentially individualistic view of free action to a view in which such action is closely bound up with participation in a certain kind of society.

Second, Marx 'naturalizes' Kant. For Kant as we have construed him, my own essence consists in possessing a will. This is defined independently of any reference to the biological human species. By contrast for Marx my individual and my communal essence are both embedded in human biology. Concomitantly, whereas for Kant freedom centrally requires respecting the will of others, that is, treating them as ends in themselves rather than merely as means, by contrast for

Marx it involves satisfying the 'needs' of others, where this centrally includes their biological needs.[17] This explains why Marx ties freedom so closely to productive activity. It may be said that the 'universality' which characterizes the communal essence of each individual is simply a naturalized form of the universality of Kant's will and that satisfying the needs of others is simply a naturalized form of treating them as ends in themselves. But Marx at least makes an attempt to rethink Kant's connection between freedom and sociality in a way that recognizes humans as part of nature.[18]

Third, Marx 'politicizes' Kant. For Kant, freedom is in principle available to everyone in every society, even if it is easier to achieve it in a society governed by Right. For everyone, no matter what their circumstances, can choose to reject their given inclinations and act instead on the laws prescribed by the nature of the will. By contrast for Marx only a communist society provides enabling conditions for freedom. Marx, unlike Kant, thereby enlists the ideal of freedom in an argument for social transformation.[19]

So far we have only outlined an understanding of Marx's conception of freedom and its relation to Kant's, but what can be said by way of assessing their relative merits? Here we might proceed by asking what makes Kant's conception of freedom attractive in the first place. The idea that for me to act freely my actions must not only be voluntary but also genuinely originate from myself, as opposed to some source outside me, is surely appealing. But why should we substitute for 'myself' in this formula the nature of the will? The deep thought behind Kant's substitution must be that each human individual is at root only an instance of agency, or willed action, as such, so that the will is the essence of each person. Therefore for an individual's actions to be genuinely free those actions must originate in the nature of agency, or of the will, as such. A parallel thought in Marx is that each of us is at root only an instance of 'intentionally producing for each other', so that intentionally producing for each other is the essence of each individual – an idea epitomized in Marx's description of humans as 'species beings'. Therefore for an individual's actions to be genuinely free they must originate in the nature of intentionally producing for each other as such. This is then spelled out in terms of expressing the individual and communal aspects of the individual's essence that we have discussed above. Thus what really differentiates Marx's conception of freedom from on the one hand Kant's and on the other hand a conception that agrees that free action is action that originates from myself but refuses to substitute any 'essence' for myself in this formula is their respective metaphysical accounts of the human self. Accordingly a serious evaluation of the relative merits of each conception will have to become an assessment of the metaphysics of human selfhood that underpins each.

Acknowledgements

For helpful comments on an earlier draft of this paper we would like to thank Meade McCloughan, Joe Saunders and Nicholas Vrousalis. All errors remain our own.

Notes

1. The term 'communal essence' may be misleading insofar as it suggests a reference to a local or national community. However, the community we have in mind in using this term is pan-human. The early Marx's commitment to such a pan-human conception of community is evidenced by his emphasis on the human species.
2. The passage does not assert that freedom *as such* can only be achieved in a communist society (the 'real community' of the passage), since Marx refers to individuals in the ruling class possessing 'personal freedom' in class societies. However, the context strongly suggests that this freedom has always been circumscribed and therefore incomplete. For this reason, we attribute to Marx in this passage the view that *genuine* freedom is only possible in a communist society.
3. However, Wood is ambiguous. Later he writes: 'Human freedom can only be attained when people's social relations are subject to conscious control' (p. 52), suggesting that exercising collective control does not constitute freedom but is rather an enabling condition of it. This falls into the 'conditions of individual freedom' account that we consider next.
4. In what follows we think of freedom primarily as a characteristic of an agent's actions (or activity), rather than a modally defined characteristic of agents. Thus, we operate with an 'exercise' rather than an 'opportunity' conception of freedom. However, derivatively we can say that an agent all of whose actions or activities over a period of time are free is free in that period of time.
5. For a *locus classicus* of the idea of freedom as self-determination see Fichte's statement in the *Foundations of Natural Right* (1796) that if a being is to ascribe 'free efficacy' to itself then it must ascribe to itself 'an activity whose ultimate ground lies purely and simply within itself' (Fichte 2000: 17).
6. For a discussion of the connection, implied in this passage, between producing for each other and Marx's claim that humans are essentially 'species beings' see Chitty 1997 and Chitty 2018: 134–8.
7. Although Marx claims that the individual and communal aspects of self-realization are complementary, this does not commit him to the implausible view that every particular act through which I express the individual aspect of my essence is also one through which I express the communal aspect or vice versa.
8. We use 'voluntary action' in a strong sense to refer to action that is done in the *absence* of coercion (i.e., in which there are no coercive pressures for the agent to act as they do), rather than in a weaker sense to mean action that is not done *out of* coercion (i.e., in which there may be such coercive pressures, but if there are the agent does not act as they do because of them but instead out of some other motivation).
9. In this respect, Marx follows Hegel, who also integrates negative (or as Hegel puts it, 'subjective') freedom into a larger account of human freedom. For discussion of this aspect of Hegel's view see Neuhouser 2000: 82–113.
10. These are strong empirical claims. Defenders of capitalism have long argued that the motivation of market participants is more diverse than Marx and Marxists suggest. For such a view, see Steiner 2014. Even if that is the case, however, Marx can still point out that capitalism encourages more egoistic forms of motivation at the expense of other-regarding concerns.
11. By 'basic needs' we mean, roughly, the things required for a minimally acceptable standard of living. By contrast, needs required for self-realization include but go beyond basic needs.

12 For further discussion of the force or compulsion involved here, see Cohen 1983. It might be argued that capitalism is compatible with voluntary productive activity, for capitalism could be combined with an unconditional basic income that enables people to meet their basic needs without having to work. Productive activity would then be voluntary. For such a view, see Van der Veen and Van Parijs 1986. However, it remains to be seen whether an unconditional income set above basic needs is compatible with capitalism.
13 This motivational assumption – that human beings are motivated to express their essence – is consonant with Marx's prediction in the *Critique of the Gotha Programme* that in the higher phase of communist society labour will become 'not only a means of life but life's prime want' (CW24: 87).
14 Here we have tacitly assumed that a communist society would exclude other forms of coercion, such as social norms.
15 For a more detailed discussion of the motivational structure of Marx's communism, which however does not address the question of freedom, see Brudney 1998: 183–19. Elsewhere Brudney criticizes Marx's view for the way that it appears to see a fortuitous alignment between voluntary activity and social needs. How, he asks, can a communist society 'ensure that while each produces as she pleases, together we generate the right mix of socially necessary outputs?' (Brudney 1998: 174; cf. Schmidt am Busch 2014). In our view, the answer is that, as Brudney himself recognizes, Marx's view is that people are motivated to provide others with the goods and services they need. Thus, there is no fortuitous alignment of producer freedom and consumer need, but a willing tailoring of producer freedom to satisfy others' needs. For further discussion, see Kandiyali 2020: 569–71.
16 In the third volume of *Capital* Marx says that the 'realm of freedom' really only begins beyond the 'sphere of material production', that is, beyond the sphere of activities that aim at the end of satisfaction of material needs (Marx 1981: 958–9). In doing so, he puts forward a view that is at odds with the view we have attributed to him here, in which freedom partly consists in activity that is directed towards the satisfaction of others' needs, including their material needs. For further discussion of this tension in Marx's thought, and for why it cannot be seen as a simple shift from the early to the late Marx, see Kandiyali 2014.
17 Of course Kant's categorical imperative includes an 'imperfect' duty to others, that one must try 'as far as he can, to further the ends of others' (*Groundwork* 430), and these ends may include the satisfaction of those others' biological needs, so the contrast with Marx that we draw here is not absolute.
18 For further discussion of this theme, and of its relation to Hegel, see Neuhouser 2020.
19 No doubt Kant's concepts of a 'kingdom of ends' and of an 'ethical commonwealth' project a society in which everyone acts in accord with the categorical imperative and so freely, but they do not describe a social structure which uniquely provides the enabling conditions for free action.

References

Brudney, Daniel (1998), *Marx's Attempt to Leave Philosophy*, Cambridge, MA: Harvard University Press.

Chitty, Andrew (1997), 'First Person Plural Ontology and Praxis', *Proceedings of the Aristotelian Society*, 97 (1): 81–96.

Chitty, Andrew (2018), 'Human Solidarity in Hegel and Marx', in Jan Kandiyali (ed.), *Reassessing Marx Social and Political Philosophy: Freedom, Recognition and Human Flourishing*, pp. 120–146 London: Routledge.
Cohen, G. A. (1983), 'The Structure of Proletarian Unfreedom', *Philosophy & Public Affairs*, 12 (1): 3–33.
Cohen, G. A. (1990), 'Self-Ownership, Communism and Equality', *Proceedings of the Aristotelian Society, Supplementary Volume*, 64: 25–61.
Fichte, J. G. (2000), *Foundations of Natural Right*, trans. Michael Baur (first published 1796–97), Cambridge: Cambridge University Press.
Hegel, G. W. F. (1991), *Elements of the Philosophy of Right*, ed. Allen W. Wood, trans. H. B. Nisbet, Cambridge: Cambridge University Press (cited by section number).
Kandiyali, Jan (2014), 'Freedom and Necessity in Marx's Account of Communism', *British Journal for the History of Philosophy*, 22 (1): 104–23.
Kandiyali, Jan (2020), 'The Importance of Others: Marx on Unalienated Production', *Ethics*, 130 (4): 555–87.
Kant, Immanuel (1998), *Groundwork of the Metaphysics of Morals*, trans. Mary Gregor (first published 1785), Prussian Academy volume 4 pagination, Cambridge: Cambridge University Press.
Marx, Karl (1973), *Grundrisse*, (written 1857–58), London: Penguin.
Marx, Karl (1976), *Capital Volume 1* (first published 1867), London: Penguin.
Marx, Karl (1981), *Capital Volume 3* (first published 1894), London: Penguin.
Marx, Karl and Friedrich Engels (1975–2004), *Marx-Engels Collected Works* (abbreviated as CW followed by volume number), London: Lawrence and Wishart.
Neuhouser, Frederick (2000), *Foundations of Hegel's Social Theory: Actualizing Freedom*, Cambridge, MA: Harvard University Press.
Neuhouser, Frederick (2020), '"Spiritual Life" as a Criterion for Social Critique', in Vitoria Fareld and Hannes Kuch (eds), *From Hegel to Marx and Back: Capitalism, Critique, and Utopia*, London: Bloomsbury.
Rousseau, Jean-Jacques (1973), *On the Social Contract* (first published 1762), trans. G. D. H. Cole, London: Dent (cited by book and chapter number).
Schmidt am Busch, Hans-Christoph (2013), '"The Egg of Columbus"? How Fourier's social theory exerted a significant (and problematic) influence on the formation of Marx's anthropology and social critique', *British Journal for the History of Philosophy* 21 (6): 1154–74.
Steiner, Hillel (2014), 'Greed and Fear', *Politics, Philosophy & Economics*, 13 (2): 140–50.
van der Veen, Robert J. and Philippe Van Parijs (1986), 'A Capitalist Road to Communism', *Theory and Society*, 15 (5): 635–55.
Wood, Allen (2004), *Karl Marx*, 2nd edition, London: Routledge.

9

Mill on freedom, normativity and spontaneity

Christopher Macleod

The influence of 'Germano-Coleridgean' thought on Mill – philosophy he associated with the nineteenth century, rather than the eighteenth century – is clearest in his practical philosophy. The ways in which Mill incorporates nineteenth-century concerns into his moral, social and political philosophy are well known. Mill's utilitarianism expands beyond its Benthamite origins by focusing on the culture of the individual; his social analysis is more firmly grounded in a historical nature of society's progression; liberty becomes in his hands a means not primarily for pursuing one's interests and desires but for their authentic development.

There are corresponding changes in Mill's theoretical philosophy, though these are less often noticed. I wish, in this paper, to highlight various advances Mill made upon his British forbearers concerning the nature of agency. In particular, I will highlight Mill's attempt to account for the existence of normativity, free will and spontaneity in the context of his associationist psychology. Each of these moves was made in response to evolving concerns of German idealists about the British empiricists' 'mechanistic' conception of mind. I will not here attempt to tell the story of the historical transmission of these concerns from German philosophy to Mill – though such a story of this sort could certainly be told.[1] Rather, I will show various ways in which Mill engaged with the problem of agency and attempted to 'elicit dynamical conclusions' from the 'mechanical premises' of associationism (*Letter to Carlyle*, XII: 221).[2]

As will be seen, Mill's attempt to grapple with these issues did not issue in entirely satisfactory results. Sometimes, philosophical progress is made by the resolution of difficulties – but sometimes simply by recognizing and taking difficulties sufficiently seriously as to be *in need* of attempted resolution. It is the latter which was the case here. Mill saw the difficulties associationism faced as an account of human agency and deserves credit for engaging with those difficulties rather than brushing them to one side. Taken together, his attempts to do justice to the fundamental *activity* of human beings show a noteworthy engagement with themes emerging from Kantian and post-Kantian schools of thought.[3]

1. The determinacy of mind

Mill's philosophical outlook is naturalistic through and through: human beings, he holds, are wholly a part of nature and are subject to natural causal laws. This applies equally to *mind* as to *body*. Mill holds that the substantive laws that govern the operation of mind can, like other causal laws, only be discovered by observation and induction. And, by observation and induction, Mill holds, it can be established that Associationism – 'the theory which resolves all the phenomena of the mind into ideas of sensation connected together by the law of association' (*Blakey's History of Moral Science*, X: 23) – is the correct theory of the human mind.

Human beings are causally receptive to the outside world – which is to say capable of *sensation*. But, equally importantly, they are capable of recollecting sensation by way of *ideas*:

> Whenever any state of consciousness has once been excited in us, no matter by what cause, an inferior degree of the same state of consciousness, a state of consciousness resembling the former, but inferior in intensity, is capable of being reproduced in us, without the presence of any such cause as excited it at first. Thus, if we have once seen or touched an object, we can afterwards think of the object though it be absent from our sight or from our touch. [...] [I]n the language of Hume, [...] every mental *impression* has its *idea*.
>
> (*System*, VIII: 852)

Ideas are excited by sensation but also by two fundamental laws of association that hold between ideas: the law of *similarity* and the law of *contiguity*. According to the first, if two ideas are similar, one idea will tend to recall the other. According to the second, when ideas are experienced contiguously – when they occur in close succession or simultaneously – again, the ideas will tend to give rise to one another even when encountered individually. Subject to various clarifications, Mill holds that all mental phenomena can be accounted for on the basis of sensation and the combination of resultant ideas by these laws.

Which ideas are combined in processes of association is clearly a matter of both the natural and the cultural order. The physical nature of fire determines that the sensation of fire is often experienced alongside the sensation of heat; as such the corresponding ideas are repeatedly experienced contiguously and become associated, and the idea of fire thereby comes to recall the idea of heat. The connection between the sensation of a particular colour and the name 'red' is not itself dictated by nature; nevertheless, when a red sensation occurs and the corresponding idea arises, the idea of 'red' is also often presented, and as such the ideas become closely associated.[4]

Strength of association is increased by the frequency with which two ideas are experienced together (*System*, VIII: 852), and it is an important feature of the associationist account that ideas can become *so* closely associated that it becomes 'impossible for us to think the one thing disjoined from the other [...] the idea called up by association become[s], in our consciousness, inseparable from the idea which suggested it' (*Examination*, IX: 178). A useful case in point is the association of our idea of *matter* with that of the *primary qualities*. The idea of matter itself, Mill indicates, is nothing but the idea of groups of 'permanent possibilities of sensation' – sensations themselves may be fleeting, but where we can *return* to groups of sensations after a period of absence, we have the ideas of 'the permanency and externality which belong to Matter'. Though our idea of matter is simply this idea of the permanent possibility of groups of sensations, Mill notes that 'as we are actually constituted' groups of sensations are united 'through the connexion which they all have, by laws of coexistence or of causation, with the sensations which are referable to the sense of touch and to the muscles; those which answer to the terms Resistance, Extension, and Figure' (*Examination*, IX: 213). The constant experience of matter alongside resistance, extension and figure, means that the ideas become so associated that we cannot imagine matter *without* these 'primary' qualities.[5]

Indeed, ideas can become so closely bound up with one another that the resulting idea is entirely novel. 'When many impressions or ideas are operating in the mind together, there sometimes takes place a process of a similar kind to chemical combination' in which a 'combination of two substances produces [...] a third substance with properties different from those of either of the two substances separately, or of both of them taken together' (*System*, VIII: 853, 371).

> Mental phenomena, joined together by association, [...] may merge into a compound, in which the separate elements are no more distinguishable as such, than hydrogen and oxygen in water; the compound having all the appearance of a phenomenon *sui generis*, as simple and elementary as the ingredients, and with properties different from any of them [...] a truth which, once ascertained, evidently opens a new and wider range of possibilities for the generation of mental phenomena by means of association.
>
> (*Bain's Psychology*, XI: 347)

The processes of association are iterative and, over time, can run deep into the human mind. Association can transform our very conception of what it *is* that we perceive; interpretations and inferences that are the products of initial observations can themselves become so associated with our perceptions as to enter into our idea of *what we observe*. To offer a familiar example: where once I repeatedly inferred from my perceived visual field that *this object is a face*, by gradual processes of association, over time, the acts of perception and inference become 'intimately blended', and I come to see the object *as a face* (*System*, VIII: 641–2). Intentional content enters *into* what I take myself to perceive.[6]

> A great part of what seems observation is really inference [...] For in almost every act of our perceiving faculties, observation and inferences are intimately blended. What we are said to observe is usually a compound result, of which one-tenth may be observation, and the remaining nine-tenths inference.
>
> (*System*, VIII: 641–2)

Close and attentive analysis of what we take to be observations *may* reveal the originally given content from which present ideas have emerged – but that field may simply be irretrievably lost in the process of associative combination and interpretation. This, of course, makes it difficult to feel confident that we are able fully to trace the paths that association has taken solely by means of introspection. Furthermore, Mill holds that some ideas which enter into combinations and become transformed by association may themselves not always rise to the level of conscious awareness – again, making them unavailable to introspection (*Notes on the Analysis,* XXXI: 117–9).

The complex and progressive nature of the process of association means that 'nothing approaching' exact prediction of effects from causes is possible in any given case. '[E]ven if our science of human nature were theoretically perfect […] still, as the data are never all given, nor ever precisely alike in different cases, we could neither make positive predictions, nor lay down universal propositions' (*System*, VIII: 846). For this reason, the generalizations that we can make will always be, at best, 'approximately true'. Despite this, however, Mill does not waver on the fact that the processes of mind are at root deterministic, in the same sense that all causal laws are deterministic. '[T]here exist uniformities of succession among states of mind' (*System*, VIII: 851).

2. Mechanism and normativity

Associationism is a causal account of mind which aims to explain all mental phenomena – the generation of simple ideas but also the complex phenomena of desire and belief. Such an account, however, clearly faces questions about whether the existence of causal explanations for belief and desire is compatible with our experience of these states as the outcome of processes of reasoning. If beliefs and desires are *causally* determined, in what meaningful sense can they be said to be the results of an agent's rational judgement? If they are generated by the association, how can we understand them as products of norm-guided inferences?

Mill takes the worry very seriously. His particular comments on the relationship between the normativity and causal determinism of belief come in the context of an examination of his father's account of belief as inseparable association. According to that theory, 'to believe a succession or coexistence between two facts is only to have the ideas of the two facts so strongly and closely associated, that we cannot help having one idea when we have the other'. To believe that *Peter is tall*, for instance, is merely to have a particularly strong and inseparable association between the ideas of 'Peter' and 'tall'. When I encounter Peter and often have the idea of tallness, I come eventually to associate those ideas so closely that I cannot help thinking of Peter without thinking of tallness – a mental state constitutive of belief.

As Mill notes, if subjective association, however strong, is taken as an *exhaustive* account of how beliefs are formed, though, it neglects the form of endorsement that is distinctive of belief as aiming at objectivity.

> [I]f belief is only an inseparable association, belief is a matter of habit and accident, and not of reason. Assuredly an association, however close, between two ideas, is

not a sufficient ground of belief; is not evidence that the corresponding facts are united in external nature. The theory seems to annihilate all distinction between the belief of the wise, which is regulated by evidence, and conforms to the real successions and coexistences of the facts of the universe, and the belief of fools, which is mechanically produced by any accidental association that suggests the idea of a succession or coexistence to the mind: a belief aptly characterized by the popular expression, believing a thing because they have taken it into their heads.
(*Notes on the Analysis*, XXXI: 162–3)

This is not to deny that particularly strong association can itself issue in belief; this, Mill holds clearly, can and does occur in some cases. '[A]n association, sufficiently strong [...] produces a kind of mechanical belief' (*Notes on the Analysis*, XXXI: 179). But beliefs which are the result of processes of reasoning do not conform to this model.

Some beliefs are the product of 'mechanical' association, but some are the products of the agent engaged in active processes of reasoning. Two things need to be done in order to understand the relationship between these two sources of belief: firstly, to establish how, notwithstanding the force of association, one can *withhold* belief from certain propositions where the relevant subjective association holds, and secondly, the nature of the process of reasons which can generate beliefs in its own distinctive fashion. On the former, Mill is clear that the process by which we can resist beliefs where association holds is itself a process which can be explained in associative terms. While a might be strongly and inseparably associated with P – such that, other things being equal I would form a belief that a is P – where *other* associations are sufficiently strong, they will call to mind conflicting ideas which neutralize the effect of that initial association.

[T]he processes by which this belief is corrected, or reduced to rational bounds, all consist in the growth of a counter-association, [...] There are two ways in which this counter association may be generated. One is, by counter-evidence; by contrary experience in the specific case, which, by associating the circumstances of the case with a contrary belief, destroys their association with the original belief. But there is also another mode of weakening, or altogether destroying, the belief, without adducing contrary experience: namely, by merely recognising the insufficiency of the existing experience; by reflecting on other instances in which the same amount and kind of experience have existed, but were not followed by the expected result.
(*Notes on the Analysis*, XXXI: 179)

This is a process of *resisting* beliefs. The process which enables us to generate *new* beliefs is also associative. By coming to associate some associations with disappointment and some with successful expectation, we associate the *circumstances* of successful association with successful association. Having associated the association of a_1 with P_1, a_2 with P_2, etc., with frustration or success, that is to say, I come in turn to associate some *conditions* of belief-formation with success – i.e., I form *rules* for the successful formation of belief.

> [A]s disappointment nevertheless not unfrequently happens notwithstanding a considerable amount of past experience on the side of the expectation, the mind is put upon making distinctions in the kind of past experiences, and finding out what qualities, besides mere frequency, experience must have, in order not to be followed by disappointment. In other words, it considers the conditions of right inference from experience; and by degrees arrives at principles or rules, more or less accurate, for inductive reasoning.
>
> (*Notes on the Analysis*, XXXI: 179)

Some rules, of course, can be learnt without instruction, though some must be imparted as explicit precepts via the process of education. Whatever their source, the rules of belief can be incorporated into our belief-forming mechanisms – and it is this process of incorporating norms of the 'Art of Thinking' (*Examination*, IX: 261) into our mental life that is constitutive of our rationality.

Mill's discussion of normativity in this context is focused largely on *theoretical* reasoning – correcting mechanical belief formation by reasoning. But the point applies also to *practical* reasoning: reasoning about which objects we ought to pursue. In somewhat simplified terms, Mill holds that initially, pleasure is the only object we desire and that other objects become desirable by association with pleasure. These processes, too, can occur by 'accidental' association, as for instance when money becomes associated with pleasure and become an object of desire beyond all rational bounds. So too can they be corrected by counter-association which can be generated by associating some *conditions* of association with insufficiency or sufficiency – building up rules which can be incorporated into our practical reasoning or the 'Art of Life' (*System*, VIII: 949).

In answer to the question of how our beliefs can be the product of the rational judgement if they are causally determined, then, Mill offers the argument rational judgement is itself an associative phenomenon built from the association of certain rules with ends. Processes of reasoning are accounted for as particularly complex forms of association – but association, nonetheless. As a way to account for the possibility of normativity within a deterministic outlook, this might strike us as unsatisfactory – for rational judgements simply turn out to be causal processes, rather than being issued from a distinctive source. Two things are perhaps worth noting, however. The first is that, of course, if seen as an attempt to conjure non-deterministic normative judgements from a deterministic mind, Mill's account of normativity is not, and could not expect to be, successful. But if seen as an attempt to show how there can be two views of the same underlying processes, it does not obviously fail. Mill offers two standpoints from which we can view reasons – they can be seen as results of processes of association or as the results of incorporating rules of belief into our mental life.[7]

The second is that although Mill seeks to retain a causal and deterministic account, he quite clearly feels the pressure of accounting for normativity against the backdrop of the potential charge of being 'mechanistic' – a term, indeed, that he applies to his father's account of belief, while correcting it. At its roots, the charge was that associationism could not account for how an agent could be actively engaged in the processes of reasoning, if their thoughts were simply the outcome of process of association. Most notably, in England, Coleridge argued against associationism – 'the scheme of pure mechanism, [...] manufacturing mind our of sense and sense out of sensation, which reduces all form to shape and all shape to impression from without' (Coleridge 2002: 145-6) – as 'neither tenable in theory, nor founded in facts' on the grounds of 'the utter incompatibility of such a law (if law it may be called, which would itself be a slave of chances) with even that *appearance* of rationality' (Coleridge 1985: 106, 116).[8] Mill aims to show how the associationist account can be retained while averting this charge of 'mechanism'.

3. Mechanism and will

Mill's deterministic account of mind inevitably gives rise to worries not just about human rationality but also about human freedom.[9] Even if it could be established that human beings can act from reasons, the question would still remain whether such action was *free*. Such worries occupied Mill deeply, during his 'mental crisis'.

> [T]he doctrine of what is called Philosophical Necessity weighed on my existence like an incubus. I felt as if I was scientifically proved to be the helpless slave of antecedent circumstances; as if my character and that of all others had been formed for us by agencies beyond our control, and was wholly out of our control, and was wholly out of their power.
>
> (*Autobiography*, I: 174-6)

The focus on *character* is perhaps worthy of comment. The proximate cause of our willing any action, according to Mill, is in all cases *desire*. Desire is thus formally characterized in Mill's work as 'the initiatory stage of Will'. '[I]n every case, the will is called into action by a motive. The motive, like all other motives, is a desire' (*Notes on the Analysis*, XXXI: 215, 248). Though Mill holds that, originally, pleasure is the only object of human desire, other objects can become objects of desire by processes of association. Initially desiring only pleasure, I can come to desire, e.g., companionship, if companionship is often enough experienced alongside pleasure – indeed, having come themselves to be objects of desire, such objects can continue to be desired even if they cease to be experienced alongside pleasure. 'Although, from some change in us or in our circumstances, we have ceased to find any pleasure in the action, or perhaps to anticipate any pleasure as the consequence of it, *we still continue to desire the action*, and consequently to do it' (*System*, VIII: 842, my emphasis). Such is the process of the formation of habits of willing, and it is only when such habits 'have become independent of the feelings of pain or pleasure from which they originally took their rise, that we are said to have a confirmed character' (*System*, VIII: 483). Although, that is to say, Mill expresses his concerns about freedom primarily in terms of the determinism of character, they can equally well be expressed in terms of the determinism of desire.

It is true, Mill acknowledges, that our actions are determined according to 'Laws of Mind' (*System*, VIII: 849). '[O]ur actions are determined by our will, our will by our desires, and our desires by the joint influence of the motives presented to us and of our individual character' (*Examination*, IX: 466). Indeed, 'if we knew the person thoroughly, and knew all the inducements which are acting upon him, we could foretell his conduct with as much certainty as we can predict any physical event' (*System*, VIII: 836–7). Yet this does not threaten our freedom. I act as I do because of the particular desires I possess, in combination with the situation I find myself in. But, *had I preferred to act otherwise*, I would have done so. Indeed, that our actions are linked to our desires in this is itself a mark of our freedom. It is exactly this connection that means that it is *not* the case that '[w]hatever our wishes may be, a superior power, or an abstract destiny, will overrule them, and compel us to act, not as we desire, but in the manner predestined' (*Examination*, IX: 465).

Nevertheless, the fact that *had I preferred to act otherwise, I would have done so*, Mill acknowledges, would be scant comfort if we had no control over those desires, for it would provide a wholly unrealizable counterfactual. But, he suggests, this is not the case, for individuals *do* have control over their character and desires. Our desires are themselves a product of forces of association, but that does not preclude one of those forces being our own desire to change.

> He has, to a certain extent, a power to alter his character. Its being, in the ultimate resort, formed for him, is not inconsistent with its being, in part, formed by him as one of the intermediate agents. His character is formed by his circumstances, (including among these his particular organisation), but his own desire to mould it in a particular way is one of those circumstances, and by no means one of the least influential.
>
> (*System*, VIII: 840)

Despite the reality of determinism, then, individuals *can* change their character and desires, if they desire to do so. Mill is deeply realistic about the nature of our ability to change, however. It cannot be achieved by a revolutionary choice of *gessinnung*,[10] but must instead involve practised and gradual retraining. This process of *re*forming our character, that is to say, draws on exactly the same processes as are involved in the initial formation of our character by education and upbringing.

> We cannot, indeed, directly will to be different from what we are; but neither did those who are supposed to have formed our characters directly will that we should be what we are. [...] We are exactly as capable of making our own character, if we will, as others are of making it for us.
>
> (*System*, VIII: 840)

Whether we *do* desire to change our character and desires remains, of course, a pivotal question, and one, again, over which we have only indirect control. Someone who does not possess the desire to change their desires will not act to do so. But 'to think that we have no power of altering our character, and to think that we shall not use our power unless we desire to use it, are very different things' (*System*, VIII: 840).

Although we act in accordance to our 'strongest present desire or aversion' (*Examination*, IX: 452), then, the process is rather more complex than we might expect. The desires that we possess form a dynamic system, capable of self-correction. Once again, then, Mill attempts to resist the idea of the human action as generated mechanically – in this case, by avoiding a model under which desires are uninterruptably direct in their determination of action. Instead, Mill wishes to show an alternative view of the relation between will and desire is compatible with associationism – one under which a more active engagement with, and reflexive detachment from, our own desires is possible. Once again, Mill attempts to retain a causal and deterministic account of mind, while incorporating a view of the human being as active.

A further aspect of Mill's account is also worthy of note, for it too sits at some distance from a mechanical view of the influence of desire on the will. While Mill certainly regards desires as determining our action, we should not think of desires as stable entities which exert a set force on the will. Rather, we are to think of our preferences as themselves live and changing, actively struggling to assert themselves and never 'for any two successive instances the same.'

> [T]he hurricane does not level the house or blow down the tree without resistance [...] Far less does victory come without a contest to the strongest of two moral, or even two vital forces, whose nature it is to be never fixed, but always flowing, quantities. In a struggle between passions, there is not a single instant in which there does not pass across the mind some thought, which adds strength to, or takes it from, one or the other of the contending powers.
>
> (*Examination*, IX: 452)

Mill resists the image of our desires as a system of point vectors which can be resolved by summation. Desires themselves are taken to be fluid states – forces which by their nature are moving rather than static. Here, too, Mill attempts to avoid the charge of 'mechanism' by showing how desires *themselves*, as well as the will they influence, are forces which must be understood in dynamic terms.[11]

4. Mechanism and spontaneity

Mill's theory of freedom, then, is compatibilist. Our actions and thoughts are determined by causal laws, but if they are caused in the right way – a result of our *own* desires, which are themselves amenable to change by us – we are free.

> [W]e shall find that this feeling, of our being able to modify our own character *if we wish*, is itself the feeling of moral freedom which we are conscious of. A person feels morally free who feels that his habits or his temptations are not his masters, but he theirs: who even in yielding to them knows that he could resist; that were he desirous of altogether throwing them off, there would not be required for that purpose a stronger desire than he knows himself to be capable of feeling.

Such compatibilist accounts are of course subject to the basic objection that although some forms of causal determination for our actions might seem preferable to others – i.e., causal determination which emanates from within our own character – nevertheless, being determined in such a manner does not amount to *freedom*. As Kant puts it, 'if the freedom of our will were none other than the latter [...] then it would at bottom be nothing better than the freedom of a turnspit, which, when once it is wound up, also accomplishes its movements of itself' (CPrR, 5:79). An individual whose behaviour was determined in this manner would ultimately be passive in the face of causal forces beyond their control.

True freedom, according to this line of thought, would require that we were capable of initiating activity in a deeper sense than the compatibilist can accommodate – originating action spontaneously.[12] Even when action arises from within our true character, if that action is determined by causal laws, 'the inner principle was determined by an external principle' rather than by 'spontaneity which is without qualification' (LM, 28: 276). 'The transcendental idea of freedom [...] is that of the absolute spontaneity of an action' (CPR A448/B476). Such spontaneity would be possible only if the will 'can be efficient independently of alien causes determining it', i.e., can act independently of the causal order (GW 4: 446).

Mill, of course, disagrees that such independence from the causal order is either necessary for freedom or indeed possible. He does, however, acknowledge that prior associationist accounts have failed to adequately acknowledge and explain the active elements of mind and have as such depicted human beings as almost entirely passive. An inability to do justice to the spontaneity of mind renders those theories incomplete because 'the necessity, incumbent on any theory of the mind, of accounting for our voluntary powers'.

> Those who have studied the writings of the Association Psychologists, must often have been unfavourably impressed by the almost total absence, in their analytical expositions, of the recognition of any active element, or spontaneity, in the mind itself. Sensation, and the memory of sensation, are passive phenomena; the mind, in them, does not act, but is acted upon; it is a mere recipient of impressions; and though adhesion by association may enable one of these passive impressions to recall another, yet when recalled, it is but passive still. [...] The mind, however, is active as well as passive; and the apparent insufficiency of the theory to account for the mind's activity, is probably the circumstance which has oftenest operated to alienate from the Association Psychology any of those who had really studied it.
>
> (*Bain's Psychology*, XI: 354)

Despite his commitment to the theory, then, Mill certainly feels the force of criticisms of association's ability to account for human activity and recognizes that an account of spontaneity is needed for a complete metaphysics of voluntary action.[13] Associationism, he holds, certainly need not be rejected, but it must be significantly *expanded* if it is to meet this challenge – for genuine spontaneity cannot itself be derived from previously recognized laws of association. 'Activity cannot possibly be generated from passive elements; a primitive active element must be found somewhere' (*Bain's Psychology*, XI: 354). As such, Mill embraces Alexander Bain's account of spontaneity as grounded in the stimulus provided by nutrition.

> He holds that the brain does not act solely in obedience to impulses, but is also a self-acting instrument; that the nervous influence which, being conveyed through the motory nerves, excites the muscles into action, is generated automatically in the brain itself, not, of course, lawlessly and without a cause, but under the organic stimulus of nutrition.
>
> (*Bain's Psychology*, XI: 354)

Mill aims to draw on a *naturalized* vision of spontaneity to support his view of the human being as active, rather than passive. The conversion of nutrition into energy offers a source of vitality which contains the seeds of an agent's ability to engage in self-movement. 'This doctrine [...] supplies him with a simple explanation of the origin of voluntary power' (*Bain's Psychology*, XI: 354).

Mill's consciousness that some theory of the origin of spontaneous action is necessary comes in the context of a growing understanding and internalization of the principle of the unity and conservation of force in Victorian British thought.[14] Mill had studied, struggled with, and come to appreciate, ideas about the unity of heat and mechanical force in early 1860s. By the end of the decade, he would note that '[w]ithin the present generation several large & comprehensive generalizations have made their way in to Science[, including] the Unity & Conservation of Force' and incorporate comments on the principle to the *System of Logic*.[15] Self-movement could not, if the lessons of conservation of force were to be learnt, be generated ex nihilo – but it could be understood as the output of a process of the transformation of energy from one form into another and transmitted to the will.

In this period, significant advances had also been made in understanding what Mill termed the 'material conditions of our mental operations' (*Bain's Psychology*, XI: 348). The science of the physiology of mind had 'assumed almost a new aspect, from the important discoveries which had been made in all its branches, and especially in the functions of the nervous system' (*Bain's Psychology*, XI: 352). Mill had therefore also become more confident that physiology could make genuine and independent explanatory contributions in attempts to understand the workings of mind. '[P]hysiology is rendering more and more probable [...] that our mental feelings, as well as our sensations, have for their physical antecedents particular states of the nerves,' and the associationism of Mill's father and of Hartley could therefore be augmented by drawing on 'the much greater knowledge since acquired of the functions of our nervous organism and their relations with the mental operations' (*Examination*, IX: 282; *Notes on the Analysis*, XXXI: 102).

Mill, with Bain, aims to incorporate these insights into associationism. The energy provided by nutrition, it was now understood, could find spontaneous outlet and generate muscular movement via the nerves – and though such drives initially result in unchecked movement rather than action, they can be marshalled by the will, via associationist forces with pleasure, into forms of action. Initially merely the uncontrolled outpourings of stimulated nerves, spontaneous movement, that is to say, can be brought under the control of our desires.

> Among the numerous motions given forth indiscriminately by the spontaneous energy of the nervous centre, some are accidentally hit on, which are found to be followed by a pleasure, or by the relief of a pain. In this case, the child is able, to a certain extent, to prolong that particular motion, or to abate it; and this, in our author's opinion, is the sole original power which we possess over our bodily motions, and the ultimate basis of voluntary action.
>
> (*Bain's Psychology*, XI: 355–6)

The form of spontaneity to which Mill here appeals – a *naturalistic* form of spontaneity – would of course not be regarded as satisfactory by those who demand that spontaneity involve an *uncaused* initiation of action. The stimulation and functioning of the nervous system which gives rise to spontaneity remains, under Mill's theory, causal and law bound. And, of course, even on its own terms, the theory leaves much to be explained – as Mill himself acknowledges. But, once again, Mill is concerned to address the criticism levelled against associationism – that it is 'mechanistic' and cannot adequately account for a central aspect of human freedom – by incorporating nineteenth-century insights into theory and attempting to derive dynamic conclusions from mechanical premises.

Notes

1 The story would most obviously involve Mill's close engagement with the works of Samuel Taylor Coleridge and Thomas Carlyle, both of whom were significant importers of German philosophical currents into England. On the historical transmission of these Kantian and post-Kantian ideas into England, see Ashton (1980) and Wellek (1931).
2 All quotes from Mill are taken from Mill (1963–91) and are given by (*short title*, volume: page).
3 I mean, therefore, to offer a picture of Mill's concerns which places him at a further distance from British Empiricism than is sometimes realized. See, i.e., Fumerton (2009: 147ff.)
4 Whether ideas are *contiguous* will clearly be subject to variation between different cultures. Mill seems to believe that whether ideas are *similar* is, in contrast, a matter of brute fact. One could of course endorse an alternative view, according to which the relations of contiguity and similarity are *themselves* associationistically malleable, meaning that the similarity relation was subject to cultural variation. Mill's observation that 'many of the complex cases of suggestion by resemblance may be analysed into the elementary case of association by resemblance, combined with an association by contiguity', however, seems to suggest that he prefers to view the relation as primitive, albeit then combined with contiguity in complex, and presumably culturally relative, ways. See *Notes on the Analysis*, XXXI: 121.
5 The point is not merely a semantic one – Mill is clear that without the sense of touch, which is the basis of our ideas of resistance, extension and figure, we could still have the idea of matter, but it would be associated with different ideas. '[W]e might, in

    this supposed case, have had an idea of Matter, that idea would necessarily have been of a very different complexion from what we now have' (*Examination*, IX: 213). The relation between meaning and association is of course a difficult one – but insofar as that distinction can be maintained, it is clear Mill sees the primary qualities not as part of the *meaning* of, but rather inseparably associated with the *idea* of, matter.
6   See Macleod (2019) for further discussion of Mill on 'seeing as'.
7   Compare, of course, Kant's transcendental idealism, under at least one interpretation. See Alison (2004: 3ff.).
8   For the German post-Kantian context that influenced Coleridge heavily in his criticism of 'mechanism', see Beiser (2003: 131–52).
9   Unlike Mill's treatment of rationality and spontaneity, his theory of free will has been discussed by various commentators. See, in particular, Ryan (1987: 103–15) and Skorupski (1989: 250–5). I aim here to expand and supplement these accounts, putting them in the broader context of Mill's concerns about activity.
10 I contrast, of course, with Kant, *Religion within the Boundaries of Mere Reason* (Rel, 6.48). References to Kant are given by Akadedmie Edition, drawing on the translations offered in Kant (1995–). I use the following abbreviations: CPR = Critique of Pure Reason; GW = *Groundwork*; ML = Lectures on Metaphysics; CPrR= Critique of Practical Reason; Rel = Religion within the Bounds of Mere Reason.
11 Given Mill's argument that the existence of free will *is* compatible with our being subject to causal forces, we might of course wonder about the origin of our particular anxiety about this issue. Mill's account is clear: our worries about the compatibility of free will and causality can be traced to the particular association of the idea of *causality* with that of *necessity*. The idea of 'necessity' 'stands for the operation of those causes exclusively, which are supposed too powerful to be counteracted at all [...] The application of the same term to the agencies on which human actions depend as is used to express those agencies of nature which are really uncontrollable, cannot fail, when habitual, to create a feeling of uncontrollableness in the former also. This, however, is an illusion' (*System*, VIII: 839). We should not confound being natural beings subject to *causal forces* with being subject to some form of *indefeasible force* which cannot be counterbalance – yet the term 'necessity' tempts us to make exactly that mistake. 'I do not believe in anything real corresponding to the phrases Necessity [...] I acknowledge no other link between cause and effect, even when both are purely material, than invariability of sequence, from which arises possibility of prediction' (*Letter to Hazard*, XVI: 1065).
12 On the Kantian notion of spontaneity, see particularly Pippin (1997).
13 It is also fitting given the centrality of the properties of activity and spontaneity as an ideal of character in Mill's ethics. (See, for instance, Riley (2015: 991–101).) It would be extremely jarring if Mill could *not* accommodate spontaneity as native to the will, given that his *On Liberty* III represents a paean to the value of an 'active and energetic' character, rich in the 'raw material of human nature' – and which bemoans the progress of bourgeois culture in which 'spontaneity is hardly recognized by the common modes of thinking as having any intrinsic worth, or deserving any regard on its own account' (*On Liberty*, XVIII: 262, 263, 261).
14 See Knight (2009) for a useful account of the progress of the science of force and energy in the period, including its connection with post-Kantian *Naturaphilosophie*.
15 See, i.e., in 1863 *Letter to J. Stuart Stuart-Glennie*, XV: 871 and *Letter to Alexander Bain*, XV: 902; in 1864 *Letter to Alexander Bain*, XV: 927–8, and *Letter to Alexander Bain*, XV: 970; in 1868/9 *Letter to Edward Livingstone Youmans*, XVII: 1570; *Theism*, X: 437; and in 1872 *System*, VII: 353.

References

Allison, H. (2004), *Kant's Transcendental Idealism: An Interpretation and Defense*, rev. edition, New Haven: Yale University Press.

Ashton, R. (1980), *The German Idea: Four English Writers and the Reception of German Thought 1800–1860*, Cambridge: Cambridge University Press.

Beiser, F. (2003), *The Romantic Imperative: The Concept of Early German Romanticism*, Cambridge, MA: Harvard University Press.

Coleridge, S. T. (1985), *Biograpia Literaria*, ed. J. Engell and W. Jackson Bate, Princeton: Princeton University Press.

Coleridge, S. T. (2002), *Opus Maximum*, ed. T. McFarlane, Princeton: Princeton University Press.

Fumerton, R. (2009), 'Mill's Logic, Metaphysics, and Epistemology', in W. Donner and R. Fumerton (eds), *Mill*, 145–95, Oxford: Wiley Blackwell.

Kant, I. (1995–), *The Cambridge Edition of the Works of Immanuel Kant*, ed. Paul Guyer and Allen Wood, Cambridge: Cambridge University Press.

Knight, D. (2009), *The Making of Modern Science*, Cambridge: Polity Press.

Macleod, C. (2019), 'Historicizing Naturalism: Mill and Comte', in J. Shand (ed.), *A Companion to Nineteenth Century Philosophy*, 140–59, Oxford: Wiley-Blackwell.

Mill, J. S. (1963–91), *The Collected Works of John Stuart Mill*, ed. J. Robson, Toronto: University of Toronto Press and London: Routledge.

Pippin, R. (1997), 'Kant on the Spontaneity of Mind', in R. Pippin (ed.), *Idealism as Modernism: Hegelian Variations*, 29–55, Cambridge: Cambridge University Press.

Riley, J. (2015), *Mill on Liberty*, Abingdon: Routledge.

Ryan, A. (1987), *The Philosophy of John Stuart Mill*, 2nd edition, Hampshire: MacMillan Press.

Skorupski, J. (1989), *John Stuart Mill*, London: Routledge.

Wellek, R. (1931), *Immanuel Kant in England, 1793–1838*, Princeton: Princeton University Press.

10

Practical grounds for freedom: Kant and James on freedom, experience and an open future

Joe Saunders and Neil Williams

1. Introduction

Neither Kant nor James was fans of what we now call compatibilism. They both complain that compatibilists employ sophisticated semantic moves to make freedom appear consistent with determinism, but in doing so, miss the real philosophical crux of the matter.

In the *Critique of Practical Reason*, Kant considers the compatibilist position that while we are 'subject to unavoidable natural necessity', we might nevertheless be free because our actions are determined by our nature, desires or character (V: 95–6). Kant is dismissive of this compatibilist stance, calling it a 'wretched subterfuge' and claiming that the freedom it affords us is 'nothing better than the freedom of a turnspit, which, when once it is wound up, also accomplishes its movements of itself' (V: 97). To call such internal determination 'freedom', he thinks, is mere wordplay:

> Some still let themselves be put off by this subterfuge and so think they have solved, with a little quibbling about words, that difficult problem on the solution of which millennia have worked in vain and which can therefore hardly be found so completely on the surface.
>
> (V: 96)

Kant rejects the compatibilist account of freedom. He thinks that both theoretical and practical philosophies require a conception of freedom which involves a robust independence from natural necessity.

James too rejects compatibilism and for similar reasons. In presenting his account of freedom, James coins the distinction between *hard* determinism and *soft* determinism. Whereas hard determinism is clear about the incompatibility between freedom and the strict necessity it takes determinism to involve, soft determinism utilizes the ambiguity of the word 'freedom' to hold that freedom is compatible with necessity. Like Kant, James thinks that this strategy is a 'quagmire of evasion under which the real issue of fact has been entirely smothered' (James 1896, WB: 117).[1] 'Freedom' used in the compatibilist sense can mean acting without external constraint, or acting in light of a necessary law, but this is not the sense of 'freedom' which the libertarian about freedom thinks is at stake (James 1896, WB: 117). James agrees with Kant in thinking that our practical and moral lives require a conception of freedom which is incompatible with determinism. In order to avoid quibbling over the word 'freedom' (and, James admits, due to 'just a dash of perversity' – 1896, WB: 138), James leaves this word aside, in favour of the word 'chance'. In doing so, his analysis of what freedom means focuses on the possibility of an open future, in which future events are not fully determined by past events or necessary laws. As we shall see, James argues that this is required to make sense of our moral agency and moral lives more broadly.

In this chapter, we compare Kant and James's accounts of freedom. Despite both thinkers' rejecting compatibilism for the sake of practical reason, there are two striking differences in their stances. The first concerns whether or not freedom requires the possibility of an open future. James holds that morality hinges on the real possibility that the future can be affected by our actions. Kant, on the other hand, seems to maintain that we can still be free in the crucial sense, even if none of our actions can have any effect on the future. The second difference between them is related and concerns the *location* of freedom. Kant views experience as determined by natural necessity, and locates freedom outside of it, in things-in-themselves. James, on the other hand, has a richer conception of experience than Kant and holds that we can locate our freedom within experience alone.

In what follows, we will briefly present Kant's position on freedom and determinism (§2), before presenting James's position (§3) and comparing them in light of these two differences (§4). In the end, we contend that James has a better account of how freedom relates to our experience, but this comes at a cost. For while Kant's account struggles with the relationship between freedom and experience, it has the advantage of insulating our freedom from potential empirical challenges.

2. Kant's 'compatibilism'

Despite what we said in our opening remarks, in his own way, Kant is a sort of compatibilist. Transcendental idealism maintains that appearances are not things-in-themselves. Appearances are governed by natural necessity, whereas things-in-themselves are not. This allows Kant to maintain that natural necessity and transcendental freedom do not contradict each other. As Allen Wood famously remarks:

> [Kant] wants to show not only the compatibility of freedom and determinism, but also the compatibility of compatibilism and incompatibilism.
>
> (1984: 74)

Transcendental idealism allows Kant to accept that the thesis of determinism and an *incompatibilist* or *libertarian* conception of freedom are compatible; because the thesis of determinism applies only to appearances, not to things-in-themselves. Kant maintains the possibility of a conception of freedom which is independent of necessity, while holding that such a conception of freedom is compatible with determinism in appearances.

The key difference between Kant and standard compatibilists here concerns their conception of freedom. As we saw above, Kant is harshly dismissive of a compatibilist conception of freedom. He wants to show how *transcendental* freedom is compatible with natural necessity. Transcendental freedom is 'a faculty of absolutely beginning a state' (A445/B473), and the 'independence of […] reason itself (with regard to its causality for initiating a series of appearances) from all determining causes of the world of sense' (A803/B831). Kant thinks that this conception of freedom is required for both theoretical and practical philosophy.[2]

Kant thinks that transcendental freedom is the real ground of imputation – that is, of regarding someone as the author of their actions (A 448/B 476).[3] He also claims that, if we were not transcendentally free, morality would not apply to us.[4] And if we think about Kant's practical philosophy, some possible connections emerge that help us understand this claim. For Kant, morality requires both the ability to refrain from acting on any particular sensible desire and also to act for the sake of the moral law. Kant worries that if we were just determined by our sensible desires, we would only ever be able to act on hypothetical imperatives (at best) and would be unable to be motivated by the moral law itself.

This conception of freedom seems to be both libertarian, and to involves a two-way power, namely the ability to both act and refrain from acting on any particular sensible desire (where such refraining and acting are regarded as free in an incompatibilist or libertarian sense). However, we should note that, as with most things in Kant, this is contested. Pereboom (2006) argues that Kant is not a *leeway* incompatibilist, where freedom involves the ability to do otherwise, but instead a *source* incomptibilist, where what is key is that freedom is located outside of experience. We shall return to consider this in more detail in the final section (§4).

This ambition, to combine a libertarian conception of freedom with natural necessity, is part of what makes Kant's theory of freedom so compelling. There are many intriguing aspects to it, including Kant's claims about the timeless nature of freedom;[5] how we come to have knowledge of freedom, given our general ignorance of things-in-themselves;[6] and how freedom and appearances interact.[7] In this chapter though, we want to focus on whether or not Kant thinks that freedom requires an open future.

For this, we turn to another key passage in the *Critique of Practical Reason*. Here, Kant has discussed how transcendental idealism distinguishes between appearances and things-in-themselves, and that while appearances are determined by natural necessity (V: 94–9), things-in-themselves are not. He then claims the following:[8]

> One can therefore grant that if […] we could calculate a human being's conduct for the future with as much certainty as a lunar or solar eclipse and could nevertheless maintain that the human being's conduct is free.
>
> (V: 99. 12–19)

We think this passage is crucial. It reveals the ambition of Kant's theory of freedom. Appearances, and everything we experience, might be determined by natural necessity and could be completely predictable. But even if that were the case, that only concerns appearances, and so we can still maintain that we are transcendentally free. This is a powerful position. It manages to insulate our freedom from the world of experience. No matter what science reports, or what psychologists discover, no matter how determined or predictable our behaviour might look, our transcendental freedom is secure.

There is much more to be said here. It might seem counter-intuitive to suggest that we can have a libertarian conception of freedom while at the same time accepting that all our actions are predictable. For this reason, some Kantians want to downplay this passage. They rightly note that Kant's claim here is hypothetical.[9] Kant claims that *if* we could perfectly predict a human being's future behaviour, transcendental idealism means that human being could still be transcendentally free. In a forthcoming paper, Lucy Allais emphasizes the hypothetical nature of this passage and also argues that perfectly predicting human behaviour is not a real possibility given transcendental idealism. Allais argues as follows:

> I take [Kant] to be saying that if we could investigate the inner determinations of the subject down to their basis we could get this kind of prediction. However, getting down to the most fundamental level is not something that it is even in principle possible to do, because transcendental idealism denies that there is such a fundamental level in appearances.
>
> (Allais, forthcoming)

Allais acknowledges that this comes at a textual cost, in that she does 'not take Kant as actually asserting what he describes in these passages'. But making this move enables Allais to develop an original account of freedom in Kant which allows for an open future. By denying that 'there is a totality of facts and a totality of laws from which it follows that there is only one way the world in space and time could unfold', Allais holds that the future is open in the sense of not fully determined by past events or necessary laws.

There are also philosophical costs to this acceptance of an open future. Kant's claim seems to offer us some serious insulation. And if we distance ourselves from it, our freedom might be hostage to the way the world is. What if our best scientific theories or psychologists got back to us, and it looked like our behaviour *was* perfectly predictable because determined by natural necessity? It seems like then Allais might have to give up on transcendental idealism and, more generally, might have to give up on transcendental freedom, and with it, crucial parts of Kant's practical philosophy.

Allais presents transcendental idealism in such a way as it allows for a genuinely open future. In the end, we side with her in wanting to have a conception of freedom which allows for our agency and choices to have some effect on future events. A satisfactory account of freedom, we think, requires a world which is open to being changed by our actions. As noted above, however, this conception of the world conflicts with some key things that Kant says about freedom. Here we turn to William James, who provides an account of freedom which explicitly foregrounds the idea of an open future. We explore this account in James (§3) before returning to contrast his position with Kant's (§4).

3. James, chance, and an open future

James lays out his position on freedom most clearly in his paper 'The Dilemma of Determinism'. There are many aspects of this paper which deserve close attention: James's pragmatic analysis of the free-will debate; his idea that the choice between determinism and indeterminism is made on passional grounds, rather than through reason; and his argument that regret is only comprehensible in an indeterminist universe. In this section – though we will touch on these points – our primary focus will be on James's metaphysical claim that indeterminism means realism about chance; and his concomitant commitment to an open future which can be made better (or worse) through our actions.

One of the first things which James does in 'Dilemma' is to sidestep ambiguities about the word 'freedom' – replacing it with the word 'chance'. This allows him to focus on the meaning of determinism rather than freedom. Determinism, James claims, whether of a materialist or idealistic stripe, is a rejection of chance. Determinism holds that past and present events are compatible with only one future outcome, such that the 'future has no ambiguous possibilities'. Indeterminism, on the other hand, holds that possibilities are genuine parts of reality such that '[o]f two alternative futures which we conceive, both may now be really possible; and the one become impossible only at the very moment when the other excludes it by becoming real itself'. Determinists, he claims, deny the reality of the possible and hold that necessity and impossibility are the 'sole categories of the real' (1896, WB: 118).

When the debate is put this way, there is no middle ground for the compatibilist to occupy:

> The issue [...] is a perfectly sharp one, which no eulogistic terminology can smear over or wipe out. The truth must lie with one side or the other, and its lying with one side makes the other false.
>
> (1896, WB: 118)

In Jamesian language, this means that the decision is *forced*, which is one of the four criteria by which he identifies a will-to-believe choice. The other criteria are also met by the free-will debate: the debate is *live* (we find each option plausible and available for our belief), *momentous* (it makes a large practical difference to our lives whether or not we believe ourselves to be free); and it is *undecided* by existing empirical evidence or intellectual argument. In fact, James claims that the decision between determinism and indeterminism is (currently) 'theoretically insoluble' (1896, WB: 124).[10] As such, our decision to be determinists or indeterminists is a choice made on passional or temperamental grounds, rather than on strictly rational ones (1896, WB: 119).[11]

James returns to his discussion around freedom and chance in his *Pragmatism* lectures, where he does say something about the meaning of freedom. One of the core tenets of classical pragmatism is that to be meaningful, a concept must have practical effects.[12] By analysing our concepts in light of the practical effects which would follow from them being true, we can get a better grasp at what is at stake in our philosophical discussions. When exploring what is practically at stake in the free-will debate, however, James makes the interesting claim that it is not moral responsibility. For both the determinist *and* the indeterminist accuse their opponents of being unable to account for moral responsibility. The determinist claims that the indeterminist must hold each free act to be a 'sheer novelty' which arises '*ex nihilo*', unconnected with any past events. As such, they suggest that such an act cannot be connected to the agent's wider character and intentions in a way that would enable them to be praised or blamed for their actions. The indeterminist, on the other hand, claims that if our actions are entirely determined by past events and necessary laws, then we cannot be held responsible for them as agents. As such, the debate between the two sides stands at an impasse (1907, P: 59–60).

James, then, rejects the idea that moral responsibility is at the practical heart of the free-will debate, holding (as various compatibilists do) that a combination of '[i]nstinct and utility' can account for and ground our practices of attributing praise and blame (P: 60). The real pragmatic difference between determinism and indeterminism concerns whether or not *novelty* – and with it moral improvement – is possible:

> Free-will pragmatically means novelties in the world, the right to expect that in its deepest elements as well as in its surface phenomena, the future may not identically repeat and imitate the past. […] It holds up improvement as at least possible; whereas determinism assures us that our whole notion of possibility is born of human ignorance, and that necessity and impossibility between them rule the destinies of the world.
>
> (1907, P: 60–1)

Pragmatically speaking then, the free-will debate once again hinges on realism about possibility. The indeterminist holds that possibilities are genuine features of reality, that some events are not entirely determined by past events but offer the potential for novel additions which may improve reality. In short, pragmatically understood, belief in freedom is essentially the belief that the future is *open* to being improved through our actions.

Although James wants to sidestep the question of moral responsibility in relation to freedom, he does still tie freedom closely to moral agency. James suggests that freedom is required for moral agency in two ways. First, that determinism leads to practically debilitating pessimism and fatalism. And second, that meliorism – the attitude in which we can, through our own efforts, improve the world – requires the belief that the future can be improved by our actions. We will take each point in turn.

Determinism, as we have seen, involves a commitment to the idea that all events are determined by past events and necessary laws. When we consider the practical effects of such a commitment, thinks James, we are faced with a dilemma. Either the determinist must adopt a kind of pessimism or subjectivism. Consider any bad event – such as James's example of a particularly callous murder. When contemplating the murder, we feel a profound sense of regret. However, as (according to the determinist) such an event was causally determined by the rest of the universe, all the events and laws of the universe resulted in this murder, and no other outcome was ever really possible. For this reason, the only rational object of our sense of regret is the universe as a whole. As a result, determinism leads us to a practically debilitating pessimism about the universe as such (1896, WB: 125–6). To avoid this pessimism, the determinist might instead adopt a kind of subjectivism. According to this view, external events – such as this particularly callous murder – are not in themselves important but instead enable us to have experiences and make judgements about them (96, WB: 129–30). Understood in this way, subjectivists adopt a kind of removed position, in which external events serve the role of data for our inquiring minds which allow us to develop moral judgements and theories. Though slightly less practically debilitating than pessimism, such subjectivism has the tendency to lead to indifference, fatalism and moral licence (1896, WB: 132). Only by turning towards the external world and adopting the view that there are moral duties independent of our feelings, 'certain works to be done' and 'certain outward changes to be wrought or resisted' can we do justice to our moral phenomenology (1896, WB: 134).[13]

In short then, to avoid the pernicious effects of determinism, and do justice to our moral phenomenology, we have to adopt a view in which we have moral duties to effect change in the world. But this is to accept indeterminism, as effecting change in the world requires a belief that the future can be shaped by our actions. Our moral lives can only make sense within a fundamentally indeterministic universe, in which our actions can make a meaningful difference to the world around us:

> I cannot understand the willingness to act, no matter how we feel, without the belief that acts are really good and bad. I cannot understand the belief than an act is bad, without regret at its happening. I cannot understand regret without the admission of real, genuine possibilities in the world. Only then is it other than a mockery to feel, after we have failed to do our best, that an irreparable opportunity is gone from the universe, the loss of which we must forever after mourn.
>
> (1896, WB: 135)

James contends that we need to be realist about chance (and about morality) in order to feel that we have moral duties which can be failed or met and in order for our feelings of success or regret to be rational. He writes:

> *That* is what gives the palpitating reality to our moral life and makes it tingle [...] with so strange and elaborate an excitement. This reality, this excitement, are what the determinists, hard and soft alike, supress by their denial that *anything* is decided here and now, and their dogma that all things were foredoomed and settled long ago.
>
> (1896, WB: 140)

Indeterminism allows for this world, and our lives, to be improved through our own actions. This is what gives any particular moral situation the sense of importance which determinism loses. Though indeterminism means an acceptance of chance and novelty, the chance in question is not random chance, but 'the chance that in moral respects that future may be other and better than the past has been' (1896, WB: 137). And the admission of this kind of chance is the only thing which makes sense of our efforts towards this improvement. James is not advocating an attitude of blind optimism in place of deterministic pessimism. Rather, James is suggesting that an indeterministic universe allows for the attitude in which we can, through our own efforts, improve the world (see 1896, WB: 84). This meliorism takes moral improvement to be a *real possibility* and our acts as potentially participating in that possibility's actualization (see 1907, P: 137–8).

So, like Kant, James holds that belief in free will or indeterminism is necessary for moral agency. However, unlike Kant, James explicitly ties moral agency to the idea of an open future. James holds that the difference between determinism and indeterminism hinges on whether or not chance and novelty are real features of the universe. Though James officially holds that the decision between these two positions is undecided by theoretical reasoning, and that it is up to individuals to adopt one or the other on passional grounds, he does his best to convince his audience of the plausibility of indeterminism. This is primarily because James thinks that indeterminism makes sense of the moral phenomenology which is central to human experience. Elsewhere, James argues that any philosophical worldview which does not give room to our 'active propensities' will give rise to a 'nameless *unheimlichkeit*' – a sense of horror that we live in a universe in which most 'intimate powers' are given no place – and will as such be a less satisfying philosophical theory (1896, WB: 71–2). We can see that determinism has this defect for James. By denying the idea that our actions can contribute to the betterment of the world we live in, and that our creative agency can contribute anything novel to reality, determinism removes our motivation to moral action and leads us to fatalism and pessimism.

Having presented both Kant and James's position on freedom, as well as the connections their conceptions of freedom have to the notion of an open future, we turn now to comparing their views.

4. Kant, James and the location of freedom

As we have seen, James connects his notion of freedom very clearly with realism about possibility. Without the possibility for our actions to alter the course of future events, freedom is (pragmatically) meaningless, and we lose motivation towards moral action. Thus, James's arguments for freedom are connected to the metaphysical pluralism and 'radical' empiricism which he presented in the last years of his philosophical career, in his *Radical Empiricism* papers (1903–4; later collected in 1912); his *Pragmatism* lectures (1907), and in *A Pluralistic Universe* (1909). James contrasted his pluralistic metaphysics with the post-Kantian idealistic traditions in Germany, Britain and

America. Whereas James viewed monistic or absolute idealism as committed to the idea that universe was necessarily one conceptual and causal whole, such that any part was determined by other parts of the universe, his own pluralism granted 'some separation among things, some tremor of independence, some free play of parts on one another, some real novelty or chance' (1907, P: 78). Clearly then, James's pluralism presents the metaphysical foundation for his earlier work on freedom, understood in terms of chance and novelty. '[C]hance', James claims, 'means pluralism and nothing more' (1896, WB: 137).

James's pluralistic metaphysics suggests that reality is fundamentally *experiential*. James's radical empiricism essays make this point explicitly. There, James argues that nothing is real unless it is directly experienceable and that anything directly experienceable was by that fact real. Contrary to Humean empiricism, and the empiricism of the logical positivists, James's radical empiricism embraces a rich conception of experience and holds that relations between objects are themselves parts of direct experience, and so by that fact real (see 1903, ERE: 6–7).[14] The important point for our purposes is that chance and novelty are directly experienced features of our lives, which gives us some reason to think they are real, according to James's pluralistic metaphysics:

> Pluralism [...] taking perceptual experience at its face-value [...] protests against working our ideas in a vacuum made of conceptual abstractions. [...] We do in fact experience perceptual novelties all the while [...] So the common-sense view of life, as something really dramatic, with work done, and things decided here and now, is acceptable to pluralism. 'Free-will' means nothing but real novelty; so pluralism accepts the notion of free-will.
>
> (1910, SPP: 73)

> New men and women, books, accidents, events, inventions, enterprises, burst unceasingly upon the world. [...] Men of science and philosophy, the moment they forget their theoretic abstractions [...] believe as naively [as anyone else] that fact even now is making, and that they themselves, by doing 'original work,' help to determine what the future shall become.
>
> (1910, SPP: 78)

James's point here is that the indeterministic and melioristic worldview is supported by human experience and that – given radical empiricism – this is a reason for holding it to be real.[15]

James presents himself in opposition to both Kant and Hume on this point. Radical empiricism rejects Hume's conception of immediate experience, in which all events and elements are discontinuous. James takes Kant and the post-Kantians to have inherited this conception: 'Kant and his successors all espoused Hume's opinion that the immediately given is a disconnected "manifold"' (1910, SPP: 101). Kant, according to James, attempts to overcome the disconnectedness of immediate experience by introducing the transcendental ego to introduce continuity (1910, SPP; 1909, PU: 38). James, on the other hand, denies Hume's picture entirely and holds that both continuities and discontinuities are part of our direct experience (see 1904, ERE: 22). Leaving aside whether or not James's interpretation of the manifold of experience and the transcendental unity of apperception is correct, there is an important contrast with Kant here. Kant conceives of experience as determined by natural necessity. Given this conception of experience, to argue that we are free in a libertarian sense, this freedom would have to be located *outside* of experience. James has a richer conception of experience, and so can locate chance, novelty and the possibility of an open future *within* experience.[16]

This is a crucial contrast. Kant accepts a conception of experience that seems to leave no room for (transcendental) freedom but then finds a way to still allow for this, through locating freedom outside of experience. And, as noted at the outset of this chapter, this has at least one real advantage. It allows Kant to maintain that we are free *no matter* what we encounter in experience. If scientific developments suggest that we are determined by natural necessity, Kant can accept these scientific findings to be true of appearances, while maintaining that we are transcendentally free. By locating freedom within our experience of chance and novelty, James does not have as much insulation. Though he recognizes the fallibilism of scientific theorizing, if empirical evidence and the best scientific models consistently provided evidence that we were determined by natural necessity, this would seriously count against the hypothesis of indeterminism.

While James does not directly address this possibility, he is more comfortable with this lack of certainty or security in general. He frequently connects the idea of chance with the idea of a gift – a gift of being something which we cannot guarantee.[17] In fact, he tells us that 'the idea of chance is, at bottom, exactly the same thing as the idea of a gift' in the sense that both are names for 'anything on which we have no effective *claim*' (1896, WB: 123; see 120). By accepting chance and novelty into our ontology, we have to accept that the future is, to some degree, out of our control. James is quite clear about this. Any person who

> uses [chance] instead of 'freedom' squarely and resolutely gives up all pretence to control the things he says are free [...] [A]ny other word permits of quibbling, and lets us, after the fashion of the soft determinists, make a pretence of restoring the caged bird to liberty with one hand, whilst with the other we anxiously tie a string to its leg to make sure it does not get beyond our sight.
>
> (1896, WB: 138)

Of course, James's meliorism holds that our agency can have real impacts on future events – but these impacts will not be perfectly predictable. Indeterminism requires, for James, the surrender of any claims to *complete* conceptual or practical control over reality.

Kant, on the other hand, is unwilling to surrender control – at least over freedom and morality. He looks to secure these features of our lives, regardless of what happens in experience. This is understandable – if science were to show that we were entirely determined by natural necessity, and we did not have the insulation which transcendental idealism provides, we would have to give up on the possibility of being transcendentally free. In turn, this would rob us both of our moral agency, as Kant conceives this as involving the ability to act independently of any sensible desires and for the sake of the moral law, but also our distinctive moral status as ends-in-ourselves, which is connected to our freedom. Kant's strategy also threatens to leave a gulf between freedom and experience in several respects. For one, it creates epistemic issues, as it is not clear how other people's freedom could be part of our experience. And it also creates metaphysical issues, concerning how freedom and experience interact. Our focus here will be on one metaphysical issue: namely whether our free action can change the future.

We have already seen that, for James, making sense of our moral agency and moral phenomenology requires an admission that future events are not wholly determined by past events and the acceptance that our agency can contribute to the betterment of reality. Does Kant, then, also need an open future to make sense of moral agency? If we understand him as a leeway compatibilist, where transcendental freedom involves the ability to do otherwise, then it might. But it is not clear how this choice could show up in experience, which remains determined by natural necessity. As we have seen, Allais (forthcoming) offers an account of Kant's transcendental idealism which does allow for an open future. But perhaps Kant does not need this. As noted earlier, Pereboom (2006) draws on certain passages (e.g., VI: 50n) to argue that Kant is a *source* rather than a *leeway* incompatibilist. This is to say that the 'key notion of freedom', for Kant, 'is not the ability to do otherwise, but rather being the undetermined source of one's actions' (Pereboom 2006: 542). What matters for the source incompatibilist is not that *experience* changes in response to our will, but that our noumenal self, our pure practical reason and the moral law are the *source* or *grounds* of our actions.[18]

Such a view would, to James, miss the point. As we have seen, determinism leads to pessimism and fatalism because it detaches our moral agency from possible experiential effects, by denying that our actions can affect experienceable change. Kant's source incompatibilism would seem to have the same defect. But Kant would dispute this. After all, Kant's practical philosophy attempts to provide us with grounds for hope, even if experience is determined.

In a previous paper (Williams and Saunders 2018), we explored Kant's conception of the highest good, and his account of the practical grounds for belief, again in contrast to James. We argued that one of the benefits of Kant's account of religious belief, and his making belief in God a practical postulate, is that it is insulated from experience. To promote the highest good (happiness in proportion to virtue) is a duty (V: 125.25). Fulfilling this duty requires the possibility of progress towards holiness and of happiness in exact proportion to virtue. While neither of these are found in experience, our duty to promote the highest good makes belief in them necessary, which gives us practical grounds to believe in both the immortality of the soul and the existence of God (V: 119–37). This is related to Kant's claim to have denied knowledge to make room for faith: theoretical reason left open whether or not there is a God or the soul is immortal, and practical reason shows that these are a priori practically necessary beliefs. We thus have practical ground to believe in God and to hope for happiness in proportion to virtue. We can have this belief, and hope to progress towards being holy, even without this progress being observable within experience. As such, Kant could push back against James's claim that we need to experience the effects of our actions in order to avoid fatalism and pessimism.

Nonetheless, James would hold there were two things missing from such an answer. Firstly, as we argued in our previous paper, pragmatists hold that beliefs are habits of action which are revisable in light of appropriate experience. While James is allied with Kant in allowing us to adopt beliefs for practical reasons, he holds that such beliefs should remain responsive to experience in ways that Kant does not. Secondly, it remains mysterious *where* freedom and the possibility of moral progress we hope for are located, if not in experience. Kant locates hope – and freedom – outside of experience, and this does not help if what you want to do is change the world as we experience it for the better. For the pragmatist, any belief which has no practical or experienceable effects (broadly interpreted) is meaningless and should as such be rejected from philosophical discourse – and the worry is that Kant's insulated conception of transcendental freedom seems to meet this description.

James's position is not without problems of its own though. So far, we have focused on the notion of an 'open future' in the sense of allowing that the future can be made better by our actions. But this is not the only way things can go. James accepts that realism about chance necessarily involves the possibility that the universe can be made *worse* by our actions, rather than better. The future is vulnerable:

> The indeterminism I defend, the free-will theory of popular sense based on the judgement of regret, represents that world as vulnerable, and liable to be injured by certain of its parts if they act wrong.
>
> (1896, WB: 136)

Holding that the universe can be improved by our actions, and that the outcome of any given event is genuinely open, also implies that we might *fail* to improve it or make it worse. This might give us a sense of uneasiness and insecurity about the future which Kant's position does not entail. This is another benefit of Kant's attempt to insulate freedom and morality. For Kant, no matter how dire things get in appearances, no matter if we've never once experienced an action done from pure duty, this does not call into question the correctness of morality (IV: 406.5 – 408.11). And no matter how bad experience looks, we still have practical grounds to believe in God, the correctness of morality, and the possibility of moral progress. James might think this is a benefit of Kant's account; looking at the benefits of absolute idealism, he suggests that the capacity to take 'moral holidays' and feel like the moral outcome of the universe is in hands other than our own might be soothing for people of certain temperaments (1907, P: 42).

But, in fact, James holds that the possibility of failure is required for moral agents to feel as if their actions truly matter:

> What interest, zest, or excitement can there be in achieving the right way, unless we are enabled to feel that the wrong way is also a possible and a natural way – nay, more, a menacing and imminent way.
>
> (1896, WB: 136)

Assurance that world is saved would have the same tendency to promote fatalism as determinism does. Both remove our agency from the actual practical and lived world of our experience. To give us the motive to act on our moral principles and ideas, we must feel that if we *don't* – if we *fail* to live up to our duty – then an 'irreparable opportunity is gone from the universe, the loss of which we must forever after mourn' (1896, WB: 135). Once again, then, whereas Kant privileges the security of freedom and our moral lives, James privileges our moral phenomenology: we have to feel as if the future hinges on our efforts, otherwise our moral lives will lose their sense of importance, and our moral agency will lose its motivation.

5. Conclusion

Both Kant and James reject compatibilism about freedom, thinking that this misses the point at stake in the free-will debate. Both hold libertarian conceptions of freedom and argue that such a conception of freedom is required to make sense of our moral agency. However, we have pointed to two key differences between them: firstly, whether or not realism about possibility or an open future is required to make sense of freedom; and secondly, where freedom and moral progress are located.

For Kant, the possibility of an open future is not necessary for freedom. Libertarian freedom is compatible with experience being completely determined by natural necessity and predictable because Kant locates freedom outside of this experience. Our freedom is, in one way or another, a property of things-in-themselves, and no amount of experience can tell against our having this kind of freedom. As such, Kant presents a position in which our freedom – and our moral agency – is insulated from any possible empirical discoveries. But for James, an open future is necessary for us to make sense of moral agency. Freedom, pragmatically analysed, *means* chance, novelty and the real possibility for us to effect change in our environment (preferably for the better). Without the capacity for our actions to make real changes within experience, our moral agency will lose motivation, and we will fall into pessimism or fatalism. James does not locate freedom anywhere other than experience. However, James has a rich-enough conception of experience, so that chance, novelty and connection can be found within it. By doing so, however, James opens himself up to the possibility that experience will, in the long run of scientific inquiry, show us to be determined and rob us of our freedom.

In short, James allows freedom to be connected to our capacity to alter future events, by making the world of experience richer than Kant's manifold of experience allows. However, this comes at the expense of insulating our freedom from the discoveries of science, as James has nowhere else to locate freedom than within experience. Kant privileges the security of our freedom and moral agency, by locating freedom in things-in-themselves, rather than the world of experience. As such, our freedom is insulated from any possible discoveries from empirical science. However, Kant pays for this insulation by making the relation between our transcendental freedom and our lived experience obscure.

Notes

1. All references to William James are to the Harvard University Press editions. For abbreviations and full references, see bibliography.
2. The Thesis of the 3rd Antinomy (A444–6/B472–4) suggests that theoretical philosophy requires transcendental freedom. And at V. 29. 24–5, Kant claims that '[transcendental] freedom and unconditional practical law reciprocally imply each other'; for the classic treatment of this relationship, see Allison's (1990: 201–13) discussion of – what he calls – the reciprocity thesis.
3. For an extended account of responsibility and imputation in Kant, see Blöser (2015: 184–8).
4. In the final section of the *Groundwork*, for instance, Kant remarks (IV: 456. 29–33): 'It is [...] not just left to the philosopher's discretion to remove the seeming conflict [between transcendental freedom and natural necessity], or leave it untouched. For if they opt for the latter, this leaves a no man's land which the fatalist is in their rights to occupy, and can then chase all morality out of its supposed property, which it would have no title to hold.'
5. For recent work on this topic, see Freyenhagen (2008), Insole (2011), Saunders (2022) and Watkins (2005: 333–9).
6. See Saunders (2016) for an epistemic challenge to Kant's theory of freedom, where he suggests that transcendental idealism precludes knowledge *of other's transcendental freedom*.
7. See Watkins (2005: 301–61).
8. For discussion of a similar claim in Mill, see McLeod's chapter in this collection.
9. See Indregard (2018: 675–6), and Allais (forthcoming).
10. We will say more about the practical effects of determinism shortly. During his late twenties, James himself suffered a depression which he partially attributed to determinism: 'I'm swamped in an empirical philosophy', he wrote to his friend Thomas Ward in 1869, 'I feel that we are Nature through and through, that we are wholly conditioned, that not a wiggle of our will happens save as a result of physical laws' (LWJ, I: 152–3). James found relief from the depressive influence of determinism through reading Charles Renouvier and adopting his voluntarist conception of free will. In 1870, he wrote: 'My first act of free will shall be to believe in free will' (LWJ, I: 147). See Perry (1935, I, Chapters XIX and XLI) for on James's depression and recovery; and Dunham (2015) for more on the relationship between James and Renouvier. For a discussion of depression and freedom in Mill, see McLeod's chapter in this collection.
11. See James's 'The Will to Believe' (1896, WB: 13–3) for his account of the legitimacy of adopting certain beliefs on passional grounds when these criteria are met. See Stern (2015) for a presentation of James's position on free will as being a will-to-believe choice; and Williams and Saunders (2018) and Willaschek (2010) for more detail on the epistemology of will-to-believe choices and another contrast with Kant.
12. This broad commitment to philosophical concepts finding their meaning in practical effects is captured by the 'pragmatic maxim' endorsed by James and first articulated by his fellow pragmatist Charles S. Peirce in 1878: 'consider what effects, that might conceivably have practical bearings, we conceive the object of our conception to have. Then, our conception of these effects is the whole of our conception of the

object' (Peirce, CP5.402). This maxim is articulated and interpreted differently by different pragmatists, as well as by Peirce himself throughout his work (see, e.g., 1903, CP5.18; 1905, CP5.412), but a commitment to some broad form of it is constant.

13 The idea that a belief in determinism has negative effects on our moral action receives some support from recent empirical work. Vohs and Schooler (2008), for instance, argue that encouraging belief in determinism increases people's likelihood to cheat. And Baumeister, Masicampo and DeWall (2009) suggest that believing that we do not have free will can increase aggression and reduce helpfulness.

14 For a detailed examination of James's metaphysics of experience, see Lamberth (1999), and for its connection with a wider empiricist and analytic tradition, see Banks (2014). For James's metaphysics of relations, and their connection with a post-Kantian tradition, see Williams (forthcoming).

15 It might be worth making a distinction here between the earlier James of the *Will to Believe* and the later James's more metaphysical work. James's concern in 'Dilemma' is with the requirement for us to believe in a libertarian conception of freedom – understood in terms of chance – in order to make sense of moral phenomena and agency. However, he did not at this stage have a metaphysical argument to the effect that we could *experience* chance and novelty or that such direct experience of novelty was indicative of its reality. This metaphysical work occupied James's last years, from his radical empiricism papers of 1903 onwards, and was still substantially incomplete by his death 1910. For a detailed exploration of how James's thought regarding the experience of agency developed over this period, see Dunham (2020).

16 We should note that, while James thinks that we can discover necessary laws within our experience, he denies that such laws are all-encompassing. For James, all theories are human tools which abstract and simplify experience to enable us to better navigate reality. Nonetheless, '[s]omething always escapes' even our best attempts at theorizing reality (1909, PU: 145). A realism about novelty in direct experience, and a recognition of the limitations of theorization for grasping reality, is what allows for true novelty on James's picture.

17 For further discussion of gifts, see Stern (2019: 66–84).

18 See Timmermann (2007: 177) for a convincing case that freedom, for Kant, does not involve the libertarian capacity to do otherwise, but instead the capacity to act for the sake of the moral law.

Bibliography

All Kant references are to the volume, page and line number of the 'Akademie Ausgabe' of *Kants gesammelte Schriften* (Berlin: de Gruyter, 1900–). Citations from the first *Critique* are given to the A and B editions and translations from *the Cambridge Edition of the Works of Immanuel Kant* edited by Guyer and Wood (1995). One exception is that, for the *Groundwork*, we use the recent translation by Bennett, Saunders and Stern (2019).

All references to William James are to the *Works of William James*, Frederick H. Burkhardt, Fredson Bowers, and Ignas K. Skrupskelis (eds.) Cambridge, MA: Harvard University Press (19 volumes, 1975–1988). The following abbreviations are used:

ERE	*Essays in Radical Empiricism*
P	*Pragmatism*
PU	*Pluralistic Universe*
SPP	*Some Problems of Philosophy*
WB	*The Will to Believe and Other Essays in Popular Philosophy*

References to James's letters use the following abbreviation:

LWJ	*The Letters of William James*, 2 vols, Henry James (ed.) Boston: The Atlantic Monthly Press, 1920.

Other Referenced Texts

Allais, L. (forthcoming), 'Kantian Determinism and Contemporary Determinism'.
Allison, H. (1990), *Kant's Theory of Freedom*, Cambridge: Cambridge University Press.
Banks, E. C. (2014), *The Realistic Empiricism of Mach, James, and Russell: Neutral Monism Reconceived*, Cambridge: Cambridge University Press.
Baumeister, R. F., E. J. Masicampo and C. N. DeWall. (2009), 'Prosocial Benefits of Feeling Free: Disbelief in Free Will Increases Aggression and Reduces Helpfulness', *Personality and Social Psychology Bulletin*, 35 (2): 260–8.
Blöser, C. (2015), 'Degrees of Responsibility in Kant's Practical Philosophy', *Kantian Review*, 20 (2): 183–209.
Dunham, J. (2015), 'Idealism, Pragmatism, and the Will to Believe: Charles Renouvier and William James', *British Journal for the History of Philosophy*, 23 (4): 756–78.
Dunham, J. (2020), 'On the Experience of Activity: William James' Late Metaphysics and the Influence of Nineteenth-Century French Spiritualism', *Journal of the History of Philosophy*, 58 (2): 267–91.
Freyenhagen, F. (2008), 'Reasoning Takes Time: On Allison and the Timelessness of the Intelligible Self', *Kantian Review*, 13 (2): 67–84.
Frierson, P. (2014), *Kant's Empirical Psychology*, Cambridge: Cambridge University Press.
Indregard, J. J. (2018), 'A Gradual Reformation: Empirical Character and Causal Powers in Kant', *Canadian Journal of Philosophy*, 48 (5): 662–83.
Insole, C. (2011), 'Kant's Transcendental Idealism, Freedom and the Divine Mind', *Modern Theology*, 27 (4): 608–38.
Lamberth, D. C. (1999), *William James and the Metaphysics of Experience*, Cambridge: Cambridge University Press.
Macleod, C. M. (2023), 'Mill on Freedom, Normativity, and Spontaneity', in J. Saunders (ed.), *Freedom after Kant*, 141–54, London: Bloomsbury.
Peirce, C. S. (1931–60), *Collected Papers of Charles Sanders Peirce*, 8 vols., ed. C. Hartshorne, P. Weiss and A. Burks, Cambridge: Harvard University Press [CP].
Pereboom, D. (2006), 'Kant on Transcendental Freedom', *Philosophy and Phenomenological Research*, 73 (3): 537–67.
Perry, R. B. (1936), *The Thought and Character of William James*, 2 vols, Boston: Little, Brown and Co.

Saunders, J. (2016), 'Kant and the Problem of Recognition: Freedom, Transcendental Idealism and the Third-Person', *International Journal of Philosophical Studies*, 24 (2): 164–82.
Saunders, J. (2022). 'Timeless Freedom in Kant: Transcendental Freedom and Things-in-Themselves', *History of Philosophy Quarterly* (2022) 39 (3): 275–292.
Stern, R. (2015), *Kantian Ethics: Value, Agency, and Obligation*, Oxford: Oxford University Press.
Stern, R. (2019), *The Radical Demand in Løgstrup's Ethics*, Oxford: Oxford University Press.
Timmermann, J. (2007), *Kant's Groundwork of the Metaphysics of Morals*, Cambridge: Cambridge University Press.
Van Inwagen, P. (1983), *An Essay on Free Will*, Oxford: Oxford University Press.
Vohs, K. D. and J. W. Schooler (2008), 'The Value of Believing in Free Will: Encouraging a Belief in Determinism Increases Cheating', *Psychological Science*, 19: 49–54.
Watkins, E. (2005), *Kant and the Metaphysics of Causality*, Cambridge University Press.
Willaschek, M. (2010), 'The Primacy of Practical Reason and the Idea of a Practical Postulate', in A. Reath and J.Timmerman (eds), *Kant's Critique of Practical Reason: A Critical Guide*, Cambridge: Cambridge University Press.
Williams, N. W. (forthcoming), 'Radical Empiricism, British Idealism, and the Reality of Relations', in S. Marchetti (ed.), *The Jamesian Mind*, London and New York: Routledge.
Williams, N. W. and J. Saunders (2018), 'Practical Grounds for Belief: Kant and James on Religion', *European Journal of Philosophy*, 26 (4): 1269–82.
Wood, A. (1984), 'Kant's Compatibilism', in A. Wood (ed.), *Self and Nature in Kant's Philosophy,* 73–101, New York: Cornell University Press.

Part Three

The twentieth century: New developments; freedom, the self and others

11

Levinas and finite freedom

James H.P. Lewis and Simon Thornton

1. Introduction

It has become natural to suppose that moral responsibility presupposes freedom. But Emmanuel Levinas has claimed the reverse: that genuine human freedom presupposes moral responsibility. This counter-intuitive claim forms an important part of Levinas's overall ethical project, which advances a bracing conception of responsibility for the other that is fundamental and infinite. Here is Levinas:

> In opposition to the vision of thinkers ... who require, among the conditions of the world, a freedom without responsibility, a freedom of play, we discern ... a responsibility whose entry into being could be effected only without any choice ... Responsibility for the other, this way of answering without prior commitment, is human fraternity itself, and it is prior to freedom.
> (Levinas 1998: 161)

This is not to say that Levinas downplays the importance of freedom for ethics, as some critics have complained. To the contrary: in one place Levinas avers that freedom constitutes 'the very humanity of man' (Levinas 1990: 71); and in another he insists that his prioritization of responsibility before freedom 'must not ... signify some limit within the substance of the free being' (Levinas 1969: 223). Rather, in his ethics, Levinas seeks to promote a novel account of human freedom that is compatible with his conception of infinite responsibility for the other. He calls it 'finite freedom' (Levinas 1969: 115ff.), and it is the task of this chapter to spell out what finite freedom means and why it matters.

There are a couple of preliminaries in order before we begin. The first concerns Levinas's famously idiosyncratic philosophical style. Our view is that the strange form that Levinas's seemingly desultory and sometimes esoteric remarks on human freedom can in fact be read, instructively, as presenting a kind of 'journey to selfhood' – one that evokes the classical genre of *Bildungsroman*. Mark C. Taylor has noted that it is characteristic of this genre that the author follows the circuitous path of the hero's *Bildung* – development, education, cultivation, self-formation. The journey usually leads through various educative experiences in the course of which the protagonist progresses from the naiveté and illusion of youth to the sobriety of mature selfhood. The experiences recounted are of interest less for their individual uniqueness than for their representative character.

(Taylor 2000: 77)

Levinas's remarks on freedom can be seen to fit readily into this mould. And yet they remain highly conceptual: they chart the journey not of a 'representative character', but rather of the *freedom* in an individual, as it passes dialectically through what we might call – paraphrasing Hegel – various conceptual 'shapes', starting with an immature conception of infinite freedom and moving step-wise to a mature conception of finite freedom. Incidentally, this is why the register of Levinas's philosophical remarks on freedom feel strangely allegorical – almost mythopoeic.¹

The second preliminary we would like to advance concerns the notions of 'immature' and 'mature' freedom just mentioned. It is worth emphasizing right away that it is plausible to suppose that the conditions and circumstances in virtue of which an individual is free can typically come in degrees. For instance, one can be more or less well informed, have a greater or lesser range of viable alternative courses of action, and so on. However, philosophical discussions of freedom have typically focused on defining only the minimum 'threshold' requirements necessary for freedom to obtain. These debates are certainly of philosophical importance because questions concerning when an agent can be held responsible, and when paternalistic intervention is legitimate, hang on whether this threshold conception of freedom is met. Yet it is also surely philosophically important to understand what is involved in those putative higher degrees of freedom towards which we just signalled – that is, to understand what it takes to be more free, and more maturely free, in ways that go above and beyond whatever is required for one to count as responsible for oneself. We believe that Levinas's conceptualization of the journey from immature to mature freedom is responsive to this latter project. Specifically, we shall suggest that despite its comparability with the well-known Hegelian rendition of this journey, Levinas's account is distinct in that it holds that the account of mature, or 'finite', freedom does not negate and replace more basic conceptions, but rather presupposes them, while further enriching the I's freedom by adding further layers.

Accordingly, in this chapter, we will show that on Levinas's view for an individual to enjoy mature freedom it is not enough for the individual to feel free from arbitrary external or heteronomous constraint or determination, as a Kantian might have it; such a view is important but immature. Beyond this, Levinas argues, for an individual to enjoy mature freedom, they must stand in certain social relations to others. But it is not sufficient for the individual to stand only in harmonious relations of love, friendship and mutual care with others, as some relational autonomists have implied (see, e.g., Mackenzie and Soljar 2000: 6); nor, however, is it sufficient for the individual to stand in ethical relations of mutual recognition with others, à la Hegel. Rather, what is finally required is that the individual stand in a specific kind of *fraternal but 'non-Utopian'*

(Levinas 2000: 10) relation with the other. This is a relation in which the individual, or the 'I', is confronted with the unbridgeable independence of the other's will from the I's world, where the other's interests are felt to be radically removed from one's own. The confrontational encounter of the autonomous I with the full extent of the freedom of the other forms the core of Levinas's concept of finite freedom. In addition to Levinas's distinctive take on the *Bildungsgeschichte* [roughly: developmental story] of freedom, then, we will show that his ultimate conception of finite freedom can be marked apart from other comparable views in the post-Kantian tradition in that it holds that the social relations that are constitutive of mature freedom can be non-utopian or antagonistic.

2. Shapeless freedom and the element

We just suggested that it may be instructive to read Levinas's remarks on freedom allegorically, as charting a formative journey through various shapes of freedom, moving from an immature conception of freedom to a mature one. Strictly speaking, though, the first shape of freedom that Levinas discusses in his 1961 masterwork, *Totality and Infinity*, is in fact defined by its *shapelessness*. In a section tellingly entitled 'The Mythical Format of the Element', Levinas invites us to imagine an idyllic form of existence, 'bathing in the element[s]' (Levinas 1969: 132) that nourish and sustain it. The elements – 'wind, earth, sea, sky, air;' the warmth of the sun (Levinas 1969: 132; 112) – are 'agreeable' and seem to respond to the I's every need; they are the source of the I's primitive 'enjoyment' (Levinas 1969: 140) and primordial '*love of life*' (Levinas 1969: 112). It is no exaggeration to say that the I relates to the elements as a foetus to the womb: it is *immersed* in the element; there is no distance between it and its element. So, for the I, the element that encompasses it naturally 'retains a certain indetermination; it has no form that would contain it, and in this sense it is content without form' (Sallis 1998: 157).

Perhaps surprisingly, Levinas suggests that a certain feeling of freedom – a feeling of 'sovereignty', as he likes to put it (Levinas 1969: 140) – might nonetheless attach to this primitive state of basking, undivided enjoyment. That is, 'freedom as a relation of life with an *other* that lodges it, and by which life is *at home with itself*' (Levinas 1969: 165). This suggestion is surprising because we might wonder whether there could be so much as 'an I' who could 'feel free' amidst the undifferentiated indeterminacy of the element. Plausibly, this is why Levinas calls the format of the element *mythical*. Stanley Cavell has observed that 'myths generally will deal with origins that no one can have been present at' (Cavell 1979: 356). Accordingly, Levinas's discussion of freedom in the element can be seen to release a fantasy of the idyllic, formless pre-history of the I as a free being. Minimally, we can image that this primordial feeling of freedom is just the happy absence of the feeling of external constraint, necessitation and determination; and the absence of any sense of want, privation or desire, too; and it depends entirely on the contingent coincidence of the I's needs with the affordances of the elements.

Of course, there is an obvious sense in which the I's mythic feeling of freedom in the element is perilously superficial. Levinas himself calls it 'virtually a null freedom', one that in fact emerges only as a 'by-product of life' (Levinas 1969: 165). For, at this stage, the 'sovereignty of the I that vibrates in enjoyment' is actually engulfed by 'influences' that 'seep into it like a sweet poison' (Levinas 1969: 164), belying the I's fledgling feeling of freedom. That is to say, the I's feeling of freedom *in* the element is in fact pervasively determined *by* the element, on which the I depends entirely. Predictably, in Levinas's myth the superficiality of the I's idyllic feeling of freedom in the element is dramatically exposed by the 'non-freedom of need' (Levinas 1969: 140), which arises when the fragile agreement of the element with the I's needs lapses into disharmony. Now, the I is confronted by the fact that 'the plenitude of its instant of enjoyment is not ensured against the unknown that lurks in the very element it enjoys, the fact that joy remains a chance and a stroke of luck'; 'the uncertainties of the future that mar happiness remind enjoyment that its independence envelops a dependence. … The freedom of enjoyment is thus experienced as limited' (Levinas 1969: 143–4). The I's primitive feeling of freedom, that is to say, is shattered when it is exposed to privation and uncertainty, and it finds itself powerless before the shockingly brutal indifference of the element.

3. Infinite freedom and the will

It is this traumatic moment – in which one not only finds oneself to *have* basic needs, determined by the element, but one also finds oneself utterly powerless to fulfil those needs for oneself, without the beneficence of the element – that precipitates the first major development in the freedom of the I: the formation of a *will*.[2] Levinas characterizes the process of will formation in terms of a 'labour' which works to 'ward off' the non-freedom of need by exercising an ability to 'dominate' or 'grasp' (Levinas 1996: 18), or otherwise take 'possession' of the element (Levinas 1969: 166), thereby 'neutralizing' the ominously 'unforeseeable future of the element' (Levinas 1969: 158).[3] And he writes of this development that for the I with a will, 'the "at home" is not contained but a site where *I can*, where dependent on a reality that is other, I am, despite this dependence or thanks to it, free' (Levinas 1969: 37). In short, the fruit of the I's labour is the *freedom* of the will, and this freedom has two main features. Firstly, in its labour of dominating, grasping, possessing the element, the will puts *distance* between the I and the element, and the element thus becomes *something genuinely other*, to which the I is related in some way. As a result, the I can begin to 'take up an attitude with regard to its very existence' (Levinas 2001: 10), which is to say, to reflect upon and endorse or otherwise identify with its choices. Secondly, the free will can manifest a capacity to, in a sense, 'control' the previously irresistible – because undifferentiated – influence of element. We shall have cause to discuss this second feature in more detail shortly. At this point it is enough to note that Levinas claims that the freedom of the will manifests a capacity 'to maintain oneself against the other, despite every relation with the other, to ensure the autarchy of an I' (Levinas 1969: 40).

Significantly, in sharp contrast to the shapelessness of freedom in the element mentioned above, the shape that freedom takes at this stage is just that: a shape. That is to say, the freedom of the will as Levinas characterizes it here comes close to a widely held *procedural* conception of freedom, as a capacity for self-government or autonomy. On this conception, the conditions of freedom are identified entirely with certain agential procedures: evaluation, endorsement, intention-formation, action.[4] Accordingly, freedom is thought to be in no wise conditioned by substantive considerations, such as 'the insecurity of the morrow, hunger and thirst [that] scoff at freedom' (Levinas 1969: 241). It is on this basis that we can begin to appreciate what Levinas might mean by '*infinite* freedom' (Levinas 1998: 124). To wit, the I's freedom can be said to be infinite, in a sense, inasmuch as it remains entirely *unconditioned* or *unlimited* by the I's finite, worldly conditions. And a fully *procedural* conception of freedom as autonomy is just that; it is concerned only with formal conditions. Freedom, on this procedural conception, is identical with the *form* of the will: it is freedom *of* the will.

In his own writings, Levinas sometimes associates this conception of infinite freedom with Fichte (see, e.g., Levinas 1998: 162), whose theory of subjectivity posits a freedom that is a kind of 'unconditionedness', a 'freedom from limitations', which, as A. W. Moore has noted, 'involve[s] an infinitude of sorts' (Moore 2012: 157). More concretely, though, Levinas develops his conception of infinite freedom historically, with reference to a spiritual development introduced with Christianity. Rightly or wrongly (we shall not argue the point here), Levinas suggests that 'the Christian notion of the soul', in allowing for the possibility that 'at any moment [the Christian] can regain [through repentance and forgiveness] the nudity he had during the first days of creation', fosters a conception of freedom 'which is infinite with regard to any attachment and through which no attachment is ultimately definitive' (Levinas 1990: 65). This freedom, in other words, is the capacity to *d*etach oneself from all finite attachments. Perhaps surprisingly, this Christian idea is well captured by Sartre, whose famous conception of radical freedom canvasses the thought that one's reflective awareness of what is psychically given involves positing one's freedom with respect to it. With reference to the relevant practice of confession, Sartre thus suggests in *Being and Nothingness*:

> The man who confesses that he is evil has exchanged his disturbing 'freedom for evil' for an inanimate character of evil; he *is* evil, he clings to himself, he is what he is. But by the same stroke, he escapes from that *thing*, since it is he who contemplates it ... In confessing it, I posit my freedom in respect to it; my future is virgin; everything is allowed to me. A person frees himself by the very act by which he makes himself an object for himself.
>
> (Sartre 1978: 65)

The capacity of the I to take up a reflective attitude with regard to its finite, worldly existence, then, is also a capacity to *detach* or *distance* itself from its finite, worldly attachments at will; it is an ability, for instance, to resist having oneself be defined by one's past or conditioned by one's circumstance, and thereby to define oneself – and there is a sort of infinitude in this.

4. A tension: Heteronomy

Sartre also famously declared that 'I am condemned to be free. This means that no limits to my freedom can be found except freedom itself or, if you prefer, that we are not free to cease being free' (Sartre 1978: 439). And, in a highly qualified way, Levinas would agree. Although Levinas will ultimately claim that this freedom, which Sartre takes to constitute the fixed plight of human existence, is yet immature, he uses comparably carceral language in suggesting that one consequence of the conception of one's freedom as infinite is, paradoxically, 'enchainment to oneself' (Levinas 2001: 89). That is to say, like Sartre, Levinas acknowledges that with freedom (so construed) comes responsibility (of sorts): one must laboriously maintain one's own 'commitment to exist'; 'one has to do something, one has to aspire after and undertake' (Levinas 2001: 89) – there is no giving up. And this can naturally sometimes lead to 'weariness' and '*ennui*' (Levinas 2001: 12). This point, shared by Sartre and Levinas, introduces the beginnings of a difficulty for infinite freedom.

The distinctive kind of *ennui* Levinas has in mind is viscerally captured in its extremity in *Crime and Punishment*. There we find Raskolnikov, having selected *murder* as the act with which to assert his freedom, recoiling from this choice in disgust. Yet, despite himself, Raskolnikov is unable to drop the idea: it was 'as if [murder] were a sort of predetermination of his fate' (Dostoevsky 1993: 60), and, after happening upon a key piece of information for his homicidal plot, he felt 'like a man condemned to death … he suddenly felt with his whole being that he no longer had any freedom whether of mind or of will, and that everything had been suddenly and finally decided' (Dostoevsky 1993: 62). In other words, because Raskolnikov had arbitrarily loaded so much meaning onto the act of murder – as the ultimate symbol of individual freedom – the patently hateful thought of actually carrying out his intention became an unbearable, unshakeable burden. He couldn't escape the fact that it was up to him whether he murdered or not. And he had very good reason not to. But, in his mind, failure to carry out his heinous intention was tantamount to surrendering his freedom and becoming no more than a 'louse' (Dostoevsky 1993: 419). In effect, Raskolnikov's free choice had become weirdly transfigured into an unavoidable and unbearable fate, where – paradoxically – its punishing fatefulness consisted precisely in its absolute freedom.

It is important to bear in mind here that Levinas goes beyond Sartre in wanting not just to acknowledge the psychic burdens of infinite freedom but also to *criticize* its conceptual immaturity – from the inside. Levinas develops this internal criticism towards the end of *Totality and Infinity*, where he claims that

> the irrational in freedom is not due to its limits but to the infinity of its arbitrariness. Freedom must justify itself; reduced to itself it is accomplished not in sovereignty but in arbitrariness. Precisely through freedom – and not because of its limitation – the being freedom is to express in its plenitude appears as not having itself reason in itself. Freedom is not justified by freedom.
>
> (Levinas 1969: 303)

Here, Levinas means to match the familiar thought that determinism constitutes a threat to freedom with its inverse: that infinite, unconditioned freedom is a threat to itself. We may extrapolate on this thought by setting up a contrast between infinite freedom *simpliciter*, on the one hand and, on the other, autonomous action, governed, constrained and justified by reason. On a Levinasian view, this contrast articulates a problematic tension that can confront the I who entertains a conception of their own freedom as infinite. The tension pertains to whether the procedures that define infinite freedom are always already rationally determined. If they are, then, in a sense, the I's infinite freedom is subject to determination by a source outside itself: reason. Rational determination is seen here as a form of heteronomy. But if the I's autonomous procedures are in no wise constrained by reason, then the free choice they make possible will be practically indistinguishable from arbitrary, whimsical plumping. And this cannot be autonomy.

Of course, Kantians will balk at the idea that governance by reason should be considered a form of heteronomy. On Kant's view, rational determination is precisely what constitutes *auto*nomy and frees the subject from the heteronomous reign of desires and passions. But note that Levinas's view has some intuitive force. In the mythical beginning of his narrative, Levinas finds the most basic sense of freedom to be the freedom to satisfy one's own desires: at this primitive stage, the subject identifies fully with their desires. Levinas then recognizes, with Kant, that one's desires ought to be constrained by reason, as wholly unconstrained infinite freedom can become the source of unbearable *ennui*. But his picture departs from Kant's in preserving the residue of that earlier feeling of freedom so that realizing that reason sometimes requires one to act contrarily to one's desires is an awkward, disappointing realization. To that extent, rational determination can feel like a heteronomous imposition to the I-*qua*-subject-of-desires. The fact that Levinas's view is able to explain this sense of disappointment as a product of the I being less than fully free is an apparent advantage that his approach has over Kant's.

Granting this, Levinas's critique of infinite freedom thus yields a problematic dilemma for the infinitely free I, between the disappointing unfreedom of heteronomous governance by a source external to the I – reason – and the wearying unfreedom associated with arbitrary choice, without the reflective processes of reasoned endorsement that alone can render a decision one's own.[5] That is, Levinas regards the I who considers themselves to be infinitely free to be mired in a palpable dilemma: it seems that the I's choices must be enslaved to reason, or they are mere whimsical acts of plumping. This is the first of two ultimately decisive criticisms that Levinas raises against infinite freedom.

5. A further tension: Social dependence

In his second criticism, Levinas questions the thought associated with conceptions of infinite freedom that the ideal state of the I's freedom involves independence from others: from their influence, from the burden of their interests, from their control. Here is Levinas:

> The encounter with the Other in Sartre threatens my freedom, and is equivalent to the fall of my freedom under the gaze of another freedom. Here perhaps is manifested most forcefully being's incompatibility with what remains veritably exterior. But to us here there rather appears the problem of the justification of freedom: does the presence of the Other put in question the naïve legitimacy of [infinite] freedom?
>
> (Levinas 1969: 303)

On the Sartrean conception of freedom under Levinas's analysis, any relations with other people pose a threat to the freedom of the I.[6] Other people, whose interests and perspectives conflict with one's own, threaten to constrain the extent to which the I is able to realize its ends. In the rhetorical question of this quoted passage, though, Levinas invites us to wonder whether this image of necessarily unremitting conflict and constraint paints a plausible picture of the role that interpersonal relations play in connection with individual freedom. His suggestion is that this picture is an expression of a deep confusion about the social nature of mature freedom. This is Levinas's second objection to infinite freedom. And his conception of *finite* freedom, which includes a positive role for interpersonal relations in the realization of human freedom, can best be presented in concert with it.

Before turning to Levinas's discussion, it is worth noting that a comparable line of thinking has been forcefully promoted in recent years by so-called relational autonomists. According to the version of autonomy developed by some feminist proponents of this view, it is argued that people do not typically live as isolated, independent individuals in the way this concept might seem to imply. We are always influenced by others. Furthermore, their interests are, often, not burdens but ends that we want to promote. And insofar as we live together with others, sharing our lives with them, it is right that to some extent the decisions we make for ourselves should be decisions that they take part in making: not to control us, but to share the deliberations regarding matters of mutual concern. What it is to be autonomous, on this view, then, is to be competent in 'creating and sustaining relations of empathy and mutual intersubjectivity' (Held 1993: 60). Similar claims, it should be added, have been made by thinkers influenced by Hegel's theory of recognition, albeit with less emphasis on empathic care. In a manner comparable to their feminist counterparts, these thinkers affirm the Hegelian view concerning what Robert Stern calls 'the sociality of freedom' (Stern 2012: 359). That is, the view that mutual recognition is constitutive of human freedom. As Robert Pippin puts it, on this view, '*subjects cannot be free unless recognised by others in a certain way*' (Pippin 2000: 156), and, correspondingly, as Stern adds, 'it is only by recognizing others as equal to ourselves that we can in fact realise [our] freedom' (Stern 2012: 358).

It will come as no surprise to those readers who have some familiarity with Levinas's work that there is some prima facie compelling evidence in support of the view that Levinas's notion of finite freedom will be relational. His most forthright statement on it, for instance, runs as follows: 'What of the notion of finite freedom? No doubt the idea of a responsibility prior to freedom, and the compossibility of freedom and the other such as it shows itself in responsibility for the other' (Levinas 1998: 122). Finite freedom, we might then plausibly suppose, labels a view according to which one's freedom constitutively involves standing in relations of responsibility with others. As such, Levinas may be understood as a relational autonomist *avant la lettre*.[7]

It is on this basis that we think it is worth canvassing a serious objection that has been put to proponents of relational autonomy, before considering Levinas's view in greater detail.[8] The objection is this. One crucial function of the concept of autonomy is that it serves to identify cases of illegitimate paternalism. That is, on a traditional construal of this aspect of individual freedom, if one makes a decision autonomously, then, *ceteris paribus*, it is illegitimate for another to intervene and overrule that decision on one's behalf. Moreover, only one sort of consideration can factor in determining whether a person's decisions are sufficiently well made to rule out the legitimacy of paternalistic intervention. Those are matters concerning how the individual made their decision: procedural considerations. Considerations about what kinds of social relations a person stands in, by contrast, are just not of the right kind to factor in determining whether their choices can legitimately be the subject of paternalistic intervention. And so, relational accounts of autonomy, the likes of which Levinas may appear to be advancing, cannot fulfil this traditional role of a concept of autonomy, to differentiate legitimate from illegitimate cases of paternalism.

This *paternalism objection* may not be one that Levinas himself explicitly considered, but, as we will show shortly, his dialectical presentation of the degrees of mature freedom provides the resources to respond to this concern. In short, he does so by allowing for a range of conceptions of freedom which can serve different functions for practical philosophy.

6. Finite freedom and antagonism

In the final stage of Levinas's dialectical *Bildungsgeschichte* of freedom, the I comes face to face with another free individual.[9] And the I's infinite freedom is thereby brought forcefully into a special kind of finite worldly context, which transforms it.

The first point to note about the face-to-face encounter is that its distinctiveness is characterized, in part, by the I's unbridgeable 'separation' from the other person (Levinas 1998: 14). Recall, in this connection, that according to Levinas's narrative the I won its infinite freedom through the labour of grasping and possessing the element, and this process constitutively involved the I distancing or detaching itself from the element, eventually coming to see the element as its *other*. One consequence of this process, according to Levinas, is the emergence in the I of a deepened 'inner life' (Levinas 1969: 54). And the action of the free will is said to consist not just in distancing the I from the element but also in bringing the previously indeterminate and uncontained element unthreateningly into the I's inner life, as part of the *I's world*: '[I]n labouring, possession reduces to the same what at first presented itself as other' (Levinas 1969: 175). We shall have to build some more complexity into this picture in a moment. But, for now, it is enough just to note that the context in which the I encounters the other is one in which the I is a separated being with an inner life.

But so is the other person. So, in the encounter with the other, the I faces something unlike anything else it has come across in the element: it faces another 'free one' (Levinas 1969: 39), with their own analogously separated inner life. Being free, the other cannot be grasped or possessed in the manner of the element; the separated other remains, uniquely, a *stranger*: 'the strangeness of the Other, his very freedom! Free beings alone can be strangers to one another. Their freedom which is "common" to them is precisely what separates them' (Levinas 1969: 74). The other, it seems, is just as inaccessible – ungraspable – to me as I take myself to be to all that is other.

There is a crucial ambivalence at play here, however. It is true that the other free being is the most distant and estranged from the I. And yet, by virtue of the freedom that they hold in 'common', the other can get *closest* to the I, in a specific way; the other can get under my skin, as it were, and pry into my inner life. The other does this, according to Levinas, in the way that they 'inhibit' the I's freedom – not merely by resisting possession but by *contesting* and *questioning* it: 'freedom … is inhibited, not as countered by resistance, but as arbitrary, guilty and timid' (Levinas 1969: 203). Or, as Levinas also puts it: under the gaze of the other person, 'my arbitrary freedom reads shame in the eyes that look at me' (Levinas 1969: 252), and, facing the other, 'freedom discovers itself murderous in its very exercise' (Levinas 1969: 84).

In order to understand this difficult line of thinking, we must first note that for Levinas the I's capacity to infinitely detach itself from all of its finite, worldly attachments and to thus build its own inner life and world opens up the possibility of the I becoming entirely *detached from reality*, lost to its own interiority: this is the *egoism* of the I (Levinas 1969: 26ff.). Consider, by way of illustration, the case of Raskolnikov once again, who, on Rowan Williams's reading, appears beholden to 'the doomed enterprise of a self-sufficient inner world' (Williams 2008: 119). As a result, Raskolnikov has gradually 'lost the capacity to hear and speak, to engage humanly with others and to change in response … The crime comes out of the intensity of an inner dialogue that is practically never interrupted by a real other' (Williams 2008: 116). Admittedly, Raskolnikov represents an extreme case of detachment from reality – but it is one which highlights what Levinas thinks of as the murderousness latent in unchecked, infinite freedom.

Levinas is suggesting, then, that in the encounter with the other the I's infinite detachment from reality can be dramatically recast as a form of criminal negligence towards all that is other. This is because, for Levinas, it is in the encounter with the other that the dangerous extent of the I's egoistical and irresponsible detachment from reality is brought to the I's own attention for the first time. To continue with the case of Raskolnikov, we can note that Raskolnikov epitomizes a state of detachment and separation: he 'kept aloof from everyone' and was 'haughtily proud and unsociable, as though he were keeping something to himself' (Doestoevsky 1993: 51). He imagined himself to be intellectually superior to his peers and with respect to the murder he had a miscellaneous assortment of ingenious justifications ready at hand. But when Raskolnikov was actually called to account for his actions and to explain himself to another person – as in his tense negotiations with the cunning inspector, Porfiry Petrovich, or in his pathetic confession to Sonya – his intricate web of inner thought became more like a labyrinth in which he was hopelessly and utterly lost. Indeed, witnessing Raskolnikov's encounters with other people, the reader is struck, first of all, by the feeling that despite the arrogant decisiveness of his action Raskolnikov had no *real* idea of what he was doing. And it is only in the encounter with the other person (especially Sonya) that Raskolnikov himself starts to become aware of his infinite detachment from reality – aware that he has become hopelessly ensnared in a labyrinth of fantastical, obsessional scheming.

On the basis of our discussion so far, we can begin to understand one plausible reason why Levinas calls the encounter with the other 'non-Utopian' (op. cit.): it often involves a painful intrusion of the other into one's inner life. Yet, by the same token, we may also be able to see why Levinas suggests that the encounter with the other person nonetheless *liberates* the I's freedom. On this point, Levinas asserts – rather breathlessly – that the encounter with the other 'frees the subject from *ennui*, that is, from the enchainment to itself, where the ego suffocates in itself due to the tautological way of identity' (Levinas 1998: 124). The encounter with the other liberates the I's freedom by reacquainting it with a reality that is other than itself. And, in so doing, it brings the I's infinite freedom down to earth, as it were, by placing it in a finite context. (This, perhaps, points to a further meaning behind Levinas's anti-Utopian language: the scene of the face-to-face encounter is not unworldly or idealistic; it *exists*.)

In addition to this, Levinas claims that the encounter with the other is also an 'investiture that liberates freedom from arbitrariness' (Levinas 1969: 84). It does this, firstly, by providing the I with an outside perspective against which it can normatively orient its own freedom. The other person, we might say, can speak what the celebrated Dostoevsky scholar Mikhail Bakhtin has called the '*penetrated word*', that is, 'a word capable of actively and confidently interfering in the interior dialogue of the other person, *helping that person to find his own voice*' (Bakhtin 1984: 242, our emphasis). That is why Levinas calls the other a 'privileged heteronomy' (Levinas 1969: 88): not because the other can determine or constrain the I's freedom, but because they make the I answerable for its own freedom; the other invites the I to give *reasons* for its actions. As Levinas puts it, the encounter with the other makes possible 'one['s] giving the world, his possession, to the other, or the positive act of the one justifying himself in his freedom before the other, that is, by apology' (Levinas 1969: 252). Confronted by the other, the I is called to arrive at a weighting of its own interests and intentions that is robust, in the sense that it could survive scrutiny by the other, who can be assumed to have interests, reasons and ends – an inner life – that are independent from the I's own. Notably, here reason may seem all the more heteronomous to the I, as it refuses to bend to the I's will, but for that very reason it is all the more liberating, as it helps the I escape its self-enchainment. In this way, the encounter with the other invests the I's freedom with a sort of normative discipline that it previously lacked.

But this is not all. The other also invests the I's freedom, according to Levinas, by 'teaching' (Levinas 1969: 171) the I that *there is* an other whose own life and ends are important in and of themselves, despite their radical separation from the I's own. As Rudi Visker has noted, this teaching is an '"investiture of freedom" because it introduced a degree of freedom I did not have before. What was inevitable and involuntary now turns out to be something about which I can decide: I can break the chains that tied me to my being and put the being of the Other above my own'

(Visker 2004: 152). Minimally, this means that in the encounter with the other the I can gain vital perspective on their own freedom, values and interests *as* finite or relative rather than infinite and absolute. Maximally, this invests the I with the possibility of volunteering their free agency to a cause that is not strictly speaking their own. The encounter with the other does not only bring the I's freedom back down to earth, it also *enriches* the possibilities for the I to exercise its freedom within that finite, peopled context.

7. Conclusion

In conclusion, we would like to draw together some strands of our discussion with a view to recommending the value of Levinas's notion of finite freedom as the culmination of a multilayered account of freedom. Its precursor, the infinite conception of freedom, is one of reflective distance or detachment from the I's finite, worldly context. The problems with this were two. First, the infinitely free individual faced a painful dilemma between heteronomy and arbitrariness. How can I be free if what I am to do is wholly determined by a factor outside myself, namely, reason? But, equally, how can I be free if my choices are arbitrary and effectively indistinguishable from pure chance? Second, this conception of freedom supposes – controversially – that I can be free entirely alone and without supportive bonds of community with others. In response to these concerns, Levinas was pushed to a conception of freedom which augments the procedures of autonomy constitutive of infinite freedom with an element of sociality. Finite freedom, so understood, is an attractive characterization of certain desiderata of human freedom that are lost from view on the individualistic, excessively procedural, orthodox views. We have argued that one distinctive contribution Levinas makes in this area consists in his suggestion that the elements of sociality conducive to mature, finite freedom need not be seen simply as ones of fraternal care or mutual recognition but can also be non-utopian, involving interpersonal antagonism. This was one of the two distinguishing features of Levinas's account that we mentioned at the outset.

However, finite freedom would itself seem to be an inadequate account of freedom if it were supposed to serve every function that has been expected of that concept. This is the force of what we earlier set out as the paternalism objection. And yet the dialectical *form* of Levinas's discussion – that of charting the maturation of freedom in the individual – points to a resolution of this concern. This is the second distinguishing feature of Levinas's account. Just as the shapes of freedom that emerge in Levinas's developmental account are distinct, so do they call for a distinct array of concepts for individual freedom. One concept is the minimal, threshold notion of what it takes to be free. Infinite freedom serves this purpose. It helps to illuminate what it takes for an individual's decisions to be their own, and to be free, in the sense that is relevant for delegitimising would-be acts of paternalistic intervention, for instance. Such freedom is a matter of individual procedures of reflection, endorsement and identification with one's choices. But of course it is possible to be more than minimally free. The objections that Levinas raised to infinite freedom can be best understood, therefore, as complaints about the immaturity of that minimal conception. Finite freedom, on this view, incorporates infinite freedom and is mature by contrast. Plausibly, this is what Levinas means when he declares his interest as that of 'reconciling autonomy and heteronomy' (Levinas 2008: 148). This dialectical structure does not sublate the earlier movements, as with Hegel, but incorporates them into a consequently enriched conception of freedom.

Notes

1   Compare Royce's (1919) analysis of Hegel's phenomenology as a *Bildungsroman*. The question of how to interpret Levinas's phenomenology of freedom permits of several further answers. For instance, one could understand the narrative as an ontogenetic account of how each individual becomes free. Alternatively, it could be read as a phylogenetic story offering an explanation of the development of individual freedom in the history of our species or our society. Our suggestion here is that the account is best understood in neither of these ways, but rather as a hypothetical fictional narrative designed to articulate the conceptual structure of freedom including its distinct layers. It is uncharitable to interpret Levinas as engaged in either ontogeny or phylogeny, since his work is too far removed from any evidence in developmental or evolutionary psychology, respectively.
2   The traumatic experience that Levinas envisions here, where the subject comes up against resistance in the world, stands in contrast to Fichte's doctrine of the *Anstoß*. For Fichte (1970: 188), the not-I is posited by the subject, whereas for Levinas the hostile and challenging elements of the world are explanatorily prior to any act of the subject (see Levinas 1998: 101 and 124).
3   Although it is oriented by the metaphor of possession and not destruction, Levinas's discussion here may be compared with Hegel's discussion of desire in his *Phenomenology of Spirit*. In that discussion, when the I is threatened by dissolution into the generality of mere 'animal consciousness', it attempts to preserve its individuality by imposing its will on the world, where, as Robert Stern puts it, 'any sense of estrangement from the world is countered by the destruction of the object, and so by the negation of its otherness in a literal sense' (Stern 2002: 73).
4   Examples of procedural accounts of autonomy, to which the present shape of freedom in Levinas' discussion bears an illuminating resemblance, include Frankfurt (1988), Watson (1975) and Dworkin (1970).
5   Interestingly, the dilemma that Levinas thus poses for infinite freedom is one that is echoed in recent work by Ruth Chang (2020: 298).
6   As Levinas knew, Sartre draws heavily on Hegel's Master/Slave dialectic in this area of his thought (see Sartre 1978: 235–44).
7   The relational autonomist whose work Levinas most closely recalls here could be Andrea Westlund (2011), who focuses on interpersonal relations of answerability and responsibility.
8   This line of criticism has been developed by Holroyd (2009).
9   Again, the move Levinas is making here bears comparison with Hegel. For Hegel, the recognition of the other as another free subject constitutes a 'decisive turning point

in the journey of consciousness' in the sense that in relations of mutual recognition, 'neither side need fear that by acknowledging the other and feeling itself bound to it (in a relationship like love, for example) "it has lost itself"' (Stern 2002: 74).

References

Bakhtin, M. (1984), *Problems of Dostoevsky's Poetics*, ed. and trans. C. Emerson, Minneapolis: University of Minnesota Press.
Cavell, S. (1979), *The Claim of Reason: Wittgenstein, Skepticism, Morality and Tragedy*, Oxford: Oxford University Press.
Chang, R. (2020), 'Do We Have Normative Powers?', *Aristotelian Society Supplementary Volume*, 94 (1): 275–300.
Dostoevsky, F. (1993), *Crime and Punishment*, trans. R. Pevear and L. Volokhonsky, New York: Vintage Books.
Dworkin, R. (1970), 'Acting Freely', *Noûs*, 4: 367–83.
Fichte, J.G. (1970), *Science of Knowledge*, trans. and ed. P. Heath and J. Lacks, New York: Appleton Century Crofts.
Frankfurt, H. (1988), 'Freedom of the Will and the Concept of a Person', in *The Importance of What We Care About*, 11–25, Cambridge: Cambridge University Press.
Held, V. (1993), *Feminist Morality*, Chicago: University of Chicago Press.
Holroyd, J. (2009), 'Relational Autonomy and Paternalistic Interventions', *Res Publica*, 15: 321–36.
Levinas, E. (1969), *Totality and Infinity: An Essay on Exteriority*, trans. A. Lingis, Pittsburgh, PA: Duquesne University Press.
Levinas, E. (1990), 'Reflections on the Philosophy of Hitlerism', *Critical Enquiry*, 17 (1): 62–71.
Levinas, E. (1996), *Basic Philosophical Writings*, ed. A. T. Peperzak, S. Critchley and R. Bernasconi, Bloomington, IN: Indiana University Press.
Levinas, E. (1998), *Otherwise Than Being; or Beyond Essence*, trans. A. Lingis, Pittsburgh, PA: Duquesne University Press.
Levinas, E. (2000), *God, Death, and Time*, trans. B. Bergo, Stanford, CA: Stanford University Press.
Levinas, E. (2001), *Existence and Existents*, trans. A. Lingis, Pittsburgh, PA: Duquesne University Press.
Levinas, E. (2008), *Outside the subject*, London: Bloomsbury Publishing.
Mackenzie, C. and N. Soljar (2000), 'Introduction', in C. Mackenzie and N. Soljar (eds), *Relational Autonomy: Feminist Reflections on Autonomy, Agency, and the Social Self*, 3–34, Oxford: Oxford University Press.
Moore, A. W. (2012), *The Evolution of Modern Metaphysics: Making Sense of Things*, Cambridge: Cambridge University Press.
Pippin, R. (2000), 'What Is the Question for Which Hegel's Theory of Recognition Is the Answer?', *European Journal of Philosophy*, 8 (2): 155–72.
Royce, J. (1919), *Lectures on Modern Idealism*, New Haven: Yale University Press.
Sallis, J. (1998), 'Levinas and the Elemental', *Research in Phenomenology*, 28: 152–9.
Sartre, J-P. (1978), *Being and Nothingness*, trans. H. Barnes, London: Routledge.
Stern, R. (2002), *Hegel and the Phenomenology of Spirit*, London: Routledge.

Stern, R. (2012), 'Is Hegel's Master-Slave Dialectic a Refutation of Solipsism?', *British Journal for the History of Philosophy*, 20 (2): 333–61.
Taylor, M. C. (2000), *Journeys to Selfhood: Hegel and Kierkegaard*, New York: Fordham University Press.
Visker, R. (2004), *The Inhuman Condition: Looking for Difference after Levinas and Heidegger*, Dordrecht: Kluwer.
Watson, G. (1975), 'Free Agency', *Journal of Philosophy*, 72: 205–20.
Westlund, A. (2011), 'Autonomy, Authority, and Answerability', *Jurisprudence*, 2 (1): 161–79.
Williams, R. (2008), *Dostoevsky: Language, Faith, and Fiction*, London: Continuum.

12

Rethinking existentialism: From radical freedom to project sedimentation

Jonathan Webber

In their works of the mid-1940s, which first gave definition to the term 'existentialism', Simone de Beauvoir and Jean-Paul Sartre both argued that human freedom is objectively valuable and the foundation of all other value. However, they did not agree about the nature of that freedom. They agreed that an individual's preferences and behaviour are ultimately explained by that person's projects, which they have chosen and can reject, rather than by innate personality traits. Where they disagreed was on how projects operate and therefore how they can be changed. Sartre's view was that projects have no inertia of their own and persist only if they continue to be endorsed. Beauvoir argued that projects become gradually sedimented with continued endorsement, increasing in both influence and inertia over time. Sartre's view entails that projects can be changed instantaneously. Beauvoir's view is that projects can only be changed through a gradual process.

Sartre used the term 'radical freedom' to describe his theory. It results from his systematic philosophical method of transcendental phenomenology. Through this method, he developed a basic ontology of being and nothingness which he thought grounded a richer ontology of being-in-itself and being-for-itself. Within that framework, he thought, projects can have no being of their own and must be supported by our intentions. Beauvoir, by contrast, did not provide her theory with a specific label. I have suggested that 'sedimentation' is an appropriate description (2018: 4–6, 60–2). She grounded this theory of project sedimentation directly in the phenomenology of lived experience, particularly as she articulated and explored it in her fictional writings. Although her theoretical writings occasionally use some of Sartre's ontological terms, she is committed neither to his specific definitions of them nor to the idea that a theory of human existence must be grounded in a basic ontology.

By the end of the 1940s, Sartre had abandoned radical freedom in favour of project sedimentation. In this chapter, we will see that he was right to do so. Project sedimentation is a theory of freedom consistent with the basic existentialist claim that the reasons for our actions depend on our chosen and revisable projects. It provides clear explanations of two things rendered entirely mysterious by Sartre's theory of radical freedom: what commitment to a project consists in and how there can be cultural values. Project sedimentation is therefore a richer and more plausible theory of both freedom and culture. However, we will also see why Sartre had preferred radical freedom in the first place: the theory of sedimentation was not available through his philosophical method until he revised that method in response to reading an anthology of negritude poetry.

1. Sartre's theory of radical freedom

Sartre articulates his theory of radical freedom in *Being and Nothingness*, a treatise that applies a philosophical method that he does not explicitly explain but that he had been carefully developing for ten years. This is a form of transcendental argumentation. The premises are intended to articulate aspects of experience as these can be understood from the perspective of the subject of that experience. The conclusion describes how reality must be, given that experience has the features described in the premises. This relation between premises and conclusion is not *logical* necessity: there is no contradiction in accepting the premises but denying the conclusion. Rather, the relation is *factual* necessity: the conclusion specifies some ontological structure required for the experience described in the premises.

For example, Sartre argues that in perception we experience the world as comprising objects that can resist our intentions, which we can interact with in some ways but not others, and that we must therefore work with to achieve our aims. This feature of perceptual experience, that its objects do not respond directly to my wishes and whims, contrasts with imaginative experience. This observation forms the premises of a transcendental argument. Sartre's conclusion is that perceptual experience has this feature because it is the revelation of a reality that exists independently of my experience of it. More concisely, he argues that the objects of perception have 'being-in-itself', since otherwise perceptual experience would not have this feature.[1]

However, we experience the world, according to Sartre, not simply as an arrangement of material objects but as a field of affordances, meanings and reasons. The park lawn is experienced not simply as a mass of grass but as a place where people might play football or lay out picnic blankets. The sign that says to keep off the grass is immediately experienced not simply as a white object with black markings on it, but as having the linguistic meaning of a command to keep off the grass, and as having the social meaning that walking across the grass might attract disapproving looks, or perhaps admiring looks from some people, and might even result in being admonished by the park attendant. It might be immediately experienced as a reason to find somewhere else to play football or eat the picnic.

Affordances (which Sartre calls *potentialités*) are features that the mind-independent reality of the lawn and the sign board have in relation to my bodily abilities. They constrain what can be done, structure the ways in which objects can resist my efforts, and are manifest in perceptual experience of those objects. Meanings (*significations*) are features of the social environment overlain on the mind-independent reality of the lawn and its sign board. They too are experienced as structuring what can be done. Reasons (*motifs*), by contrast, are experienced as having directive force, which is dependent on my own values. The sign is experienced as a reason to keep off the grass only because I value conforming to social expectations, not drawing attention to myself, or avoiding conflicts. Were you to value disobeying any authority for the sake of it, you would experience the same sign board as a reason to walk directly onto the grass, perhaps to start a game of football or spread out your picnic blanket (B&N: 78–9, 574, 585–93).

Reasons are experienced not as causes of our behaviour, but as invitations and proscriptions that can be accepted, considered, rejected or revised (B&N: 67–72). They are thus experienced as dependent on my intentions. Whereas potentialities are experienced in a way that can only be explained by their being independent of my experience, reasons are experienced in a way that can only be explained by their dependence on my experience (Webber 2019b: 333–8). Potentialities are part of the being-in-itself of the world, whereas reasons are instances of nothingness or 'negatives' (B&N: 56). Reasons reflect the values at the heart of my projects (B&N: 78–9, 574). Since those values are themselves 'ideal objects' or 'non-existents', they lack the being-in-itself necessary to resist my intentions (B&N: 574). I can act contrary to the reasons that seem to confront me and in so doing reshape my projects and the values they incorporate (B&N: 575).[2]

Sartre's theory of radical freedom does not hold, however, that revising projects is easy. One source of difficulty is that projects form a hierarchical network (B&N: 574). An alteration at one part of the network will have ramifications elsewhere. Someone who wants to change one part of the network might be unwilling to accept the ramifications of doing so, especially if those are extensive (B&N: 607–8). A second source of difficulty is bad faith. We can pursue projects that we do not wish to acknowledge. Sartre's central example is the inferiority project, the aim of proving myself inferior to other people. It is essential to this project that I do not explicitly see myself as pursuing it (B&N: 618). In such cases, one might need the help of an existential psychoanalyst to uncover the troublesome project (B&N: 619–20, 737–8). Even so, Sartre holds that projects themselves have no inertia; they cannot resist our genuine intention to change them, even where this means a thorough transformation of my entire network of projects (B&N: 621–2).

2. Beauvoir's theory of project sedimentation

'One is not born, but rather becomes, woman' (SS: 293). Beauvoir's most famous sentence opens Part One of Volume Two of *The Second Sex*, titled 'Formation', which comprises four chapters on development from infancy to womanhood. Beauvoir has made clear in the Introduction to Volume One that the entire work is premised on the existentialist conception of the individual as 'a transcendence' that develops 'through projects' as an 'expansion towards an indefinitely open future' (SS: 17). Even so, this process of becoming a woman is not a matter of freely choosing to become a woman; 'her vocation is imperiously breathed into her from the first years of her life' (SS: 289). Girls are encouraged to be pleasing in looks and behaviour, discouraged from vigorous sports and exploratory physical activities like climbing trees, and are told stories, given toys and taught games that support this developmental direction (SS: 305–7, 311, 316). This 'conditioning', sustained throughout upbringing and socially reinforced in adulthood, defines 'what is called the woman's "character"' (SS: 653).

Project sedimentation is the process of this conditioning. Children freely create their own aims, but some of these are frustrated or even punished by their social environment, whereas others are positively facilitated. There does not need to be any innate project of trying to please one's parents or society to explain why one tends towards those projects that are facilitated. Rather, it is already built in to each project that one values its aim. Where one's environment systematically facilitates some aims and frustrates others, successfully achieving one's aims effectively requires selecting aims that environment facilitates and abandoning aims it frustrates (SS: 60–2). The more one continues to pursue a particular project, on Beauvoir's view, the more that project becomes engrained in one's outlook. A woman who rejects the social expectations of womanhood still has 'a different perspective on the universe' to a man, because 'she does not have the same past as a boy' (SS: 739).

Sedimentation engrains not only the values at the core of one's projects but also the strategies for achieving those aims. Those strategies need to incorporate the social meanings of one's environment if they are to be successful. Project sedimentation, although driven by the pursuit of values chosen by the individual within a social context, therefore, brings with it a sedimentation of society's understanding of the world. For example, the formation of childhood incorporates not only the idea that boys and girls are different, but also the further idea that males are superior to females. Boys are encouraged to dominate their situations, girls to navigate theirs (SS: 311–14). They become adults who see the imposition of order as masculine and adapting to the environment as feminine, according to Beauvoir, and they live their lives accordingly (SS: 655–7, 665–70).

Beauvoir presents this theory of gender sedimentation in *The Second Sex* through phenomenological descriptions of the experiences of women and girls, in part supported by social observations that these phenomenological descriptions are intended to explain. An implicit transcendental reasoning animates the text. Project sedimentation is presented as factually necessary for women's experience to have the features described in this phenomenology. Beauvoir does not present such arguments explicitly, however; neither does she develop or deploy a basic ontology to underpin the theory of project sedimentation. She considers abstract philosophical prose unable to capture the historical temporality and individual nuance of human existence (LM: 274–5). 'A metaphysical novel that is honestly read, and honestly written', she argues, 'provides a disclosure of existence in a way unequalled by any other mode of expression' (LM: 276). Beauvoir's occasional uses of Sartre's theoretical terms are intended only to provide rough outline sketches of the metaphysical picture she develops in her literary fiction.

In my book *Rethinking Existentialism*, I argue that the central narrative of Beauvoir's novel *She Came To Stay*, published the same year as *Being and Nothingness*, is driven by her conception of project sedimentation and its contradiction of Sartre's conception of radical freedom (Webber 2018a: 57–67). The same metaphysical vision of human existence is present in Beauvoir's earlier collection of short stories, *When Things of the Spirit Come First*, written in the late 1930s. These interrelated stories focus on a group of young women as they grow into adulthood from strict Roman Catholic backgrounds. Chantal, for example, rejects everything about her upbringing, tries to treat her students as her equals and wants to help them lead liberated lives (TS: 46, 75, 82). But she is annoyed when a student treats her as an equal (TS: 59), and when one student most needs her help, in a way that conflicts with the values of her upbringing, she finds the situation appalling and the request morally disgusting (TS: 84).

3. Sedimentation and rational autonomy

Beauvoir's conception of project sedimentation is essentially that the continual pursuit of a project increases its inertia and influence over our outlook. It therefore contradicts Sartre's conception of radical freedom, which is essentially the claim that projects can have no inertia of their own. Beauvoir's conception entails that projects cannot be abandoned in the way that Sartre describes but can at best be worn away through the pursuit of contrary projects, the continual endorsement of contrary values. Chantal has endorsed values contrary to those of her upbringing. She has not yet spent much time pursuing projects that regularly reaffirm her new values so has not yet done much to erode the outlook sedimented through the many formative years of her childhood. The influence of that sedimented outlook remains visible in her irritation at her students not treating her as a superior. It later, at a time of crisis, entirely overwhelms the set of values that she now professes.

However, this is not a rejection of the existentialist idea that our character consists in the projects that we choose and can change. It is only a rejection of the idea that projects can offer no resistance to our intention to change them. Beauvoir's view is that engrained projects cannot be removed immediately but can be eroded over time. Engrained projects shape our perceptions of the world and our immediate thoughts and affective inclinations in response to situations, thereby contributing to our decisions. This does not in itself prevent us from reflecting on our values, either independently or in conversation with other people, or from learning more about the world and about other people's perspectives.[3] As a result, project sedimentation does not prevent us from formulating and endorsing values contrary to our engrained projects. This is precisely what Chantal has done. Project sedimentation only means that we must continually endorse those new values in our thought and action if they are to become our engrained outlook.

Jesse Prinz is mistaken, therefore, to describe Beauvoir as holding sedimented values to be so deeply engrained that 'we cannot imagine having different views' (2018: 94). The problem Beauvoir describes is rather that we can imagine having different views and can even prefer those views, but that this is not enough to make them our views. The root of Prinz's error here has been to understand sedimentation as primarily a social and historical phenomenon, the process by which societies encode their outlook in artefacts, culture and language, making that outlook persist across time. He reads Beauvoir as developing the conceptions of sedimentation articulated by Edmund

Husserl and Maurice Merleau-Ponty (2018: 88-9, 91-2). However, she does not use the term 'sedimentation' herself, she does not refer to Husserl anywhere in *The Second Sex*, and her conception of engrained values is distinct from Merleau-Ponty's theory of tacit knowledge (Webber 2018a: 70-1, 74-5).

Project sedimentation as Beauvoir describes it is primarily an individual process. We could call it a psychological phenomenon grounded in the way minds work. Or we could call it an existential phenomenon grounded in the ontology of human being. There is not much difference between these two descriptions, given the background existentialist theory that talk of the mind or psychology is an abstract characterization of aspects of a single embodied being. Most importantly, sedimentation is driven, on Beauvoir's view, by the individual's pursuit of the projects they have chosen. The projects that have been pursued long enough to become deeply engrained are likely to be ones that fit their social environment. They will include strategies that encode the social meanings present in the environment, along with other information about that environment. In these ways, social pressures influence the result of sedimentation, but the process itself is primarily driven by the individual's choices.

Project sedimentation is therefore compatible with individual freedom. Engrained projects are the result of our choices. We are free to formulate new projects and sediment those over time. This just means that our freedom requires sustained effort, rather than being the instantaneous 'radical freedom' that Sartre described. We are not simply shaped by social forces. Continuing social pressures, however, from mere disapproval through economic structures to outright physical violence, can make it difficult or even impossible to pursue projects that defy social expectations. For this reason, Prinz is right to identify social change as essential to overcoming the constraints of social conditioning that Beauvoir finds objectionable (2018: 103-4). However, this project of social change must be formulated and pursued despite the existing conditioning. It presupposes, therefore, that project sedimentation is consistent with the rational autonomy required to envision and act upon different values (SS: 777-80).[4]

4. Projects as commitments

Project sedimentation as Beauvoir conceives of it, therefore, is compatible with rational autonomy. It is compatible with the freedom to choose our values through rational consideration. It is compatible with our chosen values determining the reasons that we experience the world as presenting us with, the reasons to which we respond in rational action.[5] It is even consistent with experiencing those reasons not as forces pushing us around but as invitations and proscriptions that can be accepted, considered, rejected or revised. Chantal can ignore her annoyance at her student treating her as an equal and continue to encourage that behaviour through her own words and actions. Beauvoir's theory of project sedimentation, that is to say, is consistent with Sartre's description of the phenomenology of experience. The difference is that acting contrary to the reasons presented in the experience, reasons that reflect sedimented projects, reshapes those projects and the values they incorporate only if such contrary action is repeated over a sufficient stretch of time.

Beauvoir's theory is not only consistent with the phenomenology that Sartre intends his theory to explain, but also has the advantage of providing a clear account of what is involved in being committed to a project, which Sartre's theory leaves entirely mysterious. Chantal could commit to her new liberal-minded values by continuing to act on them, ignoring the minor irritations that manifest her older values, and persisting in affirming her new values even when she finds it very difficult to do so. Commitment to a project, on Beauvoir's theory, consists in choosing to do the things that will engrain that project. It is an ongoing process, one that can require overcoming an inner resistance. Given the theory of project sedimentation, it is clear how such commitment is related to the project's role in shaping the reasons we experience in the world. The more one has continued to commit to the project, the more deeply engrained it has become, so the more quickly and strongly it influences one's perception of the world and one's immediate thoughts and feelings in response to the world.

Sartre's theory of radical freedom, by contrast, seems to have no resources to explain either what commitment to a project is or why one's experience is shaped by one's projects. Commitment to a project requires that one has truly oriented oneself towards the value at its core, but it is not clear what this spatial metaphor can really indicate. Sartre gives plausible reasons why it cannot indicate an explicit rational decision. My project of staying alive, with the value of my continued existence at is core, shapes my experience of dangers and opportunities in the environment and explains some of my behaviour, even though I may never have explicitly decided to stay alive (B&N: 574). The gambler's decision to give up gambling will not prevent him from placing a bet the next time an opportunity arises (B&N: 70–2). Explicit decision is therefore neither necessary nor sufficient for commitment to a project. What is it, then, that is present in the case of my staying alive but absent for the gambler's resolution?

One difference between the two cases concerns the individual's network of projects. My project of staying alive seems integrated with my other projects. Although I might occasionally engage in mildly dangerous or unhealthy behaviour, most of my projects are at least consistent with staying alive and many of them positively require staying alive. The gambler's resolution, by contrast, might well be contrary to whatever other projects explain why that person was a regular gambler in the first place. Although this is a difference between the two cases, however, it cannot provide an account of what it is to be committed to a project. For it is essentially the idea that the project of staying alive is related in the appropriate way to other commitments, whereas the gambler's resolution is not. It thus presupposes the idea of commitment. The question of what commitment itself consists in, therefore, is left unanswered.

Without a conception of commitment, Sartre's theory cannot explain the influence of projects over experience. Reasons that reflect my project of staying alive are experienced as stronger than most, perhaps all, other reasons in my experience. Yet the values at the heart of my projects are equally non-existents. The difference in the experienced strengths of reasons must reflect a difference in degree of commitment. More generally, my experience being influenced by a particular value must refer to my commitment to that value, rather than some other value I could have had instead. Project sedimentation can explain how a value influences experience and why it does so to a greater or lesser degree: the more a project is pursued, the more it becomes integrated into one's cognitive system, so the more influence it has over perception and immediate thoughts and feelings. Sartre has no rival explanation to offer. It is not only the gambler's resolution that seems like a boneless phantom (B&N: 71). Sartre's idea of a project does too.

5. Projects and cultural values

Beauvoir's theory of project sedimentation, therefore, can explain the influence that an individual's chosen projects have over their experience and behaviour, but Sartre's theory of radical freedom cannot. This pattern is repeated with respect to the influence of an individual's social context on their projects. We have already seen how project sedimentation explains the cultural inheritance of values and social meanings: the projects most likely to become sedimented are those most fit to survive in their social environment. Sartre's theory of radical freedom, by contrast, precludes any explanation of how members of a social group might generally have projects in common. To see why, we need to consider Sartre's attempt to provide such an explanation within the theory of radical freedom in his 1946 book *Anti-Semite and Jew*. Ultimately, this attempt relies on there already being a widespread project whose prevalence cannot be explained within his theory.

Sartre's basic idea is that where a group of people have generally developed a similar set of values, a common cultural outlook, they have done so as individuals responding to common features of their situations. Jewish people live in a wider society suffused with a negative portrayal of them. Jewish people develop particular projects, argues Sartre, in response to this portrayal. Because the vice of avarice is at the centre of this anti-Semitic picture, for example, Jewish people are more likely to be generous (A&J: 95). Jewish people respond to the anti-Semitic claim that they will not integrate into the wider society by becoming ambitious to succeed within the structures of that wider society. (A&J: 96–100). But because that society sees such ambition as an exception to the rule, all Jewish people remain classified together, ensuring a common interest and solidarity no matter how diverse their careers and achievements become (A&J: 98–103).

There is much that can be said about this theory. For our purposes, what matters is that it cannot function as a theory of the origins of cultural values within Sartre's existentialism. It rests on the idea that a culture develops in response to that group of people's common situation (A&J: 93). There are two ways this could occur. One is that those people are responding to some set of reasons that they all experience in their environment. This would require, within Sartre's theory of radical freedom, some project they already have in common, since the reasons we encounter reflect our projects. We would therefore need an explanation of why they already have that project in common. The other way a culture could be shaped by a common situation is by the social meanings and pressures in that environment facilitating some projects and frustrating others. If a project is systematically frustrated by some features of the social environment, those features will be experienced as reasons to abandon that project.

Sartre's account of Jewish culture rests on the first of these two kinds of explanation. He begins his lengthy description of Jewish culture by stating that it applies 'solely to the *inauthentic* Jew (the term "inauthentic" implying no moral blame, of course)' (A&J: 93). An authentic person understands that the reasons they experience reflect values they endorse and can change, understands their projects and the values they include, and understands the context in which they are operating. Authenticity requires respecting, perhaps even promoting, human freedom. But given the enormous variety of projects that are available within that constraint, authentic people have nothing more in common. They each value human freedom and live out their own freedom in their contexts in their own ways. It is within the project of inauthenticity, which includes denying radical freedom and affirming that one's behaviour is due to a fixed nature, argues Sartre, that the anti-Semitic picture of Jewish people is a reason to behave in ways contrary to it. The aim is to demonstrate that one's innate nature is not as anti-Semitism portrays it to be (A&J: 136–8).

Common cultural values among a group of people, on this theory, result from the widespread project of inauthenticity. What explains that common cultural value? Authenticity and inauthenticity are basic attitudes to human existence, so neither could be motivated by some deeper project. If widespread inauthenticity could be explained at all, therefore, it would be by its fitness to the social environment. This would require that authenticity entails that either the aims of authenticity or the aims of other projects pursued along with it are systematically frustrated in ways that are experienced as reasons to abandon the project of authenticity. It is difficult to see how this could occur, especially given that any project available to the authentic person other than authenticity itself is also available to the inauthentic person. The frustration of such a project within the context of authenticity, therefore, could not be a reason to prefer inauthenticity. The purportedly widespread project of inauthenticity therefore seems to be a cultural value that Sartre's theory cannot explain.

Sartre could not avoid this problem, moreover, by trying to explain Jewish cultural values directly in terms of fitness to the wider social environment without reference to inauthenticity. For as he points out, anti-Semitism is a climate of hostility to Jewish people no matter what they do; 'the situation of the Jew is that everything he does turns against him' (A&J: 141).

6. Sedimentation, culture and freedom

Sartre's theory of common cultural values among Jewish people is centred on the responses of individual adults to their wider society. It makes no reference to upbringing. It makes no reference to stories, songs, games, rituals, festivals, literature, humour or other aspects of the cultural fabric. This rather impoverished picture of cultural phenomena is another result of his theory of radical freedom. If projects have no inertia of their own, if they cannot become engrained in one's outlook, then the encouragement of particular values in upbringing, such as generosity or ambition, could not exert any strong influence on the projects later chosen in adult life. A community's cultural fabric could only express common projects, as these are constrained by current circumstances. Cultural values that persist over generations would need to be explained by a persisting feature of the environment, just as anti-Semitism has been a persisting feature of the wider social context of Jewish culture.

Beauvoir's theory of the origins of gender, by contrast, is built on an account of childhood and adolescence, one that emphasizes the role of the cultural fabric in shaping that upbringing. This richer account of cultural phenomena is made available by the theory of project sedimentation. The values at the heart of the projects pursued through childhood and adolescence become deeply engrained in one's outlook, along with the social meanings those projects need to navigate. These meanings and values continue to shape one's perceptions and immediate thoughts and feelings, unless worn away by sustained pursuit of contrary projects. That same outlook shapes the cultural fabric, which in turn forms the context in which the next generation grow up. Values formed in response to a community's circumstances can themselves become sedimented through this process, long outliving their original purpose. Beauvoir's theory therefore grounds a theory of cultural inheritance, which Sartre's theory of radical freedom precludes.

The theory of project sedimentation is thus preferable to the theory of radical freedom for two reasons. One is that project sedimentation explains the inheritance of cultural values, whereas radical freedom precludes any full explanation of the existence of cultural values at all. The other is that project sedimentation explicates the idea of commitment to a project and explains how such commitment shapes the reasons we find in experience. The theory of radical freedom relies on the idea that commitment to a project shapes the reasons we experience but has no resources to clarify what commitment is or how it has this effect. Both theories subscribe to the central existentialist claim that the reasons we experience (the *motifs* that motivate our decisions and actions) depend on projects that we have chosen and can change. The theory of radical freedom adds that projects have no inertia of their own. This combination generates the problems of explaining commitment and cultural values. The theory of project sedimentation negates this second claim, thereby solving those problems.

In so doing, the theory of project sedimentation gives substance to the idea of rational autonomy. Individuals are not simply pushed around by the combination of upbringing and current environment. Rather, the environment presents reasons that the individual can accept, consider, reject or revise. These reasons reflect the individual's values, which may have been shaped by their upbringing. In responding to the reasons they experience, individuals contribute either to sedimenting their existing values or to replacing them with new values. Individuals can consciously shape their own outlooks through a sustained effort. Because this is a process of sedimentation, such an effort will have lasting effects. Therefore, we should not agree that sedimentation constrains our freedom (Prinz 2018: 94). Rather, project sedimentation *is* freedom. It is the process by which we exercise control over the roots of our behaviour. It is the method by which we shape the reasons our environment presents in our experience.

Project sedimentation is a theory of how individual freedom operates. Sartre's conception of radical freedom fails to provide such a theory. Beauvoir developed her theory of project sedimentation from at least the time of writing *When Things of the Spirit Come First* in the late 1930s, as we have seen, and it is central to her novel *She Came To Stay*, published in the same year as *Being and Nothingness*, which even dramatizes its superiority to Sartre's conception of radical freedom in explaining the role of commitment (Webber 2018a: 65–7). Given that Beauvoir and Sartre were continuously discussing their ideas with one another over this time, it seems highly likely that they compared the strengths and weaknesses of their respective ideas of freedom. In which case, why did Sartre expound the theory of radical freedom, given the superiority of the theory of project sedimentation?

7. The transformation of Sartre's philosophy

Sartre had developed his theory of radical freedom through the philosophical method that he developed for ten years up to the publication of *Being and Nothingness*. This is a form of transcendental phenomenology, which derives conclusions about the nature of reality from descriptions of experience from the perspective of the subject. The conclusions are intended to identify how reality must be for experience to have the character that it has. This method stands in a tradition of thought stemming at least from Descartes through Kant and Husserl. One feature of this tradition is its methodological solipsism: other writers can be used only as a source of inspiration; each philosopher must formulate their own descriptions of their own experience for these to be legitimate grounds for inference about the nature of reality (Husserl 1950: 2, 7). Sartre followed this prescription in the method through which he developed his ontology of values as having no being of their own and therefore offering no resistance to the subject's intentions to change them.

Beauvoir's descriptions of experiences that indicate a contrary ontology, therefore, could not directly provide Sartre with reason to abandon his theory of radical freedom in favour of that ontology. Neither could the explanatory superiority of that theory of project sedimentation. Sartre's philosophical method required his ontology to be derived from his own experience and he found nothing there that could be explained only by project sedimentation. He was aware, of course, that our intentions to change our projects are sometimes unsuccessful. The gambler who resolves never to gamble again might then place a bet at the next opportunity. However, he thought this could be accommodated by the fact that projects form a hierarchical network, so that an intended change to one project might require unwelcome changes to other projects, and the claim that we can conceal projects from ourselves in bad faith. With these points in place, it seems that he found nothing in his own experience that required him to abandon the theory of radical freedom that he had grounded in his ontology of being and nothingness.

Yet two years after publishing *Anti-Semite and Jew*, Sartre published 'Black Orpheus', an essay that embraced the theory of project sedimentation and the idea of cultural inheritance that it affords. This was written as a preface to an anthology of poetry by black francophone authors, which aimed to explore and express the 'negritude' they considered themselves to have in common. Sartre describes this negritude as something each of these poets finds 'at the bottom of his heart' (BO: 323). It is a kind of inherited essence, a way of experiencing the world that respects natural rhythms and understands through sympathy rather than analysis (BO: 294–307). This essence is a 'collective memory' passed down through culture and tradition (BO: 312). It is a project that requires commitment, but which would take a sustained effort to abandon (BO: 298–9, 319, 322–4).

Negritude poetry presented a challenge to Sartre's philosophical method. Reading this anthology made clear to Sartre that his methodological solipsism in fact impeded his ambition of discovering the universal ontology of human existence. The poetry presented a world of experience that he could not experience for himself and which supported an ontology opposed to the one he had derived from his own experience. This experience of negritude, moreover, occurs in the dissonances between the subject's experience and both the world they inhabit and the structures of the French language. These dissonances indicate an engrained cultural inheritance that does not match either the immediate environment or the French language. An engrained cultural inheritance that did match those would not be manifest in experience at all: one's perspective on the world and descriptions of it would just seem to track the way things are. Negritude poetry thereby indicated that the ontology required to explain the phenomenology of cultural inheritance could not be demonstrated on the basis of Sartre's own experience.

In response to his reading of negritude poetry, Sartre abandoned the methodological solipsism that he had tacitly deployed in all his previous philosophical work. He retained the rest of his philosophical method but now accepted that crucial aspects of the experiences of people marginalized by the cultures that shaped Europe and its languages could not be expressed literally in those languages. He further accepted two important implications of this linguistic fact: that phenomenology could not be limited to the literal description of experience in prose but must include poetry capturing experiences that cannot be described literally, and that ontological conclusions drawn by transcendental reasoning from such phenomenology of marginalized people should take priority over any contrary conclusions drawn from his own perspective.[6] It is through this revised form of transcendental phenomenology that he finally accepted the theory of project sedimentation, a theory which Beauvoir had been articulating for at least a decade.

In doing so, Sartre implicitly abandoned the basic ontology of being and nothingness which had grounded his theory of radical freedom. That basic ontology was anyway inadequate to capture his own phenomenology, though he seems not to have noticed this. For between the being-in-itself of potentiality, which structures what I can do with my environment, and the nothingness of reasons, whose directives I can ignore or refuse, the phenomenology articulated in *Being and Nothingness* posits a stratum of social meanings. These are like potentialities in that they do not depend on my commitment to them. But they are not features of the material world, since they do depend on the attitudes of my society in general or perhaps of particular people within my society. They therefore do not fit Sartre's characterization of nonexistents encountered in my experience, but neither are they features of being-in-itself. Sartre's philosophy from 'Black Orpheus' to the end of his career is shaped by his renewed method of transcendental phenomenology, which brings with it an enduring philosophical interest in poetry and an enduring commitment to the theory of project sedimentation. Whether it also leads him to a more adequate basic ontology is a question for another time.

Notes

1. For a detailed explanation of this method, its development and its deployment in *Being and Nothingness*, see Webber 2018b: 294–8; Webber 2019a: 164–74.
2. Sartre holds in *Being and Nothingness* that there are two ways of acting contrary to the reasons that seem to confront me. I can do so responding to contrary reasons that are also grounded in my projects. Or I can do so for no reason at all. This second claim, however, is incompatible with the idea of commitment to a project (Webber 2018a: 52–4). This problem is one manifestation of Sartre's failure in *Being and Nothingness* to explain how one becomes committed to a project and why that commitment influences one's experience.
3. Some projects do constrain our ability to do these things. Since our projects determine the people we meet, constrain the relationships we form and influence which media we engage with, they shape our epistemic environment. If we are not careful, our projects can leave us in an 'epistemic bubble', where we only encounter the ideas of like-minded people, though this does not prevent us from reflecting critically on our projects or on that epistemic bubble. More insidiously, our projects can lead us into an 'echo chamber', a community of like-minded people that discredits dissenting voices and discourages critical reflection. (For a careful analysis of epistemic bubbles and echo chambers, see Nguyen 2018.) However, on Beauvoir's theory of freedom, these situations that result from particular projects are not the outcome of project sedimentation itself.
4. Prinz describes Frantz Fanon as holding essentially the same conception of project sedimentation as Beauvoir (2018: 92–3) and argues that they both present their theories as exercises in consciousness raising, to confront their readers with the question of what they are doing to perpetuate or to dismantle the oppressive sedimented structures (2018: 103–4). I agree that Beauvoir and Fanon hold the same views about sedimentation and the need for social change, only disagreeing with Prinz on what those views are (Webber 2018a: 145–8).
5. In this chapter, we are concerned only with reasons in the sense of aspects of the world experienced as motivating actions (Sartre's *motifs*). We are not concerned here with the normative question of which reasons we ought to experience and act upon. Beauvoir and Sartre both consider human freedom itself to be objectively intrinsically valuable and the foundation of all other values. They hold that we ought at least to respect, perhaps even to promote, human freedom. If this is right, then we always have good reason to do so, regardless of whether the demands of that reason are manifest in our experience. To put the point another way: Beauvoir and Sartre hold that we objectively ought to have the project of authenticity, through which we would experience reasons to respect, perhaps even promote, human freedom. For detailed analyses of this ethical theory, see Webber 2018a: chapters 9 and 10; Webber forthcoming-b.
6. For a full analysis of what negritude poetry taught Sartre about language, phenomenology and ontology, and of precisely how it did so, see Webber forthcoming-a.

References

Beauvoir, Simone de. LM. (2004), 'Literature and Metaphysics', trans. Veronique Zaytzeff, in *Philosophical Writings*, by Simone de Beauvoir, ed. Margaret A. Simons, Marybeth Timmerman and Mary Beth Mader, 269–76, Urbana IL: University of Illinois Press. First published in *Les Temps Modernes* 1, no. 7 (1946): 1153–63.

Beauvoir, Simone de. TS. (1983), *When Things of the Spirit Come First*, trans. Patrick O'Brien, London: Fontana. Translation of *Quand prime le spirituel* (Paris: Gallimard, 1979).

Beauvoir, Simone de. SS. (2009), *The Second Sex*, trans. Constance Borde and Sheila Malovany-Chevalier, London: Jonathan Cape. First published as *Le Deuxieme Sexe* in two volumes (Paris: Gallimard, 1949).

Husserl, Edmund (1950), *Cartesian Meditations: An Introduction to Phenomenology*, trans. Dorion Cairns, The Hague: Martinus Nijohff. First published as *Meditations Cartesiennes: Introduction à la phenomenologie*, trans. Gabrielle Peiffer and Emmanuel Levinas, Paris: Armand Collin, 1931.

Nguyen, C. Thi. (2018), 'Echo Chambers and Epistemic Bubbles', *Episteme*, 17 (2020): 141–61. First published online 2018.

Prinz, Jesse (2018), 'Moral Sedimentation', in Gregg D. Caruso and Owen Flanagan (eds), *Neuroexistentialism: Meaning, Morals, and Purpose in the Age of Neuroscience*, 87–107, New York: Oxford University Press.

Sartre, Jean-Paul. A&J. (1948), *Anti-Semite and Jew*, trans. George J. Becker, New York: Schocken Books. First published as *Réflections sur le Question Juive* (Paris: Gallimard, 1946).

Sartre, Jean-Paul. BO. (2008), 'Black Orpheus', in Chris Turner (trans.), *The Aftermath of War (Situations III)*, 259–329, Oxford: Seagull Books. First published as the introduction to Léopold Sédar Senghor, *Anthologies de la Nouvelle Poésie Nègre et Malgache* (Paris: Presses Universitaires de France, 1948).

Sartre, Jean-Paul. B&N. (2018), *Being and Nothingness: An Essay in Phenomenological Ontology*, trans. Sarah Richmond, Abingdon: Routledge. Translation of *L'Être et le Néant: Essai d'Ontologie Phenomenologique*, revised by Arlette Elkaïm-Sartre (Paris: Gallimard, 1994; original edition: Gallimard, 1943).

Webber, Jonathan (2018a), *Rethinking Existentialism*, Oxford: Oxford University Press.

Webber, Jonathan (2018b), 'Sartre's Transcendental Phenomenology', in Dan Zahavi (ed.), *The Oxford Handbook of the History of Phenomenology*, 286–301, Oxford: Oxford University Press.

Webber, Jonathan (2019a), 'Sartre's Critique of Husserl', *British Journal for the History of Philosophy*, 28 (2020): 155–76. First published online 2019.

Webber, Jonathan (2019b), Review of *Being and Nothingness: An Essay in Phenomenological Ontology*, trans. Sarah Richmond, Abingdon: Routledge, 2018. *Mind* 129 (2020): 332–9. First published online 2019.

Webber, Jonathan (forthcoming-a), Transcendental Phenomenology Meets Negritude Poetry. Under review.

Webber, Jonathan (forthcoming-b), Existentialism Is a Kantian Humanism. Under review.

13

Murdoch and freedom

Ana Barandalla

1. Introduction

Writing in the second half of the past century, Iris Murdoch lamented the fact that the dominant concept in moral philosophy was that of freedom (IoP 2; G&G 47, 58; SoG 79–80, 80–1; AD 290). It was a descendant of Kant's own conception, but Murdoch thought it had been made extreme and had in the process engendered an impoverished and distorted conception of the individual and of moral life. The remedy was to produce a more realistic portrayal of the individual and a conception of freedom cut down to size. But she was not hopeful that this could be achieved by reverting back to Kant (SoG 83). Instead, she would employ a vast array of approaches – including the nature of language and of moral theorizing, of love, of art, of literature, and more – to build an alternative picture. In this chapter, I narrow my focus to Murdoch's concept of freedom as it relates to the concepts of the individual and of morality.

I show that the picture of the individual she developed explicitly is at odds with that implicitly contained in her account of freedom. I propose that this contradiction can be resolved by applying a constitutivist[1] spin to it. But constitutivism is built on Kantian tenets, so if my proposal is feasible, then it might be that the solution to the problem she identified in moral philosophy resided in Kant, after all.

The chapter unfolds as follows. I begin by making explicit the structure of the concept of freedom, highlighting its connection to the concepts of the individual and of morality. Next, I present Murdoch's interpretation of the prevailing conception of freedom, followed by an outline of her complaints about the notions of the individual and of morality on which it relies. I then present Murdoch's alternative picture of freedom, of the individual, and of morality. Next, I show that Murdoch's explicit conception of the individual is at odds with the conception implicit in her account of freedom. I then argue that construing Murdoch's conception of the individual in constitutivist terms resolves that contradiction. Lacking the space to explore the extent to which Murdoch's broader views would be amenable to such a measure, I finish by arguing that this constitutivist take retains the key elements which Murdoch sought to establish.

2. The structure of the concept of freedom

The concept of freedom is relational along two axes: something X is free from something Y, to do something Φ. The idea of absolute freedom is an oxymoron. If we were to say that X is absolutely free, we would mean that X is subject to no constraints whatsoever. This would include the constraints that delimit its being an X. But then there would be no X. If we allowed for those constraints by saying that X is free only from certain things, but still free to do absolutely anything, that would include freedom to rid itself from the things it is not free from, such as the things that delimit its being an X. We'd be back where we started. When we speak of freedom, then, we assume a certain thing that is free *from* certain things *to do* certain things.

A feature of this structure is that, if X is free from Y to Φ, then Y is not part of X qua Φer, nor is Y expressed in X's Φing. Only the things that are part of X qua Φer are expressed in X's Φing. For example, if I am free from my hair colour to run, then my hair colour is not part of me qua runner, nor is it in anyway manifested in my running.

It follows that what we think X is, what we think X is free from, and what we think X is free to do are intrinsically connected to each other.

In moral discourse, talk of freedom pertains to freedom of the individual qua moral agent (henceforth I'll take the qualification 'qua moral agent' as read), and our moral practices patently display those connections.

For example, if you trip and fall onto Marcus we do not judge you morally for it, but we do if you shove him out of the way. In the first case, we don't think you were free to fall onto Marcus, and we don't think your falling onto him is an expression of you – you were simply subject to causal forces. In the second case, we do think you were free to shove Marcus, and we think that the choice you made is somehow an expression of you.

We judge the individual for the things she is free to do, that is where she expresses herself, and that comprises the moral realm.

But freedom from what? Here we soon run into trouble. Our example suggests that we think that the individual is free from causal forces: where causal forces give a full account of an event, we don't think that that event was an expression of you.[2] But what are we to say about fears, desires, biases, and the like? These are causally tethered to the world. If we say that they are *not* part of the individual, we bestow a great deal of freedom on the individual, but there isn't much individual left. If instead we say that they *are* part of the individual, we secure a fuller, more recognizable individual, but we can no longer say that the individual is free from the causal realm to express herself. The individual is just one more cog in a great causal network.

Both options threaten the concept of freedom as used in moral discourse: the first renders it useless, and the second fictitious. Historically, those positions were epitomized by Kant and Hume respectively.

3. Freedom: "the movement of the lonely will"

The conception of freedom prevalent at Murdoch's time was a version of Kant's, with a handful of additional influences thrown in. It was attached to a picture of the individual which Murdoch called 'the man of modern moral philosophy' (IoP 4). A chief characteristic of this man is that he is identified as his will. Two separate doctrines supported that. The first has it that only those things with which I identify count as myself. I identify only with my will (IoP 5, 36); hence that's what I am (AD 283). The second maintains that only what is publicly observable is real (IoP 5, also 7). What is publicly observable about me is my empirical interactions with the world, 'the movement of [my] overtly choosing will' (IoP 7–8). Therefore, only my will is properly real. Hence, that's what I am.[3]

Both doctrines contrive to relegate the inner life to a tenuous existence (IoP 5) of near-irrelevance (V&C 34). My inner goings on are untouched by my will (IoP 5–6). That means that I don't identify with them, and so they don't count as me (IoP 7–8). And since the inner world is not observable to outsiders, it has but a 'parasitic and shadowy nature' on outer activities (IoP 5).

Freedom, for the man of modern moral philosophy, is 'the movement of the lonely will' (IoP 36) in the form of overt choices. He is free from his inner life. And since value – the grounds for our choices – is considered to not be in the world, but 'attached directly to the operation of the human will' (DPR 195; also SoG 80), he is free from the world too (IoP 35). This man casts his eye upon the world, value neutral and accessible to all, and pins his own value, wholly unconstrained, wherever he pleases (IoP 8).

The picture of morality accompanying this man follows from what he is thought to be. 'That which I do is that for which I am responsible and which is peculiarly an expression of myself', quotes Murdoch (sans reference) from Stuart Hampshire (IoP 5). Assuming that the realm of responsibility coincides with the realm of the moral, this means that morality comprises what are peculiarly expressions of myself, just as our moral practices reflect. In this view, expressions of myself are just expressions of my will. Since the only expression of my will is the 'bringing about of a recognizable change in the world' (IoP 5), that is what constitutes the moral realm, i.e., 'overt choices' (V&C 34; also M&E 70). The inner life, by contrast, not being something with which I identify, does not count as an expression of me; hence it falls outwith the moral sphere (IoP 8; V&C 34).

On this picture, then, *what is free* is the individual, identified as his will as expressed in overt choices; what he is *free from* is both his inner life and the world outside; what he is *free to do* is to express his will in the form of overt choices, and that makes up the moral sphere.

4. Freedom in Murdoch

Murdoch objects to the content of all components in that picture of freedom. She highlights its deficiencies through her example of M and D, mother-in-law and daughter-in-law respectively.

M does not think much of D. She finds her 'unpolished and lacking in dignity and refinement ... sometimes positively rude, always tiresomely juvenile' (IoP 17).

Being the reflective person that she is, however, M wonders whether her appraisal might not have been coloured by existing attitudes: 'I am old-fashioned and conventional. ... I might be snobbish. I am certainly jealous. Let me look again' (IoP 17).

Look again she does, and what she sees is different this time. She finds D 'to be not vulgar but refreshingly simple, not undignified but spontaneous ... not tiresomely juvenile but delightfully youthful' (IoP 17–8).

This case presents us with a number of things which we are 'irresistibly impelled to say', thinks Murdoch (IoP 21), and they all challenge the components of the prevailing account of freedom. We want to say that 'M has ... been *active*' (IoP 19, original emphasis). This challenges the idea that one expresses oneself only in overt action. We want to say that this activity is *moral* (IoP 19–20, my emphasis), thus challenging the idea that only overt action falls within the moral realm. We want to say that that activity is 'peculiarly *[M's] own*. Its details are the details of *this* personality' (IoP 23, original emphases). This challenges the idea that one is free from one's inner life to express oneself – that one's inner life is not involved in one's expression of oneself. And we want to say that the changes in M's inner life '[belong] to her', that they '[form] part of a continuous fabric of being' (IoP 22). This challenges the idea that the individual is nothing more than a will expressed in overt action.

The case of M and D, then, underlines the austerity imposed upon the conceptions of the individual and of morality by the extreme freedom assigned to the individual. But we know from Kant and Hume that if we hold on to a fuller individual we risk losing freedom. Is there not a middle way? Murdoch thinks there is (IoP 36). Let's see how she tries to find it, beginning with her conception of the individual.

5. Murdoch's individual

The preliminaries of Murdoch's conception of the individual are already contained in her observations on the M and D case. But a spot of disambiguation is needed. Murdoch claims that M's epistemic activity is an expression of M (M has been *active*, that activity is *her own*). Against her contemporaries' position that (i) I am only my will, (ii) my will expresses itself only in overt action, (iii) hence I express myself only in overt action; that claim might be taken as a challenge to (i) or to (ii). Murdoch does not address this question directly, and there is textual support for both alternatives. However, I believe that on the whole it is best interpreted as a challenge to (ii).[4] To do otherwise would require assuming an additional constituent of the individual, one which would be expressed in epistemic activity.

To be sure, Murdoch does identify another constituent to the individual, to wit, the 'fabric of being' (IoP 22), but it does not permit us to peg epistemic activity onto it in a way that would set it apart from the will. The notion of the 'fabric of being' alludes to the idea that individuals' engagements with the world do not vanish once 'completed', but that somehow they come to form part of the individuals themselves, they form something

> elusive which might be called their total vision of life, as shown in their mode of speech or silence, their choice of words, their assessment of others, their conception of their own lives, what they think attractive or praise-worthy, what they think funny.
>
> (V&C 39)

The 'fabric of being', then, is a derivative of the will. It is the accumulation of the expressions of the will, or residues thereof, and it also forms part of the context in which the will operates. This offers no support to the idea that epistemic activity is an expression of anything other than the will.

If instead we settle on the view that what is being challenged is (ii), that is, the claim that my will is expressed solely in overt action, we need not posit an additional, yet unknown, constituent of the individual. Instead we assign to the will, which is the faculty that renders overt action voluntary and attributable to the individual, the job of also rendering epistemic activity voluntary and attributable to the individual.

That view sets forth a much richer notion of the will than what was in currency. Murdoch's is no longer an isolated will 'jumping ... in and out of an impersonal logical complex' (IoP 23). Hers is a will expressed in epistemic as much as in overt activity, and its own expressions in part create the context for further expressions.[5] Identifying the individual with *this* will, then, is already to have a fuller individual.

But we've also seen that Murdoch wished to challenge the idea that overt action is free from the inner life. The idea that the 'fabric of being' functions as the context in which the will operates goes some way towards that end. But she also wants us to recognize the role that epistemic activity has in overt action too.

Murdoch stresses that epistemic activity is not only a cognitive endeavour but an evaluative one too (DPR 199, 200, 201). Our epistemic engagement with the world 'imperceptibly builds up structures of value around us' (IoP 37) by the introduction 'of a sort of seeping of colour' (DPR 200). As a result 'the world we see already contains our values' (DPR 200, also 201). This sets the tone for our decisions (DPR 200; G&G 54, 56; IoP 37 and passim). For, 'when moments of decision arrive we see and are attracted by the world we have already (partly) made' (DPR 200), 'a world which is now (for better or worse) *compulsively* present to the will' (IoP 39, original emphasis). Far from having no bearing on the choice of overt actions, then, epistemic activity is a crucial determinant of those choices.

There are a couple of further implications we can draw from the status Murdoch assigns to epistemic activity, which further shapes the emerging picture of the individual's agency. The first: To the extent that choices of overt action are preceded by deliberation, they too contribute to the 'world we see' (DPR 200), to our 'total vision of life' (V&C 39). They will come to form part of one's 'fabric of being', which in turn will influence subsequent choices. The second: Since epistemic activity involves decisions too ('M tells herself: ... Let me look again', she 'reflects deliberately about D' (IoP 17)), those must also be influenced by our 'fabric of being', as indeed M's initial appraisal of D was.

With those adjustments on board, the picture we get is one where all our activities – epistemic as well as overt – are intricately connected; they come to form who we are and set the context within which we further express ourselves.[6]

But what is underneath our epistemic activity, including its evaluative dimension? Here Murdoch draws on Freud's insights. She highlights the 'relentlessly strong selfish forces' (SoG 99), 'relentlessly looking after [themselves]' (SoG 78), 'hard for the subject to understand or control' (G&G 51; also SoG 99).

Dominant as these forces are, however, they don't have a monopoly on us (G&G 75; DPR 199, 201, 202; IoP 40). We are also attracted to the good (G&G 75), a transcendental, indefinable, and ultimately unattainable ideal (G&G 75, 62).

Our attraction to the good is manifested in our conducting our engagements with the world with 'attention' (IoP 37), that is with 'a just and loving gaze' (IoP 34; also G&G 66, 69 and passim), and a proper use of the imagination (DPR 198). By 'imagination' Murdoch means the carving of significance of what's presented to us: 'a type of reflection on people, events, etc., which builds in detail, adds colour, conjures up possibilities in ways which go beyond what could be said to be strictly factual' (DPR 198). She stresses that there is nothing nefarious with this interpretative faculty and cautions us against attempting to eliminate it – not that we could: 'To be a human being is to ... conceive of a reality which goes "beyond the facts" in these familiar and natural ways' (DPR 199).

The Freudian forces, on their part, corrupt the imagination into *fantasy*, something akin to wishful thinking (DPR 198). When dominated by those forces, we are 'reluctant to face unpleasant realities' (SoG 78) and look at the world 'through ... a cloud of more or less fantastic reverie designed to protect the psyche from pain' (SoG 78–9).

If we conduct our engagements with the world in the grip of the Freudian forces the result is 'distorted vision' (DPR 198, 199; G&G 59), that is, a distorted conception of the world, intended to console and aggrandize us (G&G 59, 64). If instead we engage with loving attention what we get is 'clear vision', we attain 'reality' (IoP 37, 38, 40; G&G 64; DPR 201).[7]

Murdoch's picture of the individual, then, is a genuine alternative to the man of modern moral philosophy. Her individual is still her will, but one now enriched with epistemic responsibilities and engaged in fruitful inner dynamics. Her expressions come to form the person that she is – her fabric of being – as well as her conception of the world, both of which in turn shape further expressions of herself. Underneath it all are forces that vie to pull her into different ways of expressing herself, and hence to cultivate different selves.

6. Murdoch's morality

This expanded picture of the individual carries a correspondingly expanded picture of morality. Morality now comprises not just overt actions, but inner goings on too, for the individual expresses herself in both (IoP 37; SoG 97; V&C 40; and passim). As for the criteria for morally good and for morally bad action, Murdoch is quite forthright. She states that 'the characteristic and proper mark of the active moral agent' is *attention*, (IoP 34); that is 'a just and loving gaze directed upon an individual reality' (IoP 34). The exercise of attention requires that we 'cease to be' (G&G 59), that we 'forget the self' (SoG 90) and that we 'silence and expel the self' (G&G 64). 'In moral life', she continues, 'the enemy is the fat relentless ego' (G&G 52) with its 'personal fantasy' (G&G 59). 'We can see in ... mediocre conduct, the intrusion of fantasy, the assertion of the self' (G&G 59).

The drama in those assertions is compelling, but we must see past it, for the self Murdoch so derides cannot be the same self without qualification. We saw her in the previous section stress that epistemic activity *cannot* but be interpretative (DPR 199). That presupposes a self.[8] And if a just and loving gaze is 'the characteristic and proper mark of the active moral agent' (IoP 34), the self that is that agent cannot be the self we are to 'silence and expel' (G&G 64). The self that Murdoch berates here, then, must be only the self that dominated by the Freudian forces, the self that succumbs to fantasy, the relentless ego.

On this view, then, your activity is morally right when it is guided by your attraction to the good and morally wrong when driven the Freudian forces.

7. Murdoch's freedom

Murdoch's statements on freedom can readily be divided into statements about what we are free from and statements about what we are free to do. She says: 'The enemy of freedom [is] fantasy' (DPR 202); 'The freedom which is a proper human goal is the freedom from fantasy' (G&G 66); 'Freedom … is the disciplined overcoming of self' (SoG 95). With fantasy being the imagination corrupted by the Freudian forces (DPR 198), and the self that is alluded to here being that in the grip of the Freudian forces, these statements can be taken to mean that what we are free from are the Freudian forces.

Murdoch also says that 'moral freedom looks … like a *mode of reflection* which we might have to achieve' (V&C 55, my emphasis), that 'freedom is … the experience of accurate vision' (G&G 67), and that it is 'concerned especially with the clarification of vision and the domination of selfish impulse' (SoG 99–100). We saw earlier (§ 5) that clear vision is the product of conducting our epistemic engagements with loving attention. On the assumption that loving attention is too the characteristic of the 'mode of reflection' of moral freedom, we can take these pronouncements to imply that what we are free to do is to engage with the world with loving attention.

Murdoch's claims on freedom, then, give us an individual free from the Freudian forces to engage with the world guided by her attraction to the good, namely, with loving attention.

This tallies with Murdoch's account of morality. You act morally when your activity is guided by your attraction to the good, and to do that you must silence the Freudian forces. In other words, the things which you must forgo to act morally are also the things which you are free from. This suggests a revision of the relation between the concepts of morality and of the self I outlined earlier (§ 2). There I said that the scope of morality comprises the individual's expressions of herself. Here we see that the scope of the moral is just the scope of the morally *right*. The morally wrong would comprise failures to express yourself, failures to guide yourself by your attraction to the good and to eschew the Freudian forces.[9]

No such matching can be found between the account of the individual implicit in Murdoch's picture of freedom and her explicit account. Murdoch's explicit account of the individual assigns to you both Freudian forces and attraction to the good. But if the Freudian forces are things you are free from to express yourself, as her account of freedom asserts, it follows that they are not part of you.

So we have a contradiction. If we tried to resolve it by rowing back from the idea that the Freudian forces are part of the individual, we would be left with an individual who is solely driven by her attraction to the good. This would surpass in inadequacy what Murdoch saw as one of the major deficiencies in current moral theory, namely, its presenting too rosy a picture of human beings (G&G 47). If, alternatively, we kept the Freudian forces as part of the individual and dropped the idea that you are free from them to conduct your engagements with the world, we would be forced to regard the expression of your Freudian forces morally on a par with the expression of your attraction to the good. It doesn't look like we can reconcile the conflicting positions.

There is an account of the individual which can dissolve that contradiction and which, I believe, befits Murdoch's views. It is an account proffered by constitutivism, especially as developed by Christine Korsgaard. In what remains I show how that would work.

8. Constitutivism

At a basic level of description, the constitutivist individual bears striking similarities to Murdoch's. According to constitutivism the individual constitutes herself in her actions; according to Murdoch, what the individual does comes to form part of herself. But constitutivism has a more developed account of what self-constitution amounts to and of its surrounding normative structure. It is in those details that we find a way out of the contradiction in Murdoch's account.

Korsgaard contends that, upon becoming aware of an impulse to do something or other – be it epistemic or overt – you face the question of whether to do that thing or not (SN 92–3). In facing that question, you are committed to being the author of its answer. That is, the answer cannot pop up, for example, in the way that an impulse does – if it did, you'd face the question of whether to do as per that impulse. Instead, the answer must come from *you* (SN 93; SC 72). As with Murdoch, what counts as you here is your will, or reason,[10] for that is what you identify with, that is where you are active (Korsgaard 2009b: 23; SC 72). So, in as much as you entertain the question of what to do, you are committed to deliberating your way to a conclusion.

Deliberation, on this view, consists in instilling upon the considerations at hand your value system, that is, the ordering of values within your value economy in relation to how much they matter to you.[11] Since deliberation is something with which you identify – it is where you are active – it follows that you identify with the instilment of your value system in your decisions. It also means that your value system is not an ordering of values which you discover but something that you yourself ratify. It is not a state of affairs; it is an activity. So when we talk about your having a value system, we talk about your ratifying a certain ordering within your values. Deliberation is the process of determining that ordering and carrying it over to your decisions. This is the sense in which, in constitutivism, you constitute yourself in your actions.

For example, suppose you're listening to the radio when on comes Mr R, whom you detest. An impulse immediately springs forth to dismiss outright anything that Mr R says. That is something that just happens to you; it befalls you. But once you become conscious of that impulse, you have to *decide* whether to act in accordance to it or not.[12] And that is something you do. In posing the question of whether to do as per your impulse to dismiss all of Mr R's utterances, you're committed to providing the answer to it – to being the author of your decision.

As you set out to address that question, you consider who you are. You might decide that you're not the kind of person who dismisses another's views out of hand; no, you're a reasonable chap; you're someone who engages with what others say, and agrees or disagrees *respectfully*. That's who you are. And in being committed to being the author of your decision, you are committed to reflecting in your decision the ordering of values comprised in that self-conception.

But it doesn't follow from your commitment to being the author of your decisions that you will. That space – the space between your commitment and whether you realize it – is, on constitutivism, the normative realm, the realm where right and wrong happen. That is because your commitment to being the author of your decisions is binding on you. On it your integrity, your unity as an agent, depends (SC 25; Bagnoli 2002: 134). If you abide by that commitment you treat yourself with respect and unify yourself. You constitute yourself properly, and your decision is therefore right. If, instead, you default on your commitment and you settle for a decision that does not reflect your value system, you disrespect yourself; you don't unify yourself. You constitute yourself badly and your decision is therefore wrong.

Back to our example. Having resolved that you're a reasonable person, and being committed to reflecting that in your decisions, you might say, 'Okay, that's who I am and I shall act accordingly, I shall listen patiently to Mr R.' Or you might instead let rip on a tirade against all to do with Mr R. It is not that you have rescinded your commitment to being the author of your decision, nor your view of yourself: those remain. Only you are acting against them, you're acting against yourself. The constitutivist would thus assess what you do here as wrong, while the previous alternative would be deemed right.

Let us now see how this picture of the individual can resolve Murdoch's contradiction.

9. Murdoch and constitutivist freedom

The conflicting claims, recall, are the following:

1. The Freudian forces are part of the individual;
2. The individual is free from the Freudian forces.

These claims stand in contradiction with each other because the things that you are free from are not part of you. Hence, claim (2) means that the Freudian forces are not part of you, while claim (1) states that they are.

Our constitutivist framework allows us to maintain both those claims. In this framework, the Freudian forces, as well as our attraction to the good, would be regarded as values broadly construed, for they both make claims on the will. The way Murdoch talks about them indicates that we much prefer to think of ourselves as responding to our attraction to the good than as responding to our attraction to the Freudian forces. This means that our attraction to the good sits at the top of our value system, and the Freudian forces at the bottom. I have explained that a constitutivist picture identifies you with the instilling of order among your values. But the instilling of order among values constitutively necessitates values. So your values are just as much a part of you as your instilling of order among them; they just play a different role.

This is analogous to how we think of other legislative units. Take a nuclear family. The unit is a family because the adults in it have cultivated certain relations between them and the children in it. The adults are the 'makers' of the family, and they, and not the children, may speak for the family. But the children are also constitutive members of it. Without the children there would be no family, for there would not be the kinds of people among whom nuclear familial relations might be established. Or take a country. Only edicts from the government count as laws of the country. Citizens' proclamations do not. And if you are a foreign dignitary and want to speak to a given country, you speak to the government of that country, not to a citizen. But citizens are constitutive members of the country too; only they play a different role to that of the government. You could not have a government without citizens to govern. As with children and with citizens, so with values. If agents are identified with the instilment of order among their values, they have to have those values to instil that order. This is not an extrinsic, instrumental condition; it is constitutive of that activity. Your Freudian forces, then, *are* a legitimate part of you.

The sense in which the Freudian forces are part of you is further refined when we consider what, on the constitutivist picture, you are *free to do*. Formally, what you are free to do is to express yourself. In the constitutivist picture, since you are identified with the activity of instilling your ordering of values in your decisions, to express yourself is a matter of instilling your ordering of values in your decisions. To express yourself is just to be yourself. Since your Freudian forces lay at the bottom of your ordering of values, reflecting their position will involve suppressing them, putting down their demand for dominance. But this does not mean that you must suppress your Freudian forces *in order to* express yourself. That would suggest that the Freudian forces have to *not be there* if you are to express yourself, and it would take us back to the contradictory position we are trying to resolve. Rather, expressing yourself *consists* in, inter alia, suppressing your Freudian forces. Again, it is the activity that counts, not a state of affairs. In this light, your Freudian forces are part of you *when they are kept subjugated* to your more important values, specifically to your attraction to the good. The same as a child is not part of a family, or a person a citizen of a state, unless they are subsumed into the relevant structures.

That picture of the individual and what the individual is free to do produces an account of what the individual is free from that evades Murdoch's contradiction. Once again, formally, what you are free from is, as it were, what you leave behind when you express yourself, what is not part of you. In our picture, what you leave behind is the satisfaction of your individual values' demands – be it the Freudian forces or your attraction to the good. As we saw above, your values are part of you when they are kept in their place, but not when they exert dominance over you. Keeping values in their place might involve subsuming them to more important values, as in the case of the Freudian forces, or upholding their superiority, as in the case of our attraction to the good. Either way, it involves restraining their push for control: *I* decide whether to do as they incite me to, not they. It is in that sense that you are free from them.

With this, the contradiction in Murdoch's account is resolved. For we can now say both that the Freudian forces are part of you and that you are free from them. They are part of you in the sense that being you involves keeping them in their place, and you are free from them in the sense that it is you, and not them, who keeps them in their place. The two statements which were before contradictory to each other are now complementary. The Freudian forces are part of you when you exercise your freedom from them, when you keep them in their place.

10. Constitutivism and Murdoch's wish list

A more thorough assessment of the merits of my proposal would involve exploring the extent to which Murdoch's broader work would be receptive to it. There, one critical question would be whether the notion of integrity employed in my proposal can be brought together with Murdoch's notion of the good. We lack the space to pursue that project. But keeping to the confines of this chapter, we can at least show that my proposal allows us to retain the key features Murdoch set out to establish.

Murdoch wanted an account of freedom suitable for a substantive picture of the individual, one that registered the opaque drives that stir us; saw us expressed in epistemic activity no less than overt activity; acknowledged our historical nature, the cumulative nature of what we do, our 'fabric of being'; recognized the close alliance between inner goings on and overt action; and allowed for a correspondingly expanded conception of the moral realm.

In the preceding two sections we have seen how the constitutivist approach fills in the details of that substantive individual, including the role that the Freudian forces play in their constitution. We also saw that the constitutivist picture regards epistemic activity as a field where the individual expresses themselves no less than in overt activity. But we've not seen how this account fares with Murdoch's notion of the 'fabric of being', nor have we drawn the picture of morality it begets. Let us turn to them now.

We might have found some of the foregoing inimical to Murdoch's notion of the 'fabric of being', to the idea that what I do comes to form part of me. Specifically, we might think that the idea that the individual constitutes herself in every act of self-expression, in every decision she makes, entails that every instance of self-constitution replaces the previous one. This would eschew the historical thrust Murdoch sought to preserve. It would not give us a 'fabric of being' so much as a slide show. However, this is not, in fact, sustained by the constitutivism presented here.

We saw that the decisions you make about what you are are binding on you (SC 25; Bagnoli 2002: 134). That means that for as long as you don't repudiate them and they remain relevant, they are authoritative to you (SC 23). Because we are almost always making decisions, we own a host of self-conceptions, suited to different circumstances (SC 21), and they will interact in productive ways with any new decisions we face. For example, your decision that you are a reasonable chap might strengthen your self-conception as a progressive (or as a conservative, depending on how you lean); that might inspire new ideas of how you might make yourself useful to society; which in turn might dilute standing militant sympathies. Each of these changes themselves will spur further changes in adjacent conceptions of yourself and of your relation to your environment, and those further still. Instances of self-constitution, then, do not replace previous ones; they add to them.

In this way, the person that you make yourself into when, against the background of Mr R on the radio, you determine you are a reasonable chap, will depend not just on this decision on this occasion but on what decisions about who you are you made on previous occasions. If on previous occasions where you were equally tempted to shout at the radio you, in the end, opted against it because you judged that that is not the person you are – because you're a reasonable chap – the person you will become now, when you make a similar decision will be different if on previous occasions you'd decided that you were *not* a reasonable chap (you might have thought that 'being reasonable' is just another name for selling out). This is how on the constitutivist account what you do comes to form part of a 'fabric of being' (IoP 22). What you are – what you make yourself into – depends partly on what person you've made yourself into before.

Notice the picture this presents of how your decisions are influenced by your inner life, another of the ideas Murdoch sought to establish. Most obviously, what you determine you are restricts what actions are appropriate for you to take. But when we consider the complex and rippling ways in which what you think you are interacts with the multitude of other existing self-conceptions, we can appreciate how certain attitudes, certain orientations to the world, would be engendered. These will influence your actions in various ways: from placing limits on the range of self-conceptions you take to be available to you, to adding saliency to some of the various actions compatible with any one self-conception, and eclipsing others. On the constitutivist picture, your inner life and your decisions are inalienably connected to each other.

As for Murdoch's ambition to incorporate the inner life into the scope of morality, we might think that the constitutivist picture presents an obstacle. Constitutivism, as outlined here, does not distinguish a moral domain, but instead presents a homogeneous normative realm. We might think, therefore, that constitutivism denies Murdoch the opportunity to assign the inner life any special status that comes with the label 'moral'. However, I think that that worry is misplaced.

The normative structure presented by our Korsgaardian constitutivism is supposed to capture the origin of normativity. Since morality, if there is such a thing, is a subset of normativity, it follows that regarding the inner life as normative activity is a necessary condition for regarding it as moral activity. In contrast with her contemporaries, constitutivism grants this necessary condition to Murdoch. To that extent at least, constitutivism is Murdoch's friend.

In any event, it so happens that what normativity is about on our constitutivist picture is a close fit to what Murdoch thinks morality is about. On our constitutivist picture normativity is about self-constitution, about what the agent makes herself into in her engagements with the world. As Murdoch sees it, morality covers 'the whole of our mode of living and the quality of our relations with the world' (SoG 97), it is something 'that goes on continually' (IoP 37), and the business of moral philosophy is 'the examination of the most important of all human activities' (SoG 78): 'to describe and analyse' the process where '[m]an makes pictures of himself and then comes to resemble the picture' (M&E 75). These remarks offer ample interpretative room. But one interpretation readily available is that the most important thing we do is coming to resemble the pictures of ourselves we create as we engage with the world. Given that on the constitutivist picture our engagement with the world is guided by conceptions of ourselves *and* it consists in staying loyal to those self-conceptions, it is hard not to conclude that Murdoch's morality and constitituvism's normativity are the same thing – that the different is merely one of terminology.

Furthermore, the standards of correctness for action endorsed by both views are also in alignment with each other. Murdoch, recall, states that moral action requires the sacrifice of the Freudian forces (§ 6). And on our constitutivist picture it is part of being an agent that you are required to reflect your value system in what you do. Given the status of the Freudian forces, that means that you are required to sacrifice the satisfaction they demand and to subjugate them to your attraction to the good. In light of the equivalence between constitutivism's normativity and Murdoch's morality highlighted above, the requirement is the same in both cases. Again, then, it seems that constitutivism and Murdoch are concerned with the same normative phenomena, albeit under different terms.

There is yet one more point of convergence between the two views which warrants mention even though we've not touched on it before. At several junctions Murdoch stresses that morality is a struggle (IoP 22, 38) and that it usually involves suffering (G&G 68). The constitutivist picture gives us a glimpse of the sense in which that is the case. In a picture where being you consists in instilling your value system upon the individual values that vie for control, to express yourself – i.e., to act morally – is to constantly constrain yourself.

11. Conclusion

Murdoch's overall aim was to produce an account of freedom suitable for a full, recognizable individual, without succumbing to determinism (IoP 36). For this she thought she needed to move away from Kant (SoG 83), the precursor of the empty man of modern moral philosophy (SoG 79–80). I have shown that she did not achieve her aim unless helped by a constitutivist conception of the individual. But the constitutivist individual I have proposed is also of Kant's lineage. She is an autonomous being; her own authority. Only this individual, unlike Murdoch's target, exercises her autonomy by fashioning herself out of the stuff given her by nature and by her surroundings, and which make for human beings as we know them. Nor is this an individual which 'thin as a needle, appears in the quick flash of the choosing will' (G&G 53). This individual is porous. Her engagement with the world is almost constant and retains what she does in the form of normative commitments that influence what else she does. The constitutivist individual affords Murdoch the account of freedom and of morality she sought. If Murdoch were to adopt it, rather than moving away from Kant, she'd be reverting back to him, shedding the various influences that she found so unfortunate and trying a different track. Although, as already adverted, we cannot here explore the full extent to which Murdoch's broader views would be receptive to a constitutivist approach, the fact that such gains would lay in store is a reason to regard that approach as a promising candidate within which to interpret Murdoch's work.[13]

Notes

1. Strictly speaking, the reading I apply is constructivist as well as constitutivist. But I'll trade accuracy for convenience and use 'constitutivism' only.
2. At least not under the description under which the causal explanation is complete.
3. We might be surprised at the idea that the will is observed, rather than inferred, but Murdoch does not pick up on this, so we must let it pass here.
4. This sides with Moran, but cf. Antonaccio.
5. See also (V&C 32), where Murdoch agrees with R. H. Hepburn's companion piece in V&C, where he includes the view that the individual creates herself through her decisions (V&C 17–18).
6. This echoes Hepburn's view, with which Murdoch agrees (V&C 32), that what the individual makes herself into through her decisions then works as a constraint on subsequent decisions (V&C 17–18).
7. This appeal to 'reality' does not evince a realist metaethic. Murdoch's characterization of 'reality' is entirely in terms of how it is reached (DPR 199, 201; IoP 38, 40).
8. Antonaccio makes a similar point (142).
9. This would saddle Murdoch with the problem of explaining how we can ever attribute bad (or wrong) actions to you if they are by definition not expressions of you. I cannot tackle this problem on Murdoch's behalf here, although an answer to it will be intimated in the constitutivist picture I present below. For a fuller treatment of that problem see Korsgaard's SC, ch.8.
10. This is a different sense of 'reason' from that used by Murdoch, who saw it as an instrumental faculty.
11. This is comprised in Korsgaard's notion of 'practical identities' (SN 100-7; SC 20-4). Bagnoli, on her part, speaks of deliberation as establishing relations with your surroundings which both inform and make claims on how you think of yourself (Bagnoli 2002: 131).
12. I am ignoring here the difference between acting in accordance with *an impulse* and acting in accordance with the *content* of a given impulse. This is crucial for a more thorough account of constitutivism, but less so for our purposes.
13. Other authors have already undertaken that task, albeit prompted by different concerns to mine. Most notable is Bagnoli in her 2012. Antonaccio, too, attributes to Murdoch a 'reflexive realism' (116 and passim), which bears, in my view, key constitutivist hallmarks. See esp. 142-5.

Bibliography

Antonaccio, Maria (2000), *Picturing the Human: The Moral Thought of Iris Murdoch*, Oxford University Press.
Bagnoli, Carla (2002), 'Moral Constructivism: A Phenomenological Argument', *Topoi*, 21: 125–38.
Bagnoli, Carla (2012), 'The Exploration of Moral Life', in Justin Broakes (ed.), *Iris Murdoch: Philosopher*, 197–226.
Broakes, Justin, ed. (2012), *Iris Murdoch: Philosopher*, Oxford University Press.
Korsgaard, Christine M. [SN] (1996), *The Sources of Normativity*, Cambridge University Press.
Korsgaard, Christine M. (1999), 'Self-constitution in the Ethics of Plato and Kant', in Christine M. Korsgaard, *The Constitution of Agency*, Oxford University Press, 100–26.
Korsgaard, Christine M. [SC] (2009a), *Self-Constitution: Agency, Identity, and Integrity*, Oxford University Press.
Korsgaard, Christine M. (2009b), 'The Activity of Reason', *Proceedings and Addresses of the American Philosophical Association*, 83 (2): 23–43.
Moran, Richard (2012), 'Iris Murdoch and Existentialism', in Justin Broakes (ed.), *Iris Murdoch: Philosopher*, 181–96.
Murdoch, Iris [V&C] (1956), 'Vision and Choice in Morality', Symposium with R. W. Hepburn, *Proceedings of the Aristotelian Society*, suppl. vol. 30, 14–58.
Murdoch, Iris [M&E] (1957), 'Metaphysics and Ethics', in *Existentialists and Mystics*, 59–76.
Murdoch, Iris [AD] (1961), 'Against Dryness', in *Existentialists and Mystics*, 287–95.
Murdoch, Iris [IoP] (1964), 'The Idea of Perfection', in *The Sovereignty of Good*, 1–45.
Murdoch, Iris [DPR] (1966), 'The Darkness of Practical Reason', in *Existentialists and Mystics*, 193–202.
Murdoch, Iris [SoG] (1967), 'The Sovereignty of Good over Other Concepts', in *The Sovereignty of Good*, 77–104.
Murdoch, Iris [G&G] (1969), 'On "God" and "Good"', in *The Sovereignty of Good*, 46–76.
Murdoch, Iris (1970), *The Sovereignty of Good*, Routledge & Kegan Paul.
Murdoch, Iris (1997), *Existentialists and Mystics: Writings on Philosophy and Literature*, ed. Peter J. Conradi, Penguin Books.

Index

action, overt 207, 208, 209, 212, 215
adolescence 200
affordances 192–3, 202
Allais, Lucy 158, 165n
Allison, Henry 27, 32, 35–6, 41, 77n, 153n, 168n
Ameriks, Karl 40, 45, 61n
anti-Semitism 198–9
Antonaccio, Maria 18 n4, n8, n13
Aristotle 117
autonomy 1, 28–30, 32–7, 43, 45, 48, 60n, 95–102, 106–8, 177, 179, 181, 182–3, 186–7, 195–6, 200, 217
autonomy, relational 176, 182–3

Bagnoli, Carla 213, 215, 218 n11, n13
Bakhtin, Mikhail 185
Beauvoir, Simone de 191, 193–7, 198, 199, 200–1, 202, 203
Beiser, Frederick 83, 108n, 153n
Bildungsgeschichte 177, 183
Bildungsroman 175, 187

capitalism 132–3
Cavell, Stanley 177
Chang, Ruth 187 n. 5
childhood 194, 195, 200, 214
Christianity 179
civil society 114, 120–4
commitment 191, 196–7, 200–1, 202
communism 129–30, 132–7
compatibilism 41, 46, 149, 155–62
constitutivism 39, 100, 146, 177, 182, 186, 205, 212–17, 218 n.1
convicting use of the law 17
Creuzer 50–2
Croce 113
cultural values 191–2, 198–200, 201–2

Descartes, René 201
deliberation 63, 67, 78n, 212, 213

desire 12–13, 18, 28, 30–1, 39–40, 127, 135, 141, 147–9, 177, 181, 187 n. 3
determinism 14, 46–8, 65–6, 84–7, 91–2, 96–106, 142–52, 159–62, 176, 177, 178, 180, 181, 186
Dostoevksy, Fyodor 180
Dworkin, Ronald 187 n. 4

egoism 133–4, 184
empathy 182
empiricism 152n, 163–4, 169n
epistemic activity 208–9, 211, 212
Erasmus, D. 16, 17–20, 23
evil 11–16, 20, 22, 21, 23
    radical evil 13–14, 19, 22

face-to-face 183, 185
Fanon, Frantz 203
Fichte 51–9, 63–78, 119–20, 138n, 179, 187 n. 2
Foster MB 123, 124n
Frankfurt, Harry 187n
freedom
    compatibilist (*see* compatibilism)
    empirical 117–19
    finite 175–6, 177, 179, 182, 183–7
    of indifference 49
    infinite 175–6, 178–82, 184–7
    libertarian 156–8, 164, 167, 169n
    mature and immature 176–7, 180, 182, 183, 186–7
    radical 179, 191–202
    as self-realization 83–4, 130–7
    transcendental 28, 36, 46–7, 53, 96, 98–9, 100–2, 107, 156–8, 164–7, 168n
free choice [Willkür] 13–14, 16–17, 22–3, 27–43, 50–1, 54–5, 58, 123
Fugate, Courtney 40–3

grace 11–13, 16–17
  co-operative grace 15, 16
  justifying grace 13
  sanctifying grace 13
Grenberg, J. 13
Guyer, Paul 24n, 27, 77n

Hampshire, Stuart 207
Hegel 113–24, 128, 176, 182, 187, 187 n. 1,
  187 n. 3, 187 n. 6, 187 n. 9
Held, Virginia 182
heteronomy 28, 36–7, 48, 95, 100, 102,
  107, 176, 180–1, 185, 186–7
Holroyd, Jules 187 n. 8
Hume 40, 163, 206, 208
Husserl, Edmund 196, 201

imputation 13–14, 16, 22, 157, 168n
individual 60n, 72, 75, 105–7, 114–24,
  127–37, 138n, 141, 148, 150, 176–7,
  180, 182–3, 186, 187n, 193–4, 196,
  199–200, 205, 212, 214, 215, 217–18

James, William 159–67
Jewish culture 198–200

Kant, I.
  Critique of Judgment 102–3, 104, 109n
  Critique of Practical Reason 14–15, 155,
    157, 165
  Critique of Pure Reason 46–7, 53, 88,
    96–9, 157
  *Groundwork for the Metaphysics of
    Morals* 24n, 32, 35, 41, 47–8, 51,
    54, 58, 58, 60n, 96–7, 99–102, 127,
    139n, 168n
  *Metaphysical Foundations of Natural
    Science* 86, 88–9
  Metaphysics of Morals 31–4, 36–7
  *Religion within the Boundaries of Mere
    Reason Alone* 11, 15, 16–17, 18,
    24n, 32–4, 51, 153n
Korsgaard, Christine 212, 213, 215, 216,
  217, 218n
Kosch, Michelle 5, 63–4, 72, 93n, 109n

Levinas, Emmanuel 175–88
Luther, M. 11, 16–22
Løgstrup, K. E. 17, 21–2

Mackenzie, Catriona 176
Marx 123–4, 127–39
meanings 192, 194, 196, 198, 200, 202
Merleau-Ponty, Maurice 196
metaphysics 60n, 96–7, 137, 150, 163–6,
  169n, 194
Mill, J.S. 141–53, 168n
Moore, A.W. 179
Montesquieu 117
morality 1, 13–14, 48, 55–6, 63–76, 100–3,
  109n, 116, 156–7, 164, 166, 168n,
  205, 206–7, 211–12
Murdoch, I. 12, 19, 25n, 205–18

nature 3, 5, 15, 32, 38, 46–7, 51–2,
  56–7, 63, 65, 68, 70–2, 74, 83–92,
  95–109, 115, 119, 131, 137, 142,
  145, 149, 153n, 168n, 199, 215,
  217
naturphilosophie 84, 102–7
negritude poetry 192, 201–2, 203
normativity 1, 144–7, 213, 216, 217
novelty 160–4, 167, 169n

open future 158–67, 193
ought implies can 11, 14–17, 19–23

passion(s) 149, 181
passional 159, 162, 168n
paternalism 176, 183, 186
pelagianism 16
Pelczynski ZA 116, 120
phenomenology 161–2, 165, 167,
  187n, 191, 194, 196–7, 201–2,
  203
Pippin, Robert 124n, 153n, 182–3
poetry 192, 201–2, 203
Plato 120
practical reason 15, 29–30, 37–42, 50, 101,
  156, 165
pragmatism 159–67
Prinz, Jesse 195–6, 200, 203
projects 191, 193–4, 195–201,
  203
prose 194, 202

radical empiricism 163–4
rational autonomy. *See* autonomy
Raskolnikov 180, 184–5

reason 18–19, 24n, 28–43, 50–1, 68–9, 75, 83, 91, 95–6, 98–101, 104, 115, 117, 144–7, 156–7, 159, 165, 180–1, 185, 186, 212, 218n
reasons 40, 145–7, 166, 185, 191, 192–3, 196–7, 198–9, 200, 202, 203
recognition 77n, 121, 176, 182, 186, 187–8 n. 9
responsibility 116, 157, 160, 175, 180, 182–3, 187 n. 7, 207
Reinhold, K. L. 13, 27–43, 59–1, 54, 58
Rousseau 115, 120, 128
Royce, Josiah 187 n. 1

Sallis, John 177
Sartre, Jean-Paul 179–80, 182, 187 n. 6, 191–3, 194–5, 196–9, 200–2, 203
Schelling 5, 52–4, 57–9, 83–94, 95–6, 102–9
self-realization 83–4, 130–7
self-sufficiency 63–76, 77–8n, 104, 121
shame 184
Soljar, Natalie 176
soul 15, 105, 119, 165, 179
sovereignty 101, 177, 178, 180
spontaneity 1, 32–6, 46, 48, 57–8, 98, 102, 107, 108n, 149–52, 153n
state, the 57, 113–24, 128, 132, 134
Stern, Robert 6n, 25n, 60n, 168n, 182, 187 n. 3, 188 n. 9

Taylor, Mark C. 175–6
teleology 102–6
Timmermann, Jens 41, 60n, 169n
transcendental arguments 77n, 192, 194, 201, 202
transcendental freedom 28, 36, 46–7, 53, 96, 98–9, 100–2, 107, 156–8, 164–7, 168n
transcendental idealism 11, 46–7, 95–6, 99, 156–8, 164–5, 168n

Ulrich, Johann August Heinrich 29, 48–50
upbringing 194, 195, 199–200. *See also* adolescence, childhood

value 193, 194–5, 15–16, 196–7, 199, 200, 201, 203, 207, 209, 212–13, 214, 215, 217. *See also* cutural values
Visker, Rudi 185–6

Watson, Gary 187 n. 4
Westlund, Andrea 187 n. 7
will [Wille] 29–43, 47, 51, 54, 177, 178–80, 182, 183, 185, 187 n. 3, 208, 209, 212
Willkür [free choice] 13–14, 16–17, 22–3, 27–43, 50–1, 54–5, 58, 123
womanhood 193–4
Ware, Owen 6n, 60n, 64, 71–3, 76–8n
Wood, Allen 5, 28, 37, 40–1, 63–4, 67, 71, 75, 77–8, 129, 138n, 156

www.ingramcontent.com/pod-product-compliance
Lightning Source LLC
Chambersburg PA
CBHW052106300426
44116CB00010B/1555